Tourism in Global Society

UNIVERSITY COLLEGE

To Sally and Joseph
And also to Anne and John G. Meethan

Tourism in Global Society
Place, Culture, Consumption

Kevin Meethan

palgrave

First published 2001 by
PALGRAVE
Houndmills, Basingstoke, Hampshire RG21 6XS and
175 Fifth Avenue, New York, N. Y. 10010
Companies and representatives throughout the world

PALGRAVE is the new global academic imprint of St. Martin's Press LLC
Scholarly and Reference Division and Palgrave Publishers Ltd (formerly
Macmillan Press Ltd).

ISBN 0–333–76057–3 hardback
ISBN 0–333–76058–1 paperback

This book is printed on paper suitable for recycling and
made from fully managed and sustained forest sources.

A catalogue record for this book is available
from the British Library.

Library of Congress Cataloging-in-Publication Data is available from the
Library of Congress.

10   9   8   7   6   5   4   3   2   1
10   09 08 07 06 05 04 03 02 01

Printed in Malaysia

Contents

Contents   vii

List of Tables

List of abbreviations

ASEAN: Association of South East Asian Nations
BTA: British Tourist Authority
CoE: Council of Europe
DCMS: Department for Culture, Media and Sport
EU: European Union
IMF: International Monetary Fund
LDCs: Less developed countries
MNCs: multinational corporations
TNCs: transnational corporations
UNESCO: United Nations Educational, Scientific and Cultural
            Organisation
WTO: World Tourism Organisation

Acknowledgements

Many people contributed to this book in one way or another. In particular though I would like to thank colleagues at the University of Plymouth who commented on earlier draft chapters, especially Sue Hemmings, Steve Miles and Malcolm Williams.

I would also like to thank the World Tourism Organisation for permission to use their data.

Chapter 1

Theorising Tourism

Introduction: why theory?

Tourism has been a significant factor in the developed economies since the mid nineteenth century, if not earlier (Feifer 1986, Löfgren 1999). Yet the development of analytical approaches, which attempt an explanation of this phenomenon, is a more recent concern. There are a number of reasons why this should be so, not the least being a tendency to view the pursuit of leisure itself and, by implication the analysis of it, as a side issue to the more serious business of industrial production. Of course, nothing ever stands still and tourism is now a globalised business, or industry. Within the social sciences there have also been substantial changes, for example, a shift towards viewing consumption, rather than production, as a serious focus of enquiry (Corrigan 1997, Miller 1995b). One of the main themes that this book will address is the extent to which such approaches can contribute to an understanding of tourism as a social phenomenon.

Of course, nothing ever springs into being without being foreshadowed, and leaving aside the genre of travel writing, the first comprehensive attempt to approach tourism from the perspective of the social sciences was provided by Dean MacCannell's book *The Tourist* (1976). Despite its faults, this book effectively opened up tourism to a more generalised and theoretically informed analysis than had previously been the case. Its continued importance can be judged by the extent to which it is cited, and the issues it raised have continued to influence both sociological and anthropological approaches towards the analysis of tourism. The next major development was the publication of John Urry's seminal book, *The Tourist Gaze* (1990) which, like MacCannell's, has also had a far-reaching

effect on the development of a theoretically informed social analysis
of tourism. Yet the world of the early twenty-first century is a very
different place to the Paris of the 1970s as much as the England of
the mid 1980s which respectively informed the work of MacCannell
and Urry. During this period we have passed from paradigms of
social analysis that grappled with modernity, to those dealing with
postmodernity and more recently, to paradigms that are beginning to
assess economic, social, cultural and political changes in terms of
globalisation.

In addition to such theoretical developments, there have also been
many important changes both within and without academia, not least
the proliferation of both vocational and degree courses in tourism,
leisure and hospitality management. Arguably one of the more under-
researched aspects or impacts of tourism is the growth of tourism
studies within higher education (Tribe 1997). Yet for all the evident
expansion of journals, books and conferences specifically devoted to
tourism, at a general analytical level it remains under-theorised,
eclectic and disparate.

The question of delimiting or creating the boundaries of tourism
as an object of academic enquiry is clearly one that needs discussion.
First there are attempts to reduce tourism to a formula or a set of
bare essentials, but this only seems to lead to rather bland and
overgeneralised statements, such as that offered by Nash and
Smith. They argue that tourism is not only found in almost every
culture, but is also 'part of some way of life and its context' (1991:
22). Rather than answering anything, this simply raises two immediate questions – what way, and what context? A more general consensus among those who have addressed the application of social
theory to tourism is that no one single approach can do justice to the
variety of activities and the variety of forms that tourism takes. In
turn this requires a theoretical, as much as a methodological, eclecticism (Dann and Cohen 1991, Ryan 1991, Tribe 1997).

One approach is to accept this as a distinct advantage. As Tribe
suggests, tourism analysis can best be described as interdisciplinary,
multidisciplinary, and 'conscious of its youthfulness' (1997: 638).
What Tribe argues is that a search for tourism as a discipline per se
should be abandoned, and that the diversity of the field is something
to be celebrated rather than denigrated (1997: 656). In many ways this
is an accurate reflection of the current state of play within tourism
analysis. While I think there is much to be said for accepting diver-

sity, after all, there is plenty of it in this book, there are also a number of problems associated with such an approach.

One possible outcome of adopting this position is the risk of falling into a form of relativism, where all that can be said is that some theories are different from others – without attempting to say what utility they may or may not have, under what circumstances they can be applied, why some theories offer better explanations than others, and why some should be rejected and so on.

Secondly, we should also be wary of the related problem of falling into a complacent attitude of simply accepting diversity rather than attempting to account for it. In short, the idea that a state of diversity is a desirable thing in itself needs to be questioned. To apply this formula is to effectively ignore that which is difficult, messy, or contradictory without subjecting it to critical scrutiny, and without sorting the good from the bad. The danger here is that the uncritical adoption of different disciplinary or analytical approaches and even methodologies may result in the worst of each discipline, not the best, coming together. Also the idea that complexity should be accepted, rather than analysed, may become uncritically accepted as the prevailing orthodoxy.

This latter point leads to a consideration of the differences between diversity at an empirical level, and diversity at a theoretical level. It is not beyond the bounds of logical possibility to account for the former without the latter, indeed the purpose of theory is precisely that, to synthesize and explain and generalise. The diversity that is current within the study of tourism from a social science perspective lies not so much at a theoretical level, where in fact it is rather thin, but rather at an empirical level. Unlike some other disciplines or fields of study the amount of empirical work, mostly descriptive, far outweighs the attempts to synthesize it into some kind of theoretical framework or even frameworks. It appears that this is a fundamental problem, which needs to be addressed rather than simply filed away under diversity or whatever. Celebrate by all means, but now it is surely time to consider what is worth keeping, and what is worth rejecting or reformulating, which conceptual tools need to be discarded or reshaped. Diversity in other words needs to be accounted for, to be discussed, to be the subject of debate, not uncritically accepted as a given or desirable state of affairs. To do so, I would argue, is to be counter-productive in terms of developing a more coherent analytical framework.

Despite my own misgivings about universal theories because they tend towards reductionism, there are a number of fundamental aspects of tourism which I think can be theorised in a more comprehensive manner than has hitherto been the case. This book approaches tourism from a perspective derived largely, but not exclusively, from two closely related social science disciplines, anthropology and sociology, which both individually and collectively have made significant contributions towards the understanding of tourism as a global social phenomenon.

Changes on the global economic and cultural stage have also had an impact on the nature of the social sciences, for although the nation state is still important, globalisation means that the traditional boundaries of social science are, rather like their subject matter, becoming revised. Sociology for example, is beginning to look beyond the confines of the nation state as the prime location of society (Robertson 1995) while anthropology has been 'coming home' for many years (Goddard et al. 1994). Both disciplines are also beginning to assess the development and impact of diasporic or transnational cultures (Clifford 1997, Hall 2000, Hannerz 1996). In addition, there have also been significant developments in the related fields of human geography and cultural studies which are also grappling with issues concerning globalisation and the significance of place in terms of cultural change (Gregory 1994, Harvey 1994, Tomlinson 1999). All of these academic fields have concerns that are to some extent common, even accounting for the different epistemological traditions between them. My approach here is to build on these developments in order to provide a more theoretically driven and interdisciplinary approach to the study of tourism.

Overall my main theme is to argue that tourism is part of the process of commodification (or commoditization) and consumption inherent in modern capitalism. Tourism is therefore best conceptualised as a global process of commodification and consumption involving flows of people, capital, images and cultures (Appadurai 1990, Clifford 1997, Frow 1997, Lanfant et al., 1995). I will also argue that the diversity of tourism that is evident in the world today can be adequately explained by adopting an approach that focuses on these dynamics.

There are also a number of subthemes, which run through this book and interrelate in a number of ways. As I mentioned above, the world has changed significantly since the first attempts to analyse tourism. Indeed, one of the great introductory clichés of tourism studies, which is nonetheless true, concerns the seemingly exponential growth of the industry in terms of its economic value and global spread (Vellas and Bécherel 1995). At this macro level, we therefore need to account for a number of factors, from the growth of multinational corporations (MNCs) and the global spread and adoption of a relatively deregulated political economy. In addition we also have to consider the ways in which nation states attempt to control and regulate the globalising trends of the tourist system for their own purposes, (Elliott 1997) such as using tourism to achieve economic growth and development.

Any book dealing with tourism as consumption must also address the issue of commodification as a central concern, that is, the ways in which material culture, people and places become objectified for the purposes of the global market. In general the debates surrounding this have been cast in negative terms. As Dann and Cohen point out, 'proponents of the "commoditization hypothesis" also appear to have succumbed to the assumption of inevitability' (1991: 160) which sees the spread of capitalist commodity relations as an all pervading and corrosive destroyer of cultures, with tourism as one of the principal causal mechanisms by which this is achieved. According to Selwyn this debate has already run its course at least in its early formulation as the inevitable destroyer of culture (1996: 15). However, I disagree, and consider that the problem here is more to do with the ways in which commodities and symbolic value have been conceptualised, particularly in models derived from Marx's notion of exchange and use value, as will be discussed in later chapters. I will argue that the processes of commodification, rather then being a side issue, are in fact central to the whole basis of tourism and, what is more, that tourism is one aspect of the global processes of commodification rather than a separate self-contained system.

A further set of issues relate to the ways in which the 'impacts' of such processes are mediated at a variety of levels and spatial scales in terms of culture, identity and locality. For all its global spread, tourism is also irreducibly associated with the specificity of places, with the processes by which sights are demarcated and set apart from the mundane (MacCannell 1976, Urry 1990b) becoming in effect the commodities to be sold in the global market place. In this sense, there is also a need to consider the ways in which the global and systemic properties of the tourist industry are manifested at the micro or local level of daily life. First are the actual patterns of demand and consumption from the tourists themselves, their motivations and values (Ryan 1991). Secondly there is also a need to consider how such demands affect host communities in terms of their cultural values (Clifford 1997, Lanfant et al., 1995) as much as the organisation of work and gender relations (Sinclair 1997). In effect, this means analysing tourism in terms of the relationships and forms of mediation between the macro level of the global tourist system, and the micro level of lived experiences. Or to put it another way, in terms of the interactions and dynamics that exist between the global and the local.

Inevitably, given the breadth of the subject matter under discussion, there are exclusions too. This book is not intended as an introduction to the application of general social theory for tourism studies, as I feel that there is nothing to be gained by reviewing in detail how different theoretical approaches such as functionalism, symbolic interactionism or structuralism for example, can be or have been applied to the study of tourism, or why many of these paradigms are simply irrelevant. Nor is there anything to be gained by simply reviewing the contribution that say anthropology or sociology or any individual discipline has contributed, all these are issues which have been dealt with elsewhere (Cohen 1984, 1988b, Crick 1989, Dann and Cohen 1991, Nash 1996, Nash and Smith 1991, Shaw and Williams 1994). Also, there is little in this book on the history of tourism which has also been adequately covered (Adler 1989, Feifer 1986, Löfgren 1999, Towner 1994, Urry 1990b). Another issue, which is not dealt with at any great length, but as and when appropriate, is that of sustainability. This seems to be one of those burgeoning sub-disciplinary fields, which again, has been extensively dealt with elsewhere (Mowforth and Munt 1997, Wahab and Pigram 1997). Inevitably though, some account of the above factors is necessary, and will be dealt with in the context of the overall arguments of this book as they arise. For the remainder of this chapter the themes outlined above will be explored in relation to the development of modernity, which will provide a theoretical overview and context for the subsequent chapters.

Conceptualising modernity

Modernity as a form not only of social order, but also as a form of conceptualising the world, is conventionally dated from the enlightenment period of the late seventeenth century. To the social theorists of the nineteenth century, the sweeping changes caused by indus- trialisation appeared to be replacing traditional forms of social organ- isation with the emergence of a capitalist system (Giddens 1991). In turn, this necessitated new ways of organising labour based on the routinisation of work, rationalisation of production, and a growing bureaucracy (Lyon 1999). Such developments have been described as a consequence of differentiation that is, the increasing specialisation of particular functions. This basic principle is premised on the idea that social relations in modernity are constituted in fundamentally different ways to those of pre-modern times. For example, whereas in pre-modern social arrangements, the domestic sphere of family and home constituted the unit of production, in modernity, work was split from the home, and became regulated as wage labour. This regulation in turn was organised around clock time, as opposed to the pre-modern seasonal rhythm of agricultural production (Lyon 1999: 29). As well as this splitting of work from the home, we can also point to the differentiation that began to occur between home and leisure.

In terms of the spatial organisation of modernity, urbanisation was a key development. This enabled factory production to increase economies of scale, as well as providing a focus for political activity through the development of forms of local government, and a source of civic identity through the provision of centralised social and leisure facilities. Urbanisation also gave rise to mass markets whose con- sumption needs were met through mass factory production. Labour relations too, went through a series of changes. Production in the factories was different from production to fulfil the needs of both individuals and families. Labour became regulated through forms of contracts, and access to commodities was regulated through a wage economy. In the classic Marxist explanation of this process, people were therefore alienated from the means of production and social relations were mediated, in effect disguised through commodity forms (Craib 1997: 92).

Both Giddens (1991) and Harvey (1989a) view the reorganisation of space and time as a key element in this process. Social relations require the coordination of large numbers of people, which can only be achieved through the extraction of social relations from local contexts, and across time. Although this may sound rather abstract, it can be explained in the following way. A tourist wishing to travel to another country purchases a ticket that indicates a specific flight, departure and arrival time. In turn, this requires coordination between the agent who sells the ticket, the airline, the airport authorities at points of both departure and arrival, the negotiation of international treaties which regulate airline routes, visa requirements, currency conversions and so on. Such coordination can only work if there is a universal system of time reckoning to which all concerned subscribe, and bureaucratic systems that can ensure coordination both within and between nation states. The important point here is the ways in which relations between people in modern forms of social organisation are not carried out on the basis of face-to-face relationships, as they allegedly were in pre-modern societies, but are increasingly mediated through rational bureaucratic forms of organisation and the regulation of wage labour.

Modernity is of course, also associated with the idea of progress and change, in particular the notion of a linear path to social development in which the pre-modern is swept aside by the progressive march of modernity which, as Harvey claims, has 'no respect for its own past' (1989a: 226). The idea that modernity constitutes a fundamental break with the past, not only of organisational forms but also in conceptual terms, also creates a distinction between the modern and the traditional. Another element to be considered is the nation state. In commonsense terms nation states tend to be viewed as 'natural' entities, which encapsulate a set of essential characteristics shared by its inhabitants, that is, a distinct national culture. Yet such assessments are in themselves products of modernity, and are usually also set in sharp contrast to the pre-modern or the primitive. The latter is confined either to history, or to other places that have yet to embark on the progressive march to modernity. In this way, both the 'primitive' and the 'traditional' become seen as the antithesis of modernity, as qualities of people and place that are survivals. As we shall see, this is a fundamental categorisation that not only underpins many forms of tourism, but also many forms of tourism analysis.

This quick dash through economic, social and cultural history is by no means intended to be anything other than broadly schematic. I have outlined certain factors at the expense of others, yet those I have isolated for particular comment have been chosen because of their relevance to the development of tourism spaces and forms of tourism commodification and consumption. Concepts of alienation, the division between past and present, the modern and the primitive still colour the ways in which many forms of tourism are thought about and analysed. Despite the tendency to think in terms of epochs, such as modernity or indeed postmodernity (see below) there is one important caveat. As with all broad classifications of history, there is a danger of assuming that for instance, modernity not only consisted of a set of definable characteristics, but more importantly, that the application of these characteristics was both universal and simultaneous. The spread of modernity, or for that matter industrial capitalism, was an uneven process, which in turn has consequences in terms of both globalisation and development, issues that will be returned to in the following chapters. For now, I would like to concentrate on the demarcation of work from leisure, a conceptual distinction which was also matched by the demarcation of leisure spaces from work spaces, and how this led in turn to the creation of modern forms of leisure space such as the seaside resorts (Corbin, 1994, Löfgren 1999, Soane 1993). Indeed the pattern that was established in these early years of mass modern tourism is one that still shapes, in part, the form of tourism in contemporary society.

Tourist spaces of modernity

Although it is possible to see the roots of modern tourism in the Grand Tours of the eighteenth century it was the development of the seaside resorts from the early nineteenth century onwards (Urry 1990b, Walton 1983, 1997) that set the dominant pattern for mass tourism. The first resorts became established as watering places for the rich and fashionable gentry and, with the advent of rail travel as day-trip destinations for the urban working classes. Increases in the real value of wages and later, the introduction of statutory holidays which eventually were also paid, meant that the majority of the urban population in the industrialised countries had both the time and means to take a holiday during the year.

The seaside resorts were clearly demarcated from the world of work both spatially, temporally, and in terms of the activities that could be pursued within them. The established pattern that holidays were taken in the summer months, in places which were removed from the world of work, and involved the conspicuous consumption of leisure was thus inextricably linked to the development of capitalism, and also mirrored the social divisions of the time. Particular resorts and destinations were associated with particular social classes. In the UK for example, Brighton was associated with the fashionable metropolitan gentry (Meethan 1996, Shields 1991) while places such as Blackpool and other resorts on the Lancashire coast became the playground for the urban working classes of the mill towns. It was not uncommon, for example, that large groups of factory workers would holiday together in the same way that they both worked and lived together (Benson, 1994: 87). While the wealthier sections of society could afford to stay in hotels, the less well off made do with cheaper lodging houses, so that even within the resorts there were clear spatial divisions that matched those of society in general. Although such patterns were by and large replicated within all the developed economies there were also significant national differences, such as those discussed by Löfgren (1999).

The growth of these seaside spaces of leisure consumption was rapid and by and large unplanned and ad hoc, often the result of speculative entrepreneurship. The urbanisation of resorts followed a radically different pattern to that of the industrialised cities, and were thus physically distinct in a number of respects as much as they were devoted to the pursuit of pleasure. Where national geography restricted access to the coast, inland spa towns and the development of winter sports resorts served much the same purpose, of demarcated spaces of tourism activity. (Corbin 1994, Soane 1993).

During the inter-war years the UK saw the growth of what Walton (1997) has termed 'bungalow towns'. These were largely the result of unplanned and speculative development in which small plots of land were sold, and on which purchasers would build their own bungalows or shacks, many of which were fashioned out of old railway carriages. Permanent, or perhaps more accurately, semi-permanent holiday homes came within the reach of a widening section of society. The appeal of this kind of do-it-yourself holidaymaking appealed, as Walton (1997) notes, to a particular section of society to whom a hankering after the simpler life, with its overtones of bohemian nonconformity and rejection of mass society was the attraction. Again, variations of such developments were found elsewhere, such as in Sweden, while in the USA and Canada, the trend had been to send children away to summer camps (Löfgren 1999).

This form of development was taken in a different direction in the UK and Germany during the 1920s and 1930s with more regimented forms of tourism in the shape of holiday camps (Benson 1994: 87,

Löfgren 1999: 241–5). Within the confines of these camps, all aspects of the holiday were catered for in standardised packages including more or less predetermined patterns of activities, overseen and regulated by the camp attendants (Urry 1990b: 36). The camps were a defined physical and social space deliberately isolated from the surrounding environment, clearly an early form of enclave development. With all needs catered for, there was little incentive for the holidaymakers to venture outside, in effect they were a predictable and risk-free environment, in which others took on responsibility for the provision of entertainment, food and childminding. Overseas travel was beyond the reach of most people, so that these tourist spaces by and large catered for national domestic markets. The development of this particular form of holidaymaking is indicative of modernity in a number of respects, most notably the spatial and social differentiation. A further aspect was the rationalisation into total holiday packages, and the controlling aspects of the camp 'overseers'. All these factors enabled economies of scale, and the holiday camps can therefore be seen as the leisure equivalent of modern, mass factory production.

Theorising tourism and modernity

The development of a specific tourist space then can be seen as a consequence of the differentiation inherent in modernity, of splitting the sphere of work from the sphere of leisure in conceptual, temporal and spatial terms. As I noted above, the first to attempt a serious and contemporary analysis of tourism as a social phenomenon was Dean MacCannell. The central theme of his book is that tourism exemplifies what he terms 'post industrial modernity' (1976: 7) which in turn, is characterised by differentiation, 'fragmentation, discontinuity and alienation that are such features of modern life' (1976: 11). Modernity is seen as the force that disrupts 'real life', that shifts people away from the 'stability of interpersonal relations' found in the 'primitive case where family structure *is* social structure' (MacCannell 1976: 1).

The non-modern, or pre-modern – which by definition is undifferentiated, becomes preserved as a plaything for the modern alienated sightseer, while tourism itself becomes a search for the authentic, the pre-modern and the primitive; a quest for heritage; a ritual response towards the alienation of modernity whose purpose is to reconstruct a 'cultural heritage or a social identity' (MacCannell 1976: 13). The tourist therefore is an alienated modern in search of the 'wholeness and structure absent from everyday contemporary life' (Selwyn 1994: 729). The tourist is not exercising choice or agency, but is rather driven by the external stimulus of modernity to respond in causally predetermined ways. As Cohen points out, analyses of this kind view the modern western tourist as an essential category (1995: 12). As such the formulation is both reductionist and an ideal typification which is seen as being universally applicable. In contrast, Cohen argues that there is no one type of 'tourist', and hence no single mode of tourist experience that may be described as universal. His solution is to propose instead different forms of tourist experiences and tourist types, some of whom may be more alienated than others. However, this does not really solve the problem in that it still accepts the notion that alienation, considered as a requisite condition of modernity, is a motivating factor and secondly, as Selwyn points out, the typologies themselves seem to have been derived as a priori categories rather than stemming from empirical observation (1996: 6).

The notion of tourism as an escape from modernity, viewed as a dystopia fuelled by the inevitable consequences of alienation, in turn gave rise to analyses which conceptualised tourism as a sacred journey, a form of secular pilgrimage directed towards the utopian authentic and primitive (Graburn 1989). This makes a binary distinction between the world of work, seen as everyday and profane, and the world of tourism, seen as different and sacred (but see Edensor (1998) on sites that are both sacred and secular). This conceptualisation is, I feel, rather limiting. The assumption that tourism is in some ways a compensatory mechanism analogous to, if not a substitute for, religious experiences is in itself questionable. Even as a metaphor its utility is rather doubtful, and there is also the problem of accounting for agency and motivation which we find in MacCannell's analysis, that is of ascribing motives to subjects/agents where none may exist. Yet there is evidence that certain forms of tourist experiences do share certain characteristics with religious sites and pilgrimages such as the reverence shown by many visitors to Elvis Presley's grave in Graceland, or to the graves of other cultural icons, or for that matter to monuments and places that encapsulate national values.

A related problem is accounting for pilgrimages themselves. These have long pre-dated the modern world, and should we regard the millions of Muslims who make the Haj to Mecca or the Christians and Jews who undertake pilgrimages to Jerusalem as tourists? Indeed many of these pilgrims may well be insulted at such a suggestion, despite the fact that the World Tourism Organisation (WTO) classifies them as such (Vellas and Bécherel 1995: 5). Even though both religious and secular elements may coexist in certain tourist sites (Din 1989), there is still a difference between those motivated to travel to sacred places out of a sense of duty and obligation, and those motivated to reside temporarily and seasonally on beaches and in resort areas. The notion of tourism as a sacred quest, even if it is subsumed under more secularised forms is conceptually limiting, if not 'banal' (Frow 1997: 65). To accept the basic metaphor – that tourism is to work what the sacred is to the profane (Graburn 1989) – is at best, partial, and at worst, obscures the complex set of relations involved at an individual level in terms of motivations and values, and at a systemic level between the tourists, the tourist industry and tourist–host relationships. The problem is that these approaches, despite attempts to open up the singular category of *the* tourist, still see tourism as the alienated modern's substitute for the real thing, the authentic other, the pristine primitive.

In this sense the analyses briefly described here offer a dystopian vision of modernity. The tourist seeks to recover, or recreate that which has been lost in the processes of differentiation. What is also of interest though, is the way that MacCannell anticipated many of the developments that are currently subsumed under the term postmodern, a concern with image, displacement, and the processes by which cultural forms are decontextualised and recontextualised as a response to the perceived conformity of modernity. However, these are matters that will be dealt with in more detail below. For now I will outline the overall structure of the arguments presented in the forthcoming chapters.

Plan of the book

Chapter two will continue the development of the themes outlined above, by examining the creation of tourist space, and the importance of symbolic value. An understanding of the processes whereby tourist spaces are both created and maintained is crucial to the understanding of tourism as a socially constructed and meaningful activity. It will be argued that since the 1970s the restructuring of the spaces of modernity have resulted in the development of a symbolic economy of space, within which the role of culture and aesthetics has become central. These new spaces are also characterised as spaces of consumption.

Chapter three will examine the global political economy of tourist space. Although, as the preceding chapters will argue, we are now dealing with a symbolic or cultural economy, this is not an entirely abstract concept. It is also important to focus on the ways in which tourism is used as a form of economic and social development, and how this links in to the development of a global economic order. In turn, this requires some analysis of the power relations of the political economy, and the uses of tourism to stimulate economic growth in both the developed and the developing economies.

In chapter four this argument will be developed through a consideration of the growing anthropological and sociological work concerned with the nature of consumption within the advanced capitalist economies of the West as well as across different cultures. It will argue that the commodification argument, despite the criticisms mentioned above, in particular, the implicit assumption that the meaning of commodities are fixed and essential, is crucial to understanding the systemic nature of tourism. It will be argued that the meanings of commodities are in fact more transient and provisional than might first appear.

In chapter five I will deal with the problem of authenticity and heritage. As I noted above, many of the earlier formulations of tourism viewed it as a destroyer of indigenous cultures, but also as a way in which the alienated moderns of the world could redeem their lost past by seeking to find the pre-modern in other cultures, as well as in the recreation of the past in their own culture. It will be argued that the uncritical assumptions that lie behind this form of theorising have seriously hindered a fuller understanding of the cultural processes involved in the development of the symbolic economy of tourism.

This theme is continued in chapter six, which examines arguments concerning the effects of globalisation on the production and consumption of culture. Two main themes can be discerned here. The first argues that globalisation and commodification are resulting in a loss of identity between cultures, which are becoming more homogenised. The second argues that, in contrast, what we see emerging are new forms of culture that are either 'hybrid' or perhaps more accurately, the result of synthesizing diverse elements. This chapter will also examine the role and development of cultural tourism in this process, and argue that cultures need to be conceptualised as dynamic systems, not as collections of self-contained essential characteristics.

Chapter seven will tackle issues of identity in relation to both culture and place, and the themes of place, identity and authenticity will be examined in relation to the socio-cultural effects of tourism development. Drawing on recent ethnographic work, this chapter will examine the complexities involved in the give and take between tourists and the host population, and the ways in which tourism may in fact generate solidarity and cultural cohesiveness among the host population, rather than destroy it.

Chapter eight will offer a final summary, and argue that the development of tourism analysis needs to proceed beyond static concepts that reduce complexity to an essential either/or choice, modernity versus the primitive, the inauthentic versus the authentic, the local versus the global. It will also be argued that tourism is best conceptualised as a global process of commodification and consumption involving flows of people, capital, images and cultures. Unlike most other forms of commodification the site of production is also the site of consumption. Tourists must travel to consume, and what they consume is their destination.

In this chapter I have sketched out the rationale and context of my approach. I have argued that to simply accept eclecticism in tourism analysis is counter-productive and that, despite the diversity of tourism, the approach I am outlining here can adequately account for diversity. In turn this means accounting for the dynamic relations between the macro level of a global tourist system and the micro level of lived experience, and the ways in which these are mediated at a number of levels and in different contexts. I also argued that tourism initially grew from the differentiation of modernity, which in turn involved the creation of specific spaces of consumption. It is this point that will now be examined in more detail in the following chapter.

Chapter 2

Creating Tourist Spaces: from Modernity to Globalisation

Introduction

Tourism creates specific forms of social space. The development of mass tourism resulted in the creation of resort areas given over, not to the pursuit of work, but the pursuit of leisure. This split in effect between 'home' and 'away' can be seen in theoretical terms as a consequence of the differentiation of modernity, of dividing society into discrete areas of social activity which were also mapped out on the actual uses of space. The relationship between forms of social organisation and the way these are worked out in spatial terms is then of fundamental importance to the analysis of tourism as a social phenomenon.

At first sight it may appear that to talk about analysing space in this way means adopting a distinctly geographical approach (Massey and Allen 1984) by examining for example, the pattern and development of tourist resort areas in terms of their evolution (Priestley 1995, Shaw and Willams 1994). Yet the important point here is not so much the physical patterns or typologies of spatial development that can be identified, that is treating space as an abstract and neutral category, but the ways in which these spatial patterns interrelate with socio-cultural values and perceptions. Issues such as these, concerning the relationship between social and spatial forms, have been of growing interdisciplinary concern over the past two decades

(Gregory and Urry 1985, Harvey 1985, 1989b, 1994). Within geography for example, humanistic approaches attempted to address the problems associated with culture and meaning in relation to their spatial elements (Agnew et al. 1984, Gregory 1994, Harvey 1989a, b, 1993, Ley 1985, Soja 1989).

While geographers were beginning to think of space in terms of concepts such as society and culture, sociologists and anthropologists were beginning to pay more attention to the importance of space in social relationships. The former (sociologists) perhaps as a reaction against treating society as if it were an abstraction in the same way that geographers had treated space, while the latter (anthropologists) arguably becoming more aware of the often implicit concern within their discipline concerning the relationship between territoriality and identity (Appadurai 1995, Clifford 1997, Ellen 1988, Lovell 1998). In short, a variety of disciplines were reaching the conclusion that spatial forms could not be divorced from the social elements which gave rise to their formations, and that to analyse society entailed some consideration of the spatial. All theories are of course a product of their times, and there is little doubt that this concern with the relationship between society and space, was prompted in large part by the related processes of economic and spatial restructuring within the advanced industrial economies.

Restructuring space

The resort areas developed as a consequence of modernity, and are linked to the processes of urbanisation and industrialisation, and the creation of both mass markets and mass consumption. As such, they were spatially demarcated both literally and symbolically from the spaces of manufacturing. With the downturn in industrial manufacturing across the developed economies which began in the 1970s, and a sectoral shift into the service economy, together with the globalisation of information technology, new forms of spatial organisation began to emerge which in turn gave rise to new forms of tourist space.

Harvey's analysis (1989a, b, 1993) of the political economy of space summarises many of these changes quite succinctly, and is worth recounting here. First, the relative locations of places within the capitalist system has been altered, places such as the former manufacturing areas are not as secure within this new system as they once were. Secondly, reduced transport costs mean that both production and marketing are now more spatially mobile than had previously been the case so that opportunities for investment are not so tied to particular localities. Investors can thus take advantage of differences in resource qualities and costs between places. Thirdly, this increases competition between places for mobile capital to the extent that the quality of life within a locality, or indeed the quality of the environment can be as much a determining factor in attracting inward investment as any other consideration. Finally, patterns of speculative investment shifted into the construction of spaces to serve both the needs of the service sector, through the building of new office space and provision for the rapidly growing leisure and retail sectors (Harvey 1993: 6–9). This latter factor was also due to the deregulation of global financial markets, and the use of information technology (Castells 1996, Borja et al. 1997). Opportunities for investment were now sought on a global and international stage. The speed at which both money and information could be transferred around the globe meant that manufacturing, which was now serving global markets, could take advantage of the lower production costs that were offered outside the developed economies. It was not only manufacturing that faced such changes as service industries too began to expand and seek new markets beyond the limitations of national boundaries (Daniels 1993: 43). The spatial forms of modernity thus faced a number of challenges.

We can begin to see how these factors came into play in relation to tourism if we examine the restructuring of the resort areas, the changing nature of the urban arena, the development of new tourist-consumption spaces. Since the 1960s the demand for the traditional seaside holiday in the UK has declined year on year, as a result of increasing competition from the Mediterranean resorts (Cooper 1997: 86) a pattern which was also replicated in other European manufacturing regions. In the USA as well, many of the established resorts, in particular hotel complexes that offered a 'total' holiday, fell into terminal decline (Löfgren 1999: 240–59). The traditional resort areas, faced by this flight to the sun, have been forced to face the need to restructure or reinvent themselves (Ashworth and Dietvorst 1995, Shaw and Williams 1994, Williams and Shaw 1997).

The holiday camps, the application of rationalisation to the production and consumption of leisure were also facing decline, changes

which were a response to changing patterns of consumer preferences. The early pattern of holidaymaking, which began in the
Victorian era as day trips, had been transformed by the mid twentieth
century into the common practice of taking an annual two-week
break in the summer months. The dominant pattern was for people
to stay in lodging houses, small hotels or the camps (Löfgren 1999,
Walton 1983). Increasing costs, coupled with the rise in car ownership meant that holidaymakers were not only less tied to one location,
but were also more inclined towards 'do-it-yourself' or self-catering
holidays. In the UK, the percentage of domestic self-catering
holidays rose from 18 per cent in 1965 to 63 per cent in 1991
(Hoseason 1992, cited in Shaw and Williams 1997). In the USA,
the pattern was somewhat different, showing a notable decline in the
traditional two-week break, and the increasing popularity of more
frequent but shorter weekend breaks (Chon and Singh 1995)

Mass tourism, and the domestic tourist spaces of modernity had
not however disappeared, but rather had relocated to the Mediterranean coast, most notably Spain for the European market (Priestley
1995) and Latin America (Chant 1992) and the Caribbean (Gayle and
Goodrich 1993) for the North-American market.

Despite national or even regional differences, the overall trend
shows greater variation in the patterns of holiday consumption. In
particular, the increasing popularity of short off-season breaks, and
the rise of new urban-based forms of tourism, has resulted in a
distinct move away from the mass provision of domestic standard
holidays into more fragmented and diversified markets.

Williams and Shaw (1997) identify some of the important elements
in this process. Although their examples are drawn from the UK
experience, they can also be applied to other countries and regions
with established resorts (Morgan 1998). Williams and Shaw argue that
there was a loss of distinctiveness between places, so that the resorts
began to resemble each other in terms of what they offered. Another
factor was an increase in other forms of tourist attractions, such as
amusement and theme parks, historic properties, museums and urban
heritage. Overseas tourism to the UK, which had been increasing
since the 1960s, also tended to be urban rather than resort based. The
countryside, which had always been defined in opposition to the city,
also came under pressure from increasing numbers of day trippers.

The shifts in the pattern of speculative property investment into
the urban leisure–retail mix outlined above also meant that the resort

areas were disadvantaged. Their infrastructure tended to be based around the movement of people by rail, and the fact that once they had arrived at a resort, they would remain within its confines. As such, they were often ill-equipped to cope with the new more diversified and mobile patterns of holidaymaking. Although some resorts fell into apparent terminal decline (Buck et al. 1988), others were more able to modify and diversify their attractions, or remained untouched by the changes in fashion (Meethan, 1996b,1998). Places such as Bournemouth, Blackpool, Brighton and Torquay still managed to maintain their pre-eminence in the resort hierarchy, partly by expanding into the conference trade. Such trends were not confined to UK resorts, and similar patterns occurred in other advanced economies. For example Atlantic City, New Jersey, which declined from the 1960s onwards, rejuvenated itself in the late 1970s by the introduction of casino gambling which resulted in significant inward investment and a reversal of its downward trend (US Department of Housing and Urban Development 1995), although this upbeat assessment has been challenged (Hannigan 1998: 163–4). In short, within the developed economies the tourist spaces of modernity were under a variety of threats. Competition was no longer between resorts within a domestic market, but between home resorts and overseas destinations. In addition another threat was that posed by the post-industrial cities and regions developing urban and heritage tourism.

Revitalising urban space

The industrial downturn which hit the manufacturing regions and localities of the developed economies during the late 1970s meant that new forms of investment and employment had to be found, and the growing tourism and leisure market began to be viewed as a sector capable of generating new forms of economic growth. The need for local and regional economies to diversify, due to the reasons outlined above, gave rise to the development of new tourist spaces, primarily based on urban heritage attractions (Judd 1995, Judd and Fainstein 1999, Law, C. 1993, Meethan 1996a, Page, 1995). Although many of the larger cities had always attracted tourists, the biggest obstacles were those of perception and image. Holidays were to be taken away from the centres of industrialisation so the divide between work space and leisure space created through the differentiation of modernity was as much conceptual and symbolic as it was actual. Certainly within the UK the idea of places such as Bradford, Scunthorpe and Manchester, all associated with industrialisation and manufacturing, being destinations for tourism was originally received with scepticism in some quarters (Buckley and Witt 1985, 1989). Clearly the general perception of these areas did not square with those of holiday resorts, and the challenge was to reverse this situation, a problem that many US cities also faced (Judd 1995: 167–77).

The successful creation or invention of these new spaces of consumption was itself part of a wider series of changes by which urban living was undergoing a process of revaluation within all the advanced industrial nations. (Bagguley, et al. 1990, M.P. Smith 1988). From the 1930s onwards cities within the developed economies have become increasingly suburbanised, a trend more pronounced in the UK and the anglophone countries such as Australia, Canada, New Zealand and the USA, rather than other European countries where distrust of the city is neither so widespread nor acute. The suburbs became the home of the urban middle class, and many inner city areas fell into a spiral of decline. During the 1970s however, the flight to the suburbs by the middle classes began to undergo a reversal as people began to move back into the inner city areas, which became known as gentrification: 'a process of the middle class replacing the working class; increasing property values; alteration in the built environment and the emergence of a new urban style of life' (Savage and Warde 1993: 80).

This revaluation of urban life coincided with the discovery or invention of heritage and urban conservation movements and the emergence of postmodernism in architecture and design. The importance of such developments for tourism should not be underestimated (Fainstein and Gladstone 1997, Judd and Fainstein 1999, Meethan 1996a, Richards 1996a). For example Zukin (1995, 1998) notes how gentrification led to the development of spaces of urban consumption which in turn are inextricably linked to 'new patterns of leisure, travel and culture' (1998: 825). Among other aspects Zukin notes how gentrification is in part a middle class desire for authenticity that emphasised an urban aesthetic of the past (1998: 831). Old properties were restored as near as possible to their original design both internally and externally which can be seen as a reaction against the perceived uniformity of mid twentieth-century architecture (which is what most people refer to as 'modern') and even to modernity itself. Such processes could also be identified in rural areas (Fees 1996, Lindknud 1998) where the problem of second-home and holiday-home ownership often became a contentious issue.

In some respects gentrification seemed to offer a solution to the problems of decaying housing stock, but the revaluation of urban space that it entailed also gave rise to new investment opportunities in the cities. The reverence for historical restoration and authenticity was more than a domestic affair. Indeed during the late 1970s and into the 1980s it became the dominant aesthetic form in public architecture, and consequently, had a considerable impact on urban design and management, which has been referred to as the 're-imagining' of the city (Ley 1989). The redundant spaces of modernity – factories, warehouses and so on, were revalued not only in terms of their newly discovered aesthetic appeal, but also for the new investment opportunities they provided for the growing leisure/tourism market. This was also a phenomenon found in all the developed economies. For example, waterfront redevelopments in the declining port cities (Hoyle et al. 1988, Judd 1995) involved the provision of new urban spaces of leisure and consumption such as those found in Liverpool (Mellor 1991) Boston (Ehrlich and Dreier 1999) Toronto (Cooper, M. 1993) which in many cases, were also linked to housing developments Sieber (1993).

Ehrlich and Dreier's comprehensive account of the development of Boston as a major urban attraction is an interesting example. Both the economy and the population of the city went into decline during the 1960s. Redevelopment tended to follow the standard pattern of the time, aptly described as 'bulldozer development' (Ehrlich and Dreier 1999: 166) in which the redundant infrastructure was simply demolished and replaced. However, such an approach began to be resisted through the formation of civic action groups, which sought to preserve the historic fabric of the city and its public spaces. The result of such action was that certain residential areas became listed in the National Register, which meant that redevelopment could not proceed without public review. Although gentrification played a role, in that we can surmise that many of these actions were by people protecting their property interests, the net result was a revaluation of urban space. Older residential districts were no longer viewed as redundant anachronisms, but rather as having value because of their historical nature. Regeneration, rather than relying on wholesale demolition and rebuilding, began to take such concerns into account.

The Faneuil Hall market area, opened in 1976, was designed as a retail area to entice shoppers back into the city centre. Interestingly, it was first thought that tourism would constitute a threat to this development, as it would 'push the merchandising toward frivolousness and sameness' (Ehrlich and Dreier 1999: 171). Twenty years after it was opened, the marketplace is the most visited attraction in the city, with tourists accounting for over one third of its customers, who provide over half the total revenue (1999: 176).

Although the specifics of the situation described here are somewhat unique, the same general pattern can be found in urban areas around the globe. What is important here is the way that the more intangible aesthetic elements of place became commodified for the purposes of economic growth, heritage and the general quality of the urban environment became added value to attract inward investment. The redevelopment of decaying urban areas into showpieces of urban consumerism also demonstrates the emergence and importance of what has been termed the tourism–shopping mix, a blurring of the boundaries between leisure and other pursuits. This became one of the principal means by which urban areas sought to regenerate their economic fortunes throughout the 1980s and 1990s. No urban area it seems can be complete without the ubiquitous shopping mall or entertainment complex. This also indicates a shift in perceptions concerning the urban form in that the problems of dealing with a decaying infrastructure were turned into opportunities for growth and development. Hannigan (1998) for example, examines developments in cities such as Baltimore, Honolulu, Miami, Boston, Milwaukee, New York, Norfolk Virginia, and St Louis. While Zukin notes that the fastest growing metropolitan areas in the USA, Las Vegas, Nevada and Orlando are also 'major tourist destinations' (Zukin 1998: 832). What all these geographically diverse examples have in common in addition to this recycling of the past was the fact that they were financed through speculative capital, and also involved the development of new forms of urban management utilising public–private partnerships. Forms of urban management began to shift away from notions of social provision for the inhabitants into more entrepreneurial forms stressing investment for wealth creation (Harvey 1993, Healey et al. 1995, Judd and Parkinson 1990, M.P.Smith 1988). Searching for new investment meant selling places, and place marketing or civic boosterism, as it became known in the USA, became common practice in all the developed economies (Frey

1994, Healey et al. 1995, Kearns and Philo 1993). Competition between places for investment as well as in the tourist markets became globalised (Gordon 1999).

These places differed from the previous pattern of tourism development in a number of ways. What they could offer in terms of tourism was not so much a substitute for the main holiday, but rather day trips and short weekend breaks. As I have noted, the single annual holiday was beginning to be supplanted by new patterns of consumption, and more specialised forms of niche marketing (Holcomb 1999: 63). Although the dominant trend was for the recycling of the past, many urban areas also embarked on prestige or flagship developments (Smyth 1994) which could include hosting large-scale events such as the Expo '86 exhibition held in Vancouver (Beazley et al. 1997) or the staging of prestige world sporting events or other 'mega events' (Roche 1996) such as the Olympic games (Holcomb 1999, Waitt 1999).

It was not only the physical environment that was regarded as an asset to attract inward investment. Many cities also embarked on cultural programmes as part of their sales pitch (Bianchini and Parkinson 1993). For example Le Galès (1993) describes how the French city of Rennes embarked on an ambitious regeneration programme designed in part to project itself as a city of commerce and culture. Booth and Boyle (1993) record the same processes in Glasgow and Atkinson (1997) also shows how tourism became a major sector in the New Orleans economy during the 1980s. Zukin (1995) also draws attention to the ways in which the economy of high culture and the arts is used in an instrumental fashion to enhance the appeal of certain spaces to speculative investors.

The revaluation of urban space also encompassed what can be termed historic cities, (Ashworth and Tunbridge 1990) whose appeal, in these heritage conscious times, was the fact that they had avoided the perceived depredations of industrialisation. Even though these tended to be viewed as places apart from modernity, the same processes of spatial commodification are evident (Meethan 1996b). These changes were not simply confined to the developed economies but are also evident in may of the newly industrialised economies of the third world, and more recently, the countries of eastern Europe (Burns 1998, Go 1997, Hall, D.R. 1991)

It is clear that the rediscovery or revaluation of urbanism which began as gentrification has had profound effects not only on the pattern of life and culture within cities, but also in terms of the opportunities it offers for new forms of tourism. Urban-based tourism is certainly better placed than the resorts to offer short-break holidays, better placed to develop the mix of leisure pursuits such as shopping and sightseeing, and therefore less likely to suffer from the effects of seasonality which affected the traditional resorts. What we see emerging then, are new forms of spatial development linked in turn to new forms of consumption which involve a revaluation of urban space, and new forms of spatial differentiation. The modernist spaces of mass tourism and mass consumption are giving way to a more diverse and fragmented situation. Although we can see that such developments are clearly linked to the political economy, and the need for economic diversification, one question immediately presents itself: that is, are we witnessing a shift from modernist to postmodernist forms of spatial development?

Postmodernism, place and aesthetics

Postmodernism is at the best of times, a rather confusing if not contradictory label. As Lyon notes, it can be seen as an idea, a cultural experience, a social condition or even a combination of all these elements (1999: 6). I do not think that much will be gained by entering the thickets of confusion that often surround this contentious term (Rose 1991). For the purposes of the arguments to be advanced here it is sufficient to draw out some of the main issues in relation to the production of space.

The term itself presupposes a break with the past. Generally this hinges on the notion that whereas modernity was characterised by differentiation, standardisation and hierarchical notions of taste and judgement, the condition of postmodernism is one where these characteristics are 'challenged' or even inverted. Norms, standards and hierarchies are no longer correct or incorrect but different and diverse. Now there certainly is a case to be made that within the field of cultural production this is an accurate description of certain trends, postmodernism seemingly reverses or de-differentiates what preceded it (Kumar 1995: 117). The development of new tourist spaces that recycle elements of the past, and pastiches of other cultures, such as those offered in Las Vegas and the Disney theme parks (Hannigan 1998, Zukin 1995) would seem evidence enough.

Space is no longer governed by a hierarchy of uses and functions in which the sphere of leisure is differentiated from the sphere of work. This hierarchy has been replaced with a more fragmented and less uniform pattern of spatial differentiation. In turn, this has been matched by consequent changes in patterns of consumer preferences, within which diversity, difference and eclecticism appear to be the key elements. Now whether or not such changes are accepted as evidence of a new epoch or not, their importance in terms of the production and uses of space cannot be discounted.

In particular, what needs consideration at this point are the ways in which space has the capacity to embody sets of values from which people derive significance and meaning. In this regard we only need to think of the ways in which the concepts of 'home' and 'away' are linked to specific forms of place, attachment, and indeed the pursuit of tourist leisure. It is also clear that the changes to the urban form across the industrialised economies described above are changes which are as much about the symbolic, that is, concerned with meaning, as a result of material and economic processes (du Gay 1997, Fainstein and Gladstone 1997, Harvey 1994, Zukin 1995, 1998). The commodification of place that revalues heritage and culture to attract investment as well as catering for tourist markets has led to what Zukin has termed a symbolic economy of space, which she describes as follows:

> the symbolic economy features two parallel production systems that are crucial to a city's material life: the *production of space*, with its synergy of capital investment and cultural meanings, and the *production of symbols*, which constructs both a currency of commercial exchange and a language of social identity (Zukin 1995: 23–4).

What Zukin is drawing attention to here is the interrelationship between the material and the symbolic, between the urban form and the meanings that are derived from it. In turn this involves the creation of coherent spatial representations or narratives which create or manipulate new patterns of consumption involving the leisure–culture–tourism nexus (Hannigan 1998, Meethan 1996a, b, Zukin 1990, 1995, 1998). But before these matters are pursued in greater detail, some initial definitions need to be made, particularly in relation to what constitutes the symbolic. For the purposes of the argument to be advanced here, symbols will be defined as forms of collective representation that act as common reference points even if this is restricted to small groups. They are in this sense inclusive, but also exclusive. Defining who you are is as much a case of defining who you are different from. Symbols also are multivocal, that is they have the capacity to carry a range of different, if not ambiguous, and contradictory meanings so that, for example, a symbol of freedom to one group may be a symbol of oppression to another. In this sense we can say that symbols are far from being neutral. Indeed, they often act as the focus for contestation or, as Harvey puts it, struggles over representation are as 'fiercely fought' as those over material resources (1993: 23). The symbolic system is therefore a system of communication, embodied in material form which can define and express social positions and distinctions (Bourdieu 1984). Although symbolic systems are modes of communication, these are not always fully articulated in the sense that languages are, rather they tend to function as condensed metaphors from which a variety of different meanings can be derived.

Take monuments for example: often built with the express intent of enshrining power, they are also part and parcel of the tourist trail. As Lefebvre notes, such spaces act as a collection of possibilities out of which new readings can be constructed, an '*horizon of meaning*: a specific or indefinite multiplicity of meanings, a shifting hierarchy in which one, now another meaning comes momentarily to the fore' (Lefebvre 1991: 222). I would suggest that space has always had the capacity for use in this way, to delimit and define the basic parameters and values of a society encoded in symbolic forms (Hannigan 1998, Rotenberg and McDonogh 1993). Such meanings though are neither fixed nor timeless. Symbolic differentiation also provides the tourist industry with the raw materials out of which tourist space can be constructed. Yet the importance of this symbolic realm is not simply that it is value added, or the icing on the cake as it were. This is not just superstructure, in the Marxist sense of the word, as the consequence of economic changes. Rather, the realm of the symbolic is in itself an integral causal factor (du Gay 1997, Fainstein and Gladstone 1997).

We can see how this works out in relation to the changes in the urban form described above. The processes of urban revaluation were in part economic, but also in part symbolic. The quality of urban life itself, expressed through gentrification and the revaluation of past architectural styles, and the development of new urban spaces of consumption came to symbolise a new urban order. This was one dominated by a new aesthetic that arguably expressed new forms of social division. In turn, this had the effect of creating new urban spaces, such as gentrified areas, which were linked to the rise of new consumption classes (Zukin 1995,1998). The high tide of modernist architecture for example, has given way to a variety of styles that offer pastiche and stylised reconstructions of imaginary other places and other times: themed shopping malls, amusement parks, pubs and other spaces of consumption (Hannigan 1998, Zukin 1995). Modernist uniformity is out, and postmodern difference is in, and as Featherstone comments, this is part of 'the concern for style, the stylization of life, the "no rules only choices" slogan of the ever-renewable lifestyle' (Featherstone 1991: 48). Such changes are both material and symbolic, and rather than seeking to reduce one to the other, both are better conceptualised as existing in a dialectical relationship to each other.

It may be tempting then to see the changes described above as conclusive evidence that we have indeed entered a new era of post-modernity. Modernism it would seem has run its course, what has replaced it is a recycling of both the past and indeed other cultures, a condition of 'hyperreality' (Hannigan 1998: 4) within which the distinction between objects and their representations is dissolved leaving everything free-floating as if 'The quest for some division between the real and the unreal, or even the true and the untrue, or the moral and the immoral, is futile' (Lyon 1999: 21). Yet such claims need to be treated with a caution. For example, Savage et al. point out that in the UK the 'audience' for postmodern culture is 'some kind of middle-class phenomenon' (1992: 129) primarily composed of urban middle-class professionals rather than a more generalized one. Yet there is little doubt that, in terms of artistic or cultural production, the emergence of postmodernism grew out of disenchantment with the totalising aesthetics of modernism. There is indeed a blurring of boundaries between what was considered to be high and low culture. The notion of the singular work of art or architecture, as the product of the lone individual, has given way to parodies and pastiches combining different styles from different epochs and from different cultures, in a seemingly inexhaustible globalised pick 'n' mix of symbolic forms.

To some, this 'end' of modernism is to be welcomed (Ley 1989). As Robins writes, many of those who espouse the cause of postmodern urbanism for example, view it as being concerned with 'the renaissance of tradition and reenchantment of place' (Robins 1993: 306). Postmodernism then appears to free us from the dead hand of uniformity, the 'disenchantment' of modernity so gloomily predicted by Weber (Craib 1997: 19). Whether or not such changes are to be welcomed or deplored is not the issue here. The important point to be taken from all this is that the processes of spatial commodification have involved the development of a new aesthetic, which in some ways constitutes a break with the past, if only because the processes of commodification have extended further into the realm of popular styles. There is also a need to be careful of assuming that the spaces of modernity were somehow devoid of any aesthetic value at all. This is far from being the case. Like many of the assertions concerning postmodernism, it is more a question of degree than of kind. To say for example that the new urban spaces of consumption are now aestheticised perhaps ignores the ways in which Victorian cities were embellished by the provision of parks, public buildings and so on, and designed in part as a display of civic pride and wealth (Barber, 1982, P. Hall, 1988, Machor 1987) Rather, they are aestheticised in a different way, in contrast to the aesthetic concerns of modernism (Rose 1991: 5).

There is no doubt that such concerns have now become more democratised and less elitist in their preoccupations, and that the development of urban areas as sites of leisure consumption has reached a new intensity. The motivations for civic embellishment have changed, it is now a matter of economic necessity for places to commodify their aesthetic attributes, which then become assets to be capitalised and exploited in the rush for growth, of which tourism is one element (Judd 1995, Judd and Fainstein 1999). In turn, this intensification of the relationship between the symbolic and the economic is no longer confined within the boundaries of nation states for internal markets, but is being fought out on a global scale.

Are such developments then, indicative of wider changes in the conceptual orientation of societies or simply the latest stylistic fad? In terms of cultural production postmodernism can indeed be fun, witty and ironic, even if ultimately parasitic. However to accept it as a form of cultural production is one thing, to accept it as an epochal shift in consciousness is another. As Elliott points out, many of the arguments made for the emergence of a postmodern era hinge on a rejection of the 'narratives' of modernity, that is, reason, science and progress, which have not delivered what they promised. As a result, modernity has become discredited (Elliott 1999: 25). To think in this way is to reject the notion that the social world can be explained in terms of universal and essential characteristics, as a quest for the unassailable truth which, in turn, is to be discovered through methods that mimic the natural sciences. Rather the focus should be on the ways in which the social world is constructed through symbolic forms. What is of prime importance are questions of social meaning, of the ways in which the social world is narrated. In turn, these are not universal categories but are specific to the places and times in which they are created. Now while I have sympathy with such approaches, which in many ways have extended the bounds of social theory, the problem lies in accepting that this is all there is. By either rejecting or underplaying the role of the political economy in favour of symbolic forms, postmodern theorising of the kind advocated by Baudrillard (1988) for example, fails to address relations between the material and the symbolic.

The definitional problems of postmodernism aside, what is certain is that we cannot conceptualise space as an abstract category, nor as an empty container in which life is organised. Instead, we need to consider it as an integral aspect of any society or culture. The uses of space can be seen as one way in which the social and cultural divisions of a society are rendered visible (Bagguley et al. 1990). If this is then coupled with the search for constructed meanings, rather than essential truths, it may appear that spatial forms can be 'read' in much the same way that a text can be. It is something to be decoded, and this decoding of space will in turn render visible underlying value systems. (Gottdeiner and Lagopoulus 1986, Lagopoulus, 1993, Rotenberg and McDonogh, 1993, Shields, 1991, Urry 1995).

One example concerns the actual use of space (Skeggs 1999). Drawing on the work of Bourdieu and Zukin, Skeggs notes that the use of leisure space involves forms of symbolic closure that precludes some groups from access. This can involve differences of gender (see also Massey 1994, McDowell 1999) ethnicity and sexuality, which are constructed not only through representational forms but also through lived experiences. People become aware of where they can and cannot go, what spaces are considered to be safe and dangerous, or the homes of others into which one should not intrude. It is also possible to extend the arguments here to encompass forms of tourist space, which are visually marked as being distinct through the creation of representations and symbols, or what Urry (1990b) termed the 'tourist gaze'.

The production of such representations is of central importance to the tourist industry, not just for the new urban destinations, but also for the more established traditional resort areas. Also, as I noted earlier, to embark on a holiday is to place trust in the coordination of people across space and time, but this trust also extends to the ways in which the destination measures up to the expectations of the tourists, to the ways in which the actual place coincides with its image. Discounting for the moment repeat visitors, each trip away from home is hedged to some degree by uncertainty. The representations of places produced by and for the tourist industry, to which we would also have to add the genres of travel writing, TV programmes and the like, are in some ways attempts to remove this uncertainty, to inform the potential visitor of what they will, or at least may, experience. At a rather general level, it is possible to view these representations as forms of social control of a rather diffuse kind. For example, both Dann (1996) and Selwyn (1993) show how representations of tourist destinations rely on certain culturally based stereotypes and received images. Now whether or not tourists actually perceive these in the same way is open to question. As Dann comments, the projected image is but the first step, which 'remains to be confirmed or invalidated by experience' (1996: 79).

In terms of analysis one problem here is that these representations can only be decoded as it were, if those who do the gazing possess the same stock of shared knowledge, have access to the same symbolic code and, moreover, draw the same conclusions. Just as there is more than one way to read a book, there is more than one way to read a place. Consumers, as I shall argue below, are not simply passive recipients. This is not to say that in analytical terms generalised forms of interpretation are impossible, but rather this requires a thorough grounding and contextualisation, and therefore we should not elevate or privilege the discourse or the forms of representation above other factors. What are important are their material realisation and the social practices, which they inform. In turn, this relates to a further problem, that of accounting for both intent and change. There is no doubt that in some cases there are attempts to deliberately communicate some intended meaning through the environment, but other meanings may well result not from deliberate intent, but from historically contingent circumstances.

Let me explain this by extending my earlier example concerning monuments. These may appear to be specifically concerned with conveying a clear and intelligible message. In turn, this may well be in a form that conceals the nature of power involved (Lefebvre 1991:143), or is a deliberate attempt to produce consensus, where conflict might exist, by providing a visible focus for collective identity. (Gillis 1994). Yet we also have to consider the possibility that over time the intended message or reading, that is, the symbolic component, has become redundant, or overlaid with new significance, or is open to a variety of conflicting interpretations at any one time. Edensor's (1998) study of tourism at the Taj Mahal shows how conflicting, and at times contradictory, readings could be encoded by the same architectural form. We can also see in relation to the medieval cathedrals of Europe, how the significance of these has changed from being places of reverence and worship, into places for the visual consumption of history by tourists. We can therefore say that spaces cannot be reduced to one 'code' or 'discourse' with prescribed meanings, even if this was intended. This latter point is, I think, of crucial significance. The values and meanings ascribed to space can only maintain their value if they are constantly remade for, as Sahlins has noted, each reproduction of a cultural system is a dialogue between received categories (the past) and contingent circumstances (the present) in which meanings are always 'at risk' (Sahlins 1987: 144). No space vanishes, rather each addition, each interpretation reorganises and redirects what is there. This can be seen in terms of gentrification and the revaluation of urban space, where the reinterpretation of problem areas into areas of opportunity changed both the economic and symbolic valuation of place. By the same token, the development of these new spaces of urban consumption contributed to a devaluation of the traditional resort areas.

Although we can point to the new patterns of more fragmented leisure consumption linked to new uses of space, and the importance of the symbolic realm in creating distinct places, the claims that we are in a period of postmodernity look somewhat over inflated. The pattern of tourist consumption established in modernity has far from vanished, rather it has shifted its location in two significant ways. First, like many forms of modern production, it has moved away from the developed economies to places that can offer some competitive advantage. These may include a more predictable climate and environment of sun, sand and sea, as well perhaps as favourable foreign exchange rates and local wage levels attractive to the tourism entrepreneurs. Secondly, it has moved away from resorts and into urban areas that, in turn, is a development relating to changing patterns of consumption. In both these ways, tourism is no different from other forms of commercial activity that seek competitive advantage in response to change. The fact that the same general trends are to be found in all the developed economies can be taken to indicate that rather than signifying a new conceptual break with the past, postmodernity 'may instead form part of a continuous modernist tradition' (Fainstein and Gladstone 1997: 130). Or as Callinicos rhetorically states:

> Has the dialectic of modernity been transcended thanks to our entry into a postmodern condition constituted by the collapse of the 'grand narratives' which offer comprehensive interpretations of the totality of human history? The short answer to this question is 'No' (Callinicos 1999: 296).

There is no need to pursue this line of reasoning any further at this particular point, other than to state that there is more than one way to account for the problem of meanings and the symbolic order, and indeed the socially constructed nature of meanings other than resorting to postmodernism (Kuper 1999). What is of importance for the purpose of the argument being advanced here are the ways in which values and meanings are both created in and derived from spatial formations, and the ways in which symbolic systems are commodified. Neither is the symbolic realm a free-floating entity which exists over and above the material conditions out of which it is constructed. If we are to talk of shifts from one mode of production to another or from one dominant organising principal to another, it is to be found, I would suggest, not in the endless rhetorical regression or hyperbolic posturing of postmodernism, but rather in the processes referred to as globalisation.

Globalisation

One of the great clichés about tourism is the apparently unassailable fact that its worldwide growth is increasing at an exponential rate, and as Held et al. point out, it is one of the 'most obvious forms of globalization' (1999: 360). Yet some thought therefore needs to be paid to initial definitions if only to avoid falling into a naive empiricism, of accepting globalisation as a self-evident and unproblematic state of affairs. Also, whereas we can generalise about modernity, we can do this with the benefit of hindsight. As Amin and Thrift (1994) argue, there is no one theory of globalisation, rather a set of concerns which involve the apparent withering away of the nation state, the rise of transnational corporations, and the spread of new technologies and electronic broadcast media. Despite these words of caution, at a base level it is possible to characterise globalisation as the increasing interconnections – economic, social and cultural – that now exist across national boundaries, and which are also impinging more and more upon the daily lives of people around the world.

As I noted in chapter one, the trajectory of modernity, or the processes of modernisation, was one of differentiation that was, by and large, organised within the boundaries of the nation state, conditions which are now beginning to be superseded. The capacity for capital to move almost instantaneously from one part of the globe to another reorders the ways in which economic relations are both conceptualised and consequently organised. Indeed, it is precisely this compression of space and time, which leads Scott (1997), for example, to argue that globalisation needs to be distinguished from both modernisation and colonialism. Globalisation therefore is not merely the sum of international or transnational connections between places, but rather implies a different order of relationships structured across space and time. As noted above, the restructuring of space was in part a response to the globalisation of economics beyond the confines of the nation state. The new urban aesthetic often involves the incorporation of commodified symbolic forms of other cultures while tourism itself involves at some level the commodification of places and, of course, the large-scale movement of people across national boundaries.

The rise of transnational corporations as major economic forces, not specifically tied to nations states, and the emergence of large-scale trading blocs such as the European Union (EU) may give the appearance that the nation state is in decline. Yet as Sklair points out, the concept of globalisation does not ignore the state, but rather adds an extra dimension of transnational practices (1994b: 167). Scholte (1996) also argues that in this respect, the state is still an important player in terms of the political economy and the competition for investment that is now fought out on an international stage (Gordon 1999). In short, globalisation implies increasing interconnectivity, increasing economic 'depth' and the extension of commodity relations into realms which were previously seen as free from such influences. Both Hoogvelt (1997) and Robertson (1995) also draw attention to the development of shared phenomenal worlds, which refers to the ways in which a form of 'global consciousness' is emerging. In other words, people are more likely than before to conceptualise economic and social relations on a global scale, for example on relation to issues of social justice, human rights and environmental issues, all of which impinge in some ways on the current patterns of tourism supply and demand, as will be discussed in the following chapters.

From this rather brief account we can see that, since the late 1970s, there have been profound changes to what we might term the global system, and in turn, we can also see how these are related to the restructuring of space as outlined at the start of this chapter. What is important in terms of tourism is that these global flows of information, capital, people and cultures are realised in specific socio-spatial forms as the development of new networks of places, and the emergence of new spaces of consumption. These are important in two ways. First, the internationalisation of businesses such as airlines, hotel chains and tour operators (Daniels 1993) that have facilitated the growth in long-haul and overseas tourism. Secondly, the impact of new technologies in facilitating both the movement of capital and people such as the development of airline and hotel-booking reservation systems (Poon 1993) and the transmission of images of people and places by satellite TV and the internet. Yet although there are clearly large-scale global processes at work here, tourism is also about the local, the specific nature of places, people and cultures

One of the notable aspects of globalisation has been the reassertion of the region or locality as the basis for social interaction and focus of both political and social identity. Such processes can also be seen to be pulling in two apparently different and arguably contradictory ways. As globalisation involves increasing interconnectivity, increasing economic 'depth', and the extension of commodity relations, it may appear that the local is therefore being subsumed into a wider economic framework. Now, in many cases it is undeniable that this is occurring. In turn, this relates to what was described in chapter one as the displacement of the local, and the extraction of social relations from both space and time. Globalisation, then, may appear as a logical continuation of such changes on a wider geographical scale. Yet the revaluation of space was also, to some degree, a reassertion of the local. Places were conserved and valued because they had avoided the depredations of modernist forms of development. So while, on the one hand, we have the rise of global forms of economic ordering, on the other, it would also appear that the local is also being reinforced, if not assuming a greater degree of prominence (Amin and Thrift 1994, Meyer and Gerschiere 1999).

A symbolic economy of space

One way of developing an analytical framework to encompass the political, economic, symbolic and the social can be found in the theoretical work of Henri Lefebvre (1991, 1996) and subsequent analyses developed from his framework (Harvey, 1989a, b, Urry 1995). Lefebvre's major work *The Production of Space* is an ambitious and complex attempt to avoid reducing the conceptualisation of space to either a container within which social activity occurs, or a philosophical abstraction (1991: 26–7).

Lefebvre makes a three-fold distinction in his analysis between spatial practice, representations of space and representational spaces. Spatial practice is concerned with 'production and reproduction, and the particular locations and spatial sets of characteristic of each social formation' (Lefebvre 1991: 33). Spatial practices then are the realm of the economic, in the strict sense of that term. They are the factors that determine in part the uses of space and their accompanying social formations. For example, the development of resorts as distinct places of leisure consumption can be seen as an aspect of the differentiation of modernity. In this sense we can then talk of the spaces of modernity as particular forms of spatial practice, as well as considering the new forms of globalisation as giving rise to new spatial practices.

Representations of space are the space of 'planners, urbanists, technocratic subdividers and social engineers' which tend 'towards a system of verbal (and therefore intellectually worked out) signs' (Lefebvre 1991: 38). What Lefebvre is drawing attention to here are the ways in which spaces are conceptualised in terms of policies and planning, as much as those of various academic disciplines. The most significant point here is that of bureaucratic management, that is, attempts to control, direct or mediate the dominant form of spatial practice. In terms of tourism this would encompass not only policy-makers at a variety of spatial scales – national, regional and local – but also the workings of tourism transnationals. It is also at this level that we could locate the production of certain forms of narratives which encapsulate selected readings of the environment, as in promotional literature, brochures, itineraries and so on.

The final element of this triad, representational spaces, is concerned with its inhabitants and users, 'space as directly *lived* through its associated images and symbols [which]... tend towards more or less coherent systems of non verbal symbols and signs' (Lefebvre 1991: 39). In other words, representational spaces are those which are partly imagined, and which can provide the focus for identity. In terms of tourism space this would encompass sets of values and meanings, the symbolic element that is derived from the experiences of tourists as much as the inhabitants. It is these systems, derived from lived experience, which in turn are the raw materials that are commodified to produce tourist space. It is also at this level that struggles over the symbolic construction of space are struggles to objectify meanings, to impose upon, or appropriate from the environment a particular order, a dynamic process of contestation and appropriation through which particular interests are maintained and legitimised.

In terms of the overall production of tourist space, the triad can be applied as follows. Within the restrictions of the global economy, policies and marketing strategies assign symbolic and aesthetic value to the material attributes of space. In turn, these representations or narratives of people and place assume an exchange value as the objects of consumption becoming commodities to be traded and consumed in the same way as the material services and goods which are associated with them. Such changes also impinge on, and are affected by, changes in localised practices, The development of tourist space means change at the level of lived experience for those whose space of home, or of work, is the space of leisure for others. The production of tourist space therefore involves the material environment and the socio-economic circumstances which give rise to its form as well as encapsulating symbolic orders of meaning for both hosts as much as guests. What is at stake here are different forms of knowledge, different ways of thinking about the organisation of the social world and people within it and different ways of deriving meaning from the environment.

A distinct advantage of Lefebvre's three-fold distinction is that it conceptualises the production and consumption of space as a continuous and dynamic process of interaction and change at both a macro and micro level, without reducing one to the other. At the same time, this formulation can also account for the specificity and importance of local relations and the capacity of people to think and act. That is, it allows for the symbolic and imaginary nature of spatial formations, the gazes of tourism, and the forms of knowledge they generate, and indeed the localised forms of knowledge that permeate daily life, to be taken into account without separating them off from broader issues concerning the political economy, and the management and control of space. It also means that the realm of the imaginary, of representations should not be idealised as either discourse or 'text' existing above and beyond material practices.

This latter point is the most important. Lefebvre's theoretical approach is concerned with the realisation of socio-spatial relations as a form of practice, for, as he comments, this triad 'loses all force if it is treated as an abstract "model". If it cannot grasp the concrete...then its import is severely limited' (Lefebvre 1991: 40) That is to say, the production and consumption of space cannot be reduced to a mere side effect of society or culture, and must be grasped through the practices that give rise to it. Another advantage is that this formulation, which sees the production of space as a continuous process of change and adaptation, avoids many of the problems of analysing space and indeed tourism as comprising of a set of either/or choices which, as the following chapters will demonstrate, appears to be a common feature.

To analyse space then means focusing on the material production of places, of sites, of economic and social practices as much as the symbols and representations they give rise to, and which are also derived from them. (Harvey 1989a, b, 1993, Lefebvre 1991, 1996). Such an analytical framework implies a similarity, or homology, between the realm of socio-economics – capital and commodities – and that of communication – signs and symbols – both of which can be conceptualised in terms of production – circulation – and consumption. The construction of space therefore involves the production and circulation of commodities which are both material and symbolic (Bourdieu 1984, Baudrillard 1988, Harvey 1989a, b, Featherstone 1991, Lagopoulus 1993, Zukin 1995).

Conclusion

Accounting for the importance of space and the related problem of meaning in the environment is a complex undertaking. As I have been arguing, although it is possible to see many of the changes outlined here in terms of the political or global economy, I have argued too that the aesthetics of place are also a major factor in the commodification of space. I also outlined the idea that these changes could be accounted for by seeing the production of space as a form of symbolic economy. As this chapter has shown, patterns of leisure and tourism have changed significantly in the past two decades. We can point to an increase in day trips, short breaks and the flight to the sun; the decline of seaside resorts and the growth of new spaces of consumption, all of which have had their impact on the creation and maintenance of tourism. To talk of tourist space as if it were a single form of spatial production would only underplay the complexities involved in both its conceptualisation at a theoretical level and its realisation in specific forms.

The interrelation between spatial and social structures also requires approaches that can account for the ways in which values are both imposed upon, and derived from the environment, in other words, a symbolic system. As I have pointed out, this can be conceptualised as a shift from modernity to postmodernity yet as I have argued, there is a danger here of reducing the complexities of spatial formation and consumption to a culturally determined and reified set of 'readings'. This is not to say that the environment cannot therefore be 'decoded', nor that, for example, tour operators and others select aspects of the environment to be valued. In turn, this is carried out through a socially determined set of practices, that Urry identified as the tourist gaze. Rather, it is to draw attention to other related material processes that are just as salient. It is also clear from the above that the recent socio-spatial reorganisation evident throughout the world is bound up with the globalisation of capital, the development of information technologies and mass transport. Yet it is not just capital that has become more globalised. Cultures and people too are also more mobile than at any previous time in history.

Finally, the arguments advanced in this chapter can be summarised as a set of interlinked propositions as follows: first, the material order of space is also a social order that encapsulates both material and symbolic elements. Secondly, tourism is irreducibly associated with the production and consumption of specific socio-spatial forms. Thirdly, the production of tourist spaces is a general process of commodification mediated at various spatial and institutional levels, from the global and transnational to the national, regional and local. Lastly, such processes need to be considered as dynamic systems of change. In the next chapter, these issues will be addressed in terms of the globalisation of the political economy in relation to tourism development.

Chapter 3

Tourism Development and the Political Economy

Introduction

The development of tourism spaces can be viewed as part of a more general process of modernity, of the increasing differentiation of functions in both space and time. In the previous chapter I drew attention to the processes of spatial restructuring in the advanced capitalist economies, and how many of the developments associated with the revaluation of space tended to be analysed in terms of the values and meanings that are derived from spatial formations. Many of these arguments were seen to be rooted in what has been termed the shift from modernism to postmodernism, and I also criticised some of these approaches for paying insufficient attention to the ways in which economic processes shape the form of spatial development and the creation of tourism spaces. I argued that by applying Lefebvre's analytical triad, it is possible to account for production of space as a dynamic process which encompasses both material and symbolic elements without reducing one to the other. Finally, I suggested that the exponential growth of tourism in terms of its geographical spread as much as the numbers involved may appear as evidence for what is commonly referred to as globalisation. This chapter will examine the production of tourist space in relation to the global spread of capitalism and the role of the political economy. In other words, it will focus on the spatial practices of global capitalism

41

and their relationship to the forms and patterns of tourist development.

Tourism: modernisation or underdevelopment?

The restructuring of global space is in part the result of changes to the pattern of economic growth and investment which is now played out on a global scale. Spatial practices are no longer confined within the boundaries of nation states, and tourism is no exception. It was during the late 1960s that tourism, as a distinct form of development, first emerged on the global stage (de Kadt 1979). Initially, this involved a shift from the developed economies into the less developed countries (LDCs) in Latin America (Chant 1992) and the Caribbean (Gayle and Goodrich 1993) as well as the more economically peripheral European economies such as Greece (Leontidou 1990) and Spain (Pearce 1989).

In the initial stages of its global spread, tourism, as much as many other forms of economic development, may have appeared as a path to modernity for many of the LDCs. For example during the 1960s many of the newly independent former colonial states embarked on programmes of industrialisation and infrastructural development programmes of modernisation designed to equip them with the necessary means of ensuring their economic as well as political freedom. Unlike other forms of development, tourism has one obvious attraction to LDCs in that it is an industry 'without chimneys' which requires relatively low capital investment (Harrison 1994: 233–6). In addition, tourism is also a means of earning foreign currency and, as such, it counts as an invisible export earner and can be seen as a relatively low-cost means of balancing payments. (Archer and Cooper 1998, Harrison 1997) In some cases, receipts earned from overseas tourism can be considerable. In the Caribbean for example, Gayle and Goodrich (1993) point out that the economic gains of tourism are substantial. In both Jamaica, (Gayle 1993) and Barbados (Palmer 1993) tourism contributes more than any other sectors to foreign exchange earnings and Cuba also sees tourism as a means of earning convertible currency (Espino 1993). It is this earning potential that makes tourism attractive for many LDCs.

As with other forms of modernity or modernisation, mass tourism was, at least in the early phases of expansion, the accepted model. Yet the tourism spaces created are of a different kind to those in the advanced capitalist economies in a number of respects. First, they did not cater for internal domestic markets, at least in their early manifestations. In this sense what occurred was the export of leisure from the developed economies to the less developed economies. Secondly, many resort developments were built as enclaves. Now although this may be seen as the replication of resort developments in the industrialised economies as, after all they too were kept spatially and socially distinct, spatial segregation could also act to highlight both social and economic differences between the host population and the guests. In some cases though, such separation could be deliberately planned precisely as a means to limit 'outside' influences on the host population (Pearce 1989: 95).

This first phase of expansion was followed by the development of tourism in South East Asia, which catered for the rapidly expanding long-haul markets, and began to displace the Mediterranean and Caribbean as new mass destinations (Ioannides 1998: 155). Competition on the global stage was intensified with the further spread of free-market capitalism following the collapse of the old Soviet-dominated system in eastern Europe (D.R. Hall 1991). Tourism in these countries, often termed transitional economies, had developed along a path broadly similar to those in the western democracies. Resorts were spatially distinct, and catered for their domestic markets (Böröcz 1996) but with some significant differences. Overseas tourism outside the Soviet bloc was severely restricted, as was inbound tourism, and the use of leisure time, like all aspects of life, came under centralised state control. As had happened in Western Europe some years previously, many of the old manufacturing industries were closed down, and tourism was seen as a means of generating new forms of employment and wealth.

The appeal of tourism as a means to generate wealth appears to be an attractive proposition, due to its seemingly exponential growth, its potential as an invisible export earner and its relatively low costs. Yet calculating the economic impacts of tourism is fraught with difficulties, not the least being that tourism consists of a bundle of services and products which, unlike some other forms of commodity production, are not easily disaggregated. As Walton notes, economic assessments usually seek to account for the multiplier effect by distinguishing between direct, indirect and induced impacts (Walton 1993: 240). Direct refers to the actual income generated from the tourists. Indirect refers to the secondary effects generated by the supply of goods and services to meet the needs of the tourist sector, including labour costs, and induced refers to the spread and distribution of monies earned by those who benefit from both the direct and indirect effects. Yet assessments in terms of such cost–benefit models can often ignore the complexities of relationships between the economic and the social as, for example, in the changes that may occur in patterns of work and gender relations (Sinclair 1997) These however, are issues that will be returned to in later chapters. For now it is sufficient to concentrate on some of the theoretical issues raised by tourism as a form of modernisation, and its counterpart underdevelopment, both of which approaches still have resonances within the tourism literature (Harrison 1997).

Wall offers a useful overview of approaches towards development. He identifies four main themes, modernisation, dependency, neoclassical counter-revolution and alternative (1997: 35). In this section I will examine the first two. Modernisation assumes that development occurs on a linear or evolutionary basis, and that less developed societies can catch up with the developed world given the right conditions, which should be encouraged through strategic development organised at a state level. In terms of tourism, this form of development assumes, for example, that the building of large hotels or resort areas will act as a catalyst to promote some form of 'trickle down' effect, which will then benefit the overall economy. Also, the development of a modern infrastructure, such as airports, roads and so on, will also benefit the economy as a whole. There are, however, certain problems in this scenario. The first is the possibility that any profits accrued will leak from the national economy overseas. The second is that economic developments may only benefit existing national or more localised elites. In both cases, the economic relationships will be uneven, if not exploitative, and the indigenous economy may suffer as a consequence of catering for the needs of the developed world.

Such an approach therefore assumes that the spread of modernity in itself is both desirable and achievable, and in turn, traditional values and cultures could be viewed as inimical to progress (R.E.Wood 1993). Development in these terms is therefore viewed as the spread of a system of universal values, or rather, of providing the underdeveloped nations and regions with the means by which universal goals of economic growth and prosperity can be achieved.

These kinds of assessments of the desirability of economic development as such tend to be endorsed by many, including the World
Tourism Organisation (WTO). A shortcoming of these approaches is
however, as Böröcz argues, that tourism is viewed as the 'agent of
change' at a national level, as if it is 'a benevolent external factor that
is completely independent of any global, regional or subnational
structural process or constraint' (Böröcz 1996: 16). Development is
thus seen as being a neutral mechanism, a simple means to an end
which at a more abstract level, stresses the utopian ideals of modernity as a form of universal progression.

Dependency theory, on the other hand, tended to view ties to the
developed western economies as being essentially negative, if not
dystopian, seeing global economic relationships in terms of first
world–third world or centre–periphery models (D Pearce 1989: 10–
14). There were of course political considerations involved. Economic ties between the developed capitalist economies and the
developing world were to be encouraged partly as a bulwark against
that other competing global paradigm of the mid twentieth century,
communism. Barriers to development were conceptualised not as
some form of internal dynamic, such as tradition versus modernity,
but rather as neo-colonial forms of exploitation, of which tourism
was but one particular manifestation. The obvious ties of political
dependency may have vanished, but these were replaced with less
obvious forms of economic and perhaps even cultural control. Such
approaches drew attention to the reliance on foreign investment
capital and loans and in particular the problem of leakage, that is
the expropriation of profit from the underdeveloped world to the
developed world, all of which resulted in ties of subordination and
dependency. Colonialism as a political entity may have been a thing
of the past, but this was presumed to have been replaced by economic relationships of a neo-colonial kind.

In terms of tourism development, two frequently cited examples
of this kind of analysis are provided by Britton (1982, 1991) who
adopts a neo-Marxist approach to the political economy of tourism,
arguing that third world countries suffer from structural distortions
to their economies as the indigenous economy is undermined and
redirected to serve the interests of external markets (1982: 333).
Surplus value is expropriated or, alternatively, is appropriated by
internal elites so the benefits of tourism development are unevenly
distributed. In short, the presumed 'trickle down' effect predicted by

modernisation does not occur. Although Britton is correct in drawing our attention to the wider processes of the political economy of tourism development, more recent research as much as theoretical development has called these earlier analytical frameworks into question.

Böröcz makes the point that both tourism as development and tourism as dependency both present a partial and lopsided view of events. The first because it privileges the role of the nation state, and the latter for failing to recognise that tourism may play a positive role, and that people are not necessarily the passive recipients of cultural imperialism (1996: 17). A further problem is that both modernisation and, by implication its inverse counterpart, dependency theory are conceptually locked into dividing the globe into first, second and third worlds (Kelly 1999: 242) a situation which arguably is no longer so cut and dried (Appadurai 1990, Meyer and Gerschiere 1999, Held et al. 1999). As an example, Hoogvelt argues that segments of the third world have been brought into the economic core, while at the same time segments of the first world are being relegated to peripheral status (1997: 145). In addition, we also have to account for the transitional economies of the former Soviet bloc, which are different again. This is not to argue that the problems identified by earlier theoretical models such as modernisation or dependency have vanished. There is no doubt that some global economic relationships are decidedly unequal (Held et al. 1999: 213) and the universal claim that modernisation, at least in terms of the western model, is the passport to development is questionable. Also, there is no doubt that in certain circumstances tourism development has had negative effects, and may indeed involve some notion of subordination, or some measure of dependency.

The apparent appeal of modernisation or dependency models lies in the fact that they reduce complexity to a simple binary either/or choice, as if one were invited to be either an advocate for a totalising modernity that sweeps all in its path, or a critical analyst decrying the iniquitous spread of capitalism. The situation now, I would argue, is less stark and more complex. The apparent certainties of both these positions simply do not fit the contemporary world. Models of centre–periphery have, as Harrison (1997) writes, largely been superseded by arguments relating to the nature and spread of globalisation.

In the preceding chapter I sketched out the main elements of globalisation, such as increasing economic ties which, in turn, have also brought about changes in the structure of labour markets (Held et al. 1999, McDowell 1999). Not only are workforces required to be more flexible, that is less tied to one specific job or location, but they are also more mobile. One of the key features of globalisation are the flows of migrant workers, not only from rural to urban locations, but also from the LDCs to the developed world (Eade 1997) and also within regions. As Hoogvelt (1997) argues, such developments are more than economic. In particular relations between the centre and the periphery (to the extent that these terms were useful in the first place) are no longer defined only in geographical terms but also, as I will argue later, in cultural terms. In terms of tourism we can also see shifts in the pattern of global distribution.

Table 3.1   International tourist arrivals, 1980–95

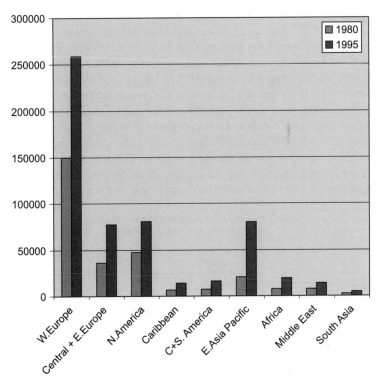

Source: World Tourism Organisation 1997

Table 3.1 shows the overall growth rates in international tourist arrivals between the years of 1980 and 1995. Although there has been an overall increase in the total number, the largest receiving regions are North America and Western Europe. Yet the biggest regional increase is in the South East Asia Pacific region. As Wall and Nuryanti also point out, most of this is intra-regional. In addition, there has also been substantial growth in domestic tourism within this region. (1997: 70).

The intra-regional flow of tourists can be gauged by comparing the total number of arrivals with region of origin. Although selected for illustrative purposes, what table 3.2 indicates is that intra-regional growth is becoming more significant. In short, tourists are no longer exclusively 'exported' from the West to other locations or regions, although there is still a disparity between the developed and the less developed economies, which becomes clear if we look at the balance between incoming and outgoing tourists.

As table 3.3 shows, both Japan and Malaysia have greater flows of tourists going out of the country than coming in. Another factor that needs to be considered is that these countries also have their own internal market dynamics to cater for. What we can see emerging is a transformation in the pattern of tourist flows which is, so to speak, no longer one-way traffic. Another important factor here is that many criticisms of tourism, based on the notion that it exports *western* values and ways of life, no longer reflect these changes in tourism patterns. In other words, the new order of globalisation appears to cut across and redefine the old pattern of geographical and cultural fixities to the extent that models of centre and periphery, modernisa-

Table 3.2   Visitor numbers and region of origin,
1991–5 (000s, selected countries)

	Japan		Malaysia		Thailand	
Region of origin	1991	1995	1991	1995	1991	1995
South Asia/Pacific	2159	2069	4968	6660	3117	4520
North Europe/Americas	1260	1215	556	540	1535	1427
Subtotal	3419	3284	5524	7200	4652	5947
Total*	3533	3345	5847	7469	5087	6951

* Includes visitors from other regions
Source: World Tourism Organisation 1997

Table 3.3 Inbound and outbound tourist flows,
1991–95 (000s, selected countries)

| | 1991 | | 1995 | |
	inbound	outbound	inbound	outbound
Japan	3533	10634	3345	15298
Malaysia	5847	16082	7469	20642
Thailand	5087	1014	6951	1820

Source: World Tourism Organisation 1997

tion and underdevelopment are no longer able to deal with the complexities of the contemporary situation. Clearly there are a number of factors at work here, not least changes to the global economy.

Globalisation and economic deregulation

From the late 1940s, the global economic order had been underpinned by the Bretton Woods agreement of 1944 which saw the establishment of the International Monetary Fund (IMF) and the World Bank. This agreement, and the institutional mechanisms to which it gave rise, was an attempt to regulate the world economy but, however, excluded the communist countries. International capital was to be subordinate to national interests by giving the latter preference over the former. This in turn was seen as a way to ensure economic prosperity and full employment within the member states. By the late 1960s, the system was beginning to come under strain due in part to the rise of private international finance (Held et al. 1999: 199–201). The 1973 rise in oil prices followed by the international debt crises of the 1980s signalled the final end of this post-war system. (Amin and Thrift 1994, Bornschier 1999, Wall 1997). The result of such changes was a restructuring of relations between the state and capital, and the rise and dominance of neo-liberal economic policies on the global stage. From the late 1970s, there was a distinct trend among the developed industrialised economies in response to such changes.

Whereas previously the general trend was for regulation through policies such as nationalisation, during the 1980s the new economic orthodoxy saw a number of states withdrawing from regulatory and management roles (Bornschier and Chase-Dunn 1999, Held et al. 1999) which became known variously as 'Thatcherism,'

Reaganomics' or the 'New Right'. What these approaches shared
were an emphasis on deregulation, especially of the international
financial markets, and a downplaying of the state in favour of private
enterprise (Corner and Harvey 1991, McGrew 1992, M.P. Smith
1988, Van der Hoeven and Sziracki 1997). As an example, the
introduction of this neo-liberal economic orthodoxy into the UK
during the 1980s was an attempt to reduce the state burden of public
expenditure and foster a spirit of entrepreneurialism which, coupled
with policies directed towards the maintenance of preserving a
national heritage, also gave rise to opportunities for tourism growth.

   In contrast to the earlier system, such approaches emphasise a
diminished role for the state, and argued that the role of government
was to ensure 'sound finance' and maintain a correct 'business
climate' (Hoogvelt 1997: 135). The role of the state was recast
from social provider to economic enabler. Nationalisation, a common practice in many of the LDCs as much as the developed
economies, was being overtaken by privatisation. The final collapse
of the old Soviet bloc accelerated the global adoption of this new
orthodoxy of free market ideology and tourism was as much part of
this as anything else. As Hall (1991) argues, the development of
international tourism in eastern Europe is seen not only as a means
to earn hard currency, but also as a mechanism of economic restructuring through privatisation to encourage a greater degree of indigenous entrepreneurship.

Tourism multinationals

One of the features of contemporary globalisation is the growth and
influence of multinational corporations (MNCs). Both the number
and importance of these have increased significantly since the 1970s,
most notably in terms of finance capital, and especially during the
deregulation of the 1980s (Bornschier and Chase-Dunn 1999). In this
section I will briefly examine the role of hotel chains, and tour
operators as examples. Griffiths' (1998) assessment of the UK hotel
industry shows how transnational consortia are becoming ever more
important on the global stage. Accor, one of the largest groups,
operates approximately 25,000 hotels in 70 countries (Griffiths
1998: 27) while Holiday Inn, arguably the biggest brand name, operates 1571 hotels with a total of 2.3 million rooms. In 1996 this was

purchased by the UK brewing and leisure group, Bass PLC (1998: 28) who, in 1998, also purchased the Inter-Continental chain from the Japanese Saison Group (1998: 70). As he points out, this is part of a growing trend towards the globalisation of the hotel industry (Griffiths 1998: 66). Both Sinclair and Vokes (1993) and Harrell and Chon (1997) also draw attention to the significance of MNCs and hotel ownership in the Asia–Pacific region. In the late 1980s and early 1990s hotel space in the region grew dramatically. Many hotel consortia were especially concerned with building in 'gateway' cities in order to secure a foothold and would later develop in secondary cities and resorts areas. This resulted in complex franchising agreements that often cut across national boundaries and also saw the emergence of regionally based consortia (Sinclair and Vokes 1993, Sinclair and Stabler 1997: 136–7) which have the added advantage over independent operators of being able to utilise economies of scale and product branding (Vellas and Bécherel 1995: 102–6).

A case in point is that of CDL Hotels International, owners of the London based Millennium and Copthorne brands. The majority shareholder is the Singapore based City Developments Ltd. CDL Hotels International began in 1989, and has now expanded to own 64 hotels with 16,400 rooms in 12 countries, including the gateway cities of Singapore, London, New York, Paris, Hong Kong and Sydney. Most of these properties were acquired in the early 1990s as part of a deliberate global strategy to diversify into three geographical regions, Asia, Australasia and Europe/North America. This was for two reasons, first, in order to compensate for the fluctuations in national and regional economic cycles and secondly, to engage in the 'cross selling' of its hotels on a global basis, that is, promoting European and North American destinations in Asia, and vice versa. (CDL Hotels International 1999). What this shows is a clear example of the movement of investment capital on a global basis in order to seek regional and local advantages, while at the same time achieving higher profits through global economies of scale. What is of interest here is that capital investment and expansion can no longer be considered a western phenomenon, indeed the flow of profits is from the USA and Europe to Singapore. In the new order of globalisation, the old patterns and flows can be, and are being, reversed.

Tour operators can be regarded as the 'wholesalers' of the tourist industry (Vellas and Bécherel 1995: 169). That is to say, many of them deal in bulk hotel bookings that are then sold on through agents, the suppliers, to individual holidaymakers. Although they are therefore significant players, their influence varies greatly from country to country. One example to illustrate the pattern of relationships that exist between these wholesalers and suppliers is given by March's case study of Japanese wholesalers and Australian suppliers. As he notes, the Japanese market is of crucial importance to the Australian tourist industry, yet access to this market has to be negotiated through a tightly structured system of wholesalers dominated by a few large players, out of which eight are responsible for nearly 65 per cent of visits to Australia (March 1997: 56). In turn, this resulted in some suppliers being dependent on the wholesalers, and some destinations being more dependent on the Japanese market than others. A similar point is made by Curtin and Busby who note that the flow of tourists to some of the smaller destinations is controlled by global tour operators (1999: 137). As the examples given in this section show, MNCs are clearly important components of the global tourist economy. Yet we also have to bear in mind that the economic relationships between the MNCs and other interests are complex. It is not so much a matter of controlling the market as perhaps responding to demand, as Curtin and Busby note, 'markets are never constant, they alter and change rapidly, as mass operators expand into specialist markets and specialist markets offer products that are gradually evolving into mass markets' (Curtin and Busby 1999: 141).

The examples discussed here also indicate difficulties in conceptualising global–local relationships in terms of the actions of MNCs alone. For many of these larger corporations, the local may well be a nation state, or even a transnational region (Amin and Thrift 1994, Dirlik, 1999). Airlines for example, although not dealt with here, are regulated through international agreements and treaties negotiated by nation states or even trading blocs such as the European Union which are as much to do with controlling borders and flows of migrants (Held et al. 1999: 314) as much as the issuing of tourist visas. National and regional policies will also have some effect in shaping the form and development of tourist space and the flows of both investment capital and people, as one of the main incentives for governments to pursue tourism development policies is the lure of foreign exchange earnings. Despite globalisation the state has clearly not withered away, rather its role can be crucial in mediating and directing the political economy. MNCs may exert considerable economic leverage, more so perhaps in relation to LDCs, (Harrison 1994: 241) but they are not doing so in a totally unfettered marketplace. The example of the Australian suppliers and Japanese wholesalers also shows that economic ties of dependency are not simply matters of the developed economies imposing on the less developed ones. Ties of dependency can also exist across sectors of the developed economies, and indeed between different regions and localities within national economies. In practice, what globalisation adds is the dimension of transnational practices in the policy arena (Sklair 1994a, b) so that national, regional and local policy decisions are now having to be made in the light of the global political economy, and are having to reconcile the interests of the MNCs with different and perhaps conflicting, national, regional and local agendas.

Mediating globalisation: power and policies

In terms of tourism, as Hall and Jenkins have argued, the role of state institutions has tended to be underplayed, despite its rather obvious importance. However, as they also note, the institutional arrangements within states varies considerably (1995: 18). The main issue, in terms of the global political economy though, is the degree to which the state either pursues interventionist policies, or deregulates and opens up development to the play of market forces, even if these are mediated at a number of spatial and administrative levels. The analysis by Qiu Zhang et al. (1999) of Chinese tourism policy from the late 1970s onwards shows that even the more centralised economies are not immune from this trend. The institutional setting can also affect policies at a more localised level. As I have argued elsewhere (Meethan 1998) regional as well as local policymaking can also play an important role and, as C.M. Hall points out, even local states are now 'international actors in tourism' (1998: 216). So although it is possible to talk in terms of the global political economy, there is always the possibility that sub-national institutional arrangements can attempt to control the trajectory of globalisation through localised solutions.

Things therefore, are often not as clear cut as they first appear, even at the level of the nation state, indeed as Douglass (1994) argues, the role of state in the global political economy can appear to be rather paradoxical. Basing the analysis on evidence from Hong Kong, South Korea, Singapore and Taiwan, Douglass notes that these countries were pursuing active and strong state interventionist roles while at the same time attempting to deregulate. This in itself calls into question theories which argue that in terms of economic growth, the state has little autonomy from capital (Douglass 1994: 544). Like many other current analytical concepts, often prefixed by 'post', deregulation implies an undoing or dissolving of old certainties. This does not mean that the state as such is withering away, rather its role has changed.

One recent example of this overall trend, from interventionist to market-led is offered by Clancy's analysis of tourism development in Mexico. He outlines how, until the late 1960s, Mexican tourism was market driven. In this sense it followed a pattern of indigenous development proceeding in an ad hoc and unplanned fashion, with few internal constraints, similar in some respects to the development of the early tourism spaces outlined in chapter two. From the late 1960s onwards, there was shift into a more strategic approach which resulted in multiyear plans being drawn up by the Tourism Ministry (Clancy 1999: 10).

Clancy argues that these are best seen in the light of wider development plans in which tourism was viewed as a means to balance the economy by enhancing export earnings as well as promoting regional development. This took the form of planned resorts on beach sites to cater for an 'international class' of mass tourists. (Clancy 1999: 11). State involvement included the planning, buying and selling of land, and developing the infrastructure including hotels, as well as offering financial incentives to the private sector through the form of subsidised loans.

Following the debt crisis that hit Mexico in 1982, there was some privatisation of state holdings. The pattern of growth and development though shows that both internal as much as external factors played a significant role. The fact that there were few internal constraints in the early phase of development also needs to be balanced against the fact that is was 'the international industry that influenced ownership and control patterns' (Clancy 1999: p13). Because Mexico wished to attract the international mass market, it needed to attract international hotels. As a consequence, many of the new hotels were part-owned and-controlled by non-Mexicans by the 1980s. However, there have also been some significant changes since. Indigenous growth has been fuelled by industrial conglomerates entering the hospitality sector through forming strategic alliances with major international players.

There are certain important points to be drawn from this particular case. First, as Clancy makes clear, the tourism industry in Mexico is largely the result of planned state action. Also, this cannot be easily accounted for by either modernisation or dependency theories. It could be argued that Mexico, however, is somewhat atypical, and there are clearly degrees of control and influence in terms of state and TNC relationships. These examples presented here call into question the idea that, under the conditions of globalisation, the state is less important. Richter's study of the countries that constitute the Association of South East Asian Nations (ASEAN) records that all had government-owned airlines, and pursued centralised and elite-driven policies. R. E. Wood (1984) records that Hong Kong, Indonesia, Singapore Thailand and Taiwan opted for mass tourism development. In contrast, Walton (1993) draws attention to the fact that all the ASEAN countries, with the exception of Brunei, promoted a different form of tourism later in the 1980s as they attempted to shift 'upmarket' to attract the higher-spend, long-distance tourists.

As Sassen and Roost point out, what is occurring, especially in relation to privatisation, is a transfer of power to the private sector which relies on different forms of regulation. Such changes do not diminish the role of the state, but recasts it in a 'complex set of intersections and negotiations' (Sassen and Roost 1999: 151). Although Douglass' analysis does not directly concern tourism as such, it provides evidence that globalisation is not such a monolithic and totalising force as it appears on the surface, and as Harrison remarks, globalisation is neither automatic nor even in its spread and effects (1997: 169). The state may well have to reconfigure its policies, it is far from being written out of history. This latter point is taken up by R. E. Wood (1984) who argues that certain states in South East Asia, including those mentioned by Douglass, have pursued active tourism development policies, with the state picking up the costs of infrastructural development, while most investment has been from overseas. In short, they have been pursuing a mixed economy of tourism development that brings together both the state and private investment capital. What these examples suggest is that what is required is a consideration of the interplay between the state and the global tourist industry, as well as the need for internal comparisons between tourism policy and other economic policies. In short, tourism cannot be considered in isolation from the global structures of the tourism industry, the global political economy, or indeed the state itself, but is an integral component of globalised neo-liberal spatial practices.

As the material outlined so far has shown, there are levels and degrees of tourism planning from the global operations of the MNCs, to the state, and finally, the local. This also indicates that the processes of tourism planning have to account for a number of complexities that are no longer confined within the boundaries of nation states. As Clancy (1999) has argued, it may not be best to view tourism planning as an activity in its own right, but rather as one aspect of the overall planning of any economy, whether developed or undeveloped.

Localising development

Although, as we have seen, there is considerable variation in the patterns of recent tourism development which are mediated by a number of factors, from the global to the state, one of the dominant themes to emerge is a set of criticisms aimed against mass tourism, and a consequent move into more diversified and fragmented markets. In many ways, such changes can be conceptualised as a critique, or reaction against the totalising effects of modernity similar in many ways to the issues surrounding the re-enchantment of place discussed in chapter two. As I also pointed out, one of the apparent paradoxes of globalisation is the way that it appears to be pulling in two directions at once, on the one hand towards the creation of a global system of deregulated neo-liberal economics, while on the other, towards forms of cultural fragmentation or de-differentiation leading to the assertion of nations, regions and locales as foci of identity in an apparently rootless global world. In other words, there exists a series of tensions between the dominant form of global spatial practice, representations of space defined at a national level and the representational spaces of localities and lived experiences (Friedman 1999a, Kong 1999).

Tourism is no exception to these trends and, in the past decade or so, many alternative models that emphasise both local solutions to development and a concentration on more specialised targeted or niche markets have emerged. As Nash outlines, such approaches assume that mass tourism – the harbinger of modernity – is the dominant model to which they are contrasted (1996: 23). These are what Wall (1997) typifies as alternative forms of development which seek solutions which are not imposed from above, but are allowed to develop from a more localised or indigenous base. In some ways a response to the globalising tendencies discussed in the previous sections, such developments can also be viewed as a response to a number of issues subsumed under the label of sustainability. As I mentioned in the opening chapter, the issue of sustainable tourism has created a substantial literature and set of sub-specialisms. I do not intend to provide a comprehensive review of these themes, rather I will sketch out the main arguments in relation to the issues raised in this chapter.

At a general level the concept of sustainability is a critique of industrial modernisation. It means balancing the present consumption and use of environmental resources to predicted patterns of future use, in order that demand does not outstrip the capacity of these resources in the long term. As Nash points out, such an interpretation is very close to the idea of carrying capacity that is frequently employed within tourism analyses. Yet, as he also states, 'what is a limit for one people, is not necessarily a limit for another' (Nash 1996: 126), and that all forms of development require some degree of economic growth.

This position can be explained if we look at some examples of what have become known as 'alternative' tourism which have been variously glossed as 'Ecotourism, nature tourism, appropriate tourism, ethical tourism and responsible tourism' (Wall 1997: 37). Hawkins and Khan for example, argue that developments such as ecotourism are often described as being 'in harmony with nature, as opposed to the more traditional "mass" tourism activities' (Hawkins and Khan 1994: 191–2). But all tourism development must have some market in mind, those attracted to ecotourism for example, are a relatively small market segment: 'Eco tourism involves primarily affluent people travelling from developed countries to developing countries. These ecotourists are from a relatively higher income group with more leisure time and money to spend' (1994: 193).

One problem here, as Weaver (1998) outlines, is that ecotourism could be seen as an instrument of modernisation, and, as such, may be viewed as unsustainable. It also involves a high degree of aesthetic

appreciation which, as I noted in chapter two, is now a central
element within contemporary patterns of consumption and commodification. What is occurring here is that this process is being
extended not only to the natural environment (Urry 1990b) but
also to the less developed regions of the globe. As tourism continues
to grow, the demand for ecotourism may therefore intrude on areas
that have so far been ignored, and are therefore relatively 'unspoilt'.
One possible consequence is that the management of the environment for outside interests, however well intentioned, may conflict
with local needs. In situations such as this, sustainability may appear
to be a contradiction in terms, and to some, ecotourism is equally
damned as no more than a cynical marketing ploy. The most severe
criticism of this form of development is provided by Wheeler (1994,
1997). According to Weaver, this means regarding ecotourism as
'inherently misrepresentative and dishonest' (Weaver 1998: 23) as,
to put it simply, business and nature do not mix. According to
Wheeler himself ecotourism is merely 'short term business practice'
(Wheeler 1997: 48), that is, it caters for niche markets.

Although Wheeler's critique of ecotourism may strike some as
unnecessarily cynical, it nevertheless raises some important issues.
We should not fall over ourselves to embrace alternatives simply
because they are labelled as such, nor for that matter should we reject
them for the same reason. Indeed a greater degree of cynicism could
be attached to tour companies and operators who add the eco label
simply as a form of product branding (Curtin and Busby 1999). In
economic terms, applying the green label of sustainability may act as
a justification for further growth and development, as economic
growth itself may be seen as that which needs sustaining, rather
than the environment itself. Abram for example comments that in
many cases 'the state has attempted to re-route environmental arguments through the discourse of sustainability' (Abram 1998: 14).

Although the concept of sustainability was first applied to the
environment, it has more recently become broadened to include
the control and management of less tangible resources such as
culture, which in turn are seen as resources to be frozen in time
and isolated from modernity (Butcher 1997). As Harrison points out,
the actual undeveloped nature of many third-world economies may
well be what makes them attractive in the first place (1994: 236). A
similar point is also made by Friedman who observes that: 'The
representation of other worlds, other scenes, the primal fantasies of

world travel, are embedded in the institutional organisation of the tourist industry and motivate much of its activity' (Friedman 1995: 76). Such concerns relate to issues raised in the previous chapter concerning the commodification of space. After all, it is the environment, people and culture, in the broadest senses of those terms, which constitute the materials out of which representations of space are constructed. If people and their cultures are commodified for the purposes of tourism, then they too must logically be seen as a resource that needs to be sustained. For example, Pigram and Wahab (1997) regard the important question as being 'whether tourism growth must inevitably lead to resource degradation and alienation of participants and host communities' (1997: 4). What is of interest here is the way in which the concept of alienation is simply assumed as a given and perhaps necessary consequence of tourism development.

As Nash points out, issues of sustainability have tended to become a catch-all term that encompasses many forms of 'alternative' development (1996: 126). The critique of modern industrial development that underpins the sustainability argument can also be subsumed under the mantle of local involvement in the planning and implementation of development policies. Arguments against big business can easily translate into arguments against big government. Rather than large-scale development, we have instead approaches that emphasise the small scale – local and community involvement. As I noted above, the pursuit of neo-liberal economics is based in part on the orthodoxy of deregulation, of removing the perceived restraints which impede economic growth. Although this is often seen as acting in the interests of global finance, a related approach is to argue for the incorporation of local people into the planning process. Such models of participatory development are not only seen to be desirable ends in themselves, but are also seen as ways to ensure that the more negative effects of tourism are at least managed, and that development itself will benefit those who need it most (Din, 1997, Marien and Pizam 1997). Din takes the view that modernity, if it is to be more than an outside imposition, needs to be indigenized, and that tourism development can only really succeed if the needs and wishes of local people are respected and accounted for (1997: 78–9).

One example is of the kind discussed by V. L. Smith (1994). Her analysis concentrates on small-scale family-operated tourism enterprises such as inns and guest houses. The positive advantages for this form of development, she argues, are that proprietorship confers social status. The encouragement of indigenous entrepreneurship is seen as a way to stop the expropriation of profit from the third world to the first and, in this sense, it leads to a form of empowerment at a local level. Local ownership also allows business equity to be built up, and family ownership is seen as a way to guarantee employment. Set against this, are a number of disadvantages. Opportunities for ownership are not equally accessible. Indeed, developments may well be to the benefit of local elites, and thus 'disrupt' traditional structures. Successful businesses also require adequate training. In eastern Europe for example, when political and economic liberalism occurred, there was no indigenous entrepreneurial sector which could take advantage (D.R. Hall 1991: 11). Even in the developed economies of the West, entrepreneurship is not a 'natural' but a learned set of skills (Shaw and Williams 1997, 1998) which needs to be encouraged in order for indigenous economic growth to proceed, which in turn is part of the orthodoxy of neo-liberal economics (OECD 1990: 11, Din 1997: 76–7).

Once more we are dealing here with the apparent paradox of globalisation, in which the local assumes a greater degree of autonomy from the state, and in terms of the apparent rejection of modernity, while, on the other hand, it is all the more closely bound in to the global system itself. Although the form of development that Smith is outlining has some advantages over the massive scale of earlier forms of resort development, there are a number of issues which need considering. First, sustainability is not a self-explanatory concept and needs to analysed like many other concepts in terms of its use and deployment, not as an essential category (Mowforth and Munt 1997). Sustainability can also be used in different ways, most importantly perhaps as a form of environmental protection, as a form of cultural protection, or even as a justification for economic growth. Secondly, alternative tourism may be little more than reflecting the wants of particular consumer niches underpinned by a romanticised view of nature (Urry 1990b) combined with a western moral agenda. This could be seen as a desire for the otherness of places untainted by modernity that can also be discerned within some regions of the developed world (Meethan 1998). Alternative approaches then can assume a mantle of self-righteousness (Weaver 1998: 10–11) that Nash also identifies as the implicit moral agenda of alternatives (1996: 23). Attempts by the less developed countries to modernise may be viewed as forms of anti-environment-alism (Abram 1998: 11) or perhaps even as the 'selling out' of their unique cultural identity. Third, and relating to both the above points, is the nature of scale. Alternative approaches are seen as being deliberately small scale, and therefore should involve the 'grassroots', or include community involvement.

The notion of community itself is a slippery term to say the least (Crow and Allen 1994) which is not only rooted in a nostalgic yearning for the simple life (MacDonald 1997b: 132–5), but also often ignores issues of conflict by assuming social homogeneity as given (Taylor and Davis 1997). In addition, they also presuppose some innate primordial attachment of a people to a locality, especially when dealing with exoticised other cultures (Selwyn 1993). As such, we can see these developments as a rejection of the presumed totalising tendencies of modernity, and the embracing of small-scale difference and variety. Now there is certainly a case to be made that, in certain circumstances, such developments may well be the most appropriate choice. Mass tourism has undoubtedly had negative impacts in some regions and localities, but to simply assume there-fore that large is bad and small is good is no more than a naive reductionism.

What all these new trends emphasise or capitalise on is difference contrasted to similarity both in terms of underlying ideologies and their marketing appeal. Policies based on neo-liberalism emphasise privatisation and deregulation and a diminished role for the state, thus opening up the possibilities that locally organised and small-scale enterprises can flourish. Such enterprises in turn need to emphasise a singularity of place and difference which, coupled with a western dislike for the presumed totalising effects of modernity, gives alternative forms of tourism a folksy, ethnic appeal. Earlier theories of development, both modernisation and centre–periphery, were based on the idea of some universally applicable model, which was analysed in terms of being either positive or negative. On the other hand, both the neo-liberal and alternative forms of development – even if they proceed from different bases, both reject universalism and concentrate instead on more localised solutions, even if this is only made possible through the extension of neo-liberal economics. Yet such alternatives would not be possible without a global system of transport and infrastructure capable of moving people from one destination to another. Such developments are by their nature therefore selective, and many of these alternative forms of tourism development can be viewed as forms of market segmentation rather than a panacea for the ills of modernity.

However, such qualifications and criticisms should not result in a wholesale rejection of alternatives. Sustainability is important in terms of the political economy regardless of whether or not it is ultimately achievable, contradictory or irresolvable. Economics is not simply about the maximisation of profit in the sense that it is not a neutral activity, but is related to patterns of social life and the ways in which human activity is conceptualised and acted upon (Sahlins 1976). Even if a 'weak' version of sustainability, such as slow but steady economic growth rather than attempting to maximise in the short term, becomes the accepted orthodoxy then it will inevitably have an impact on the form and shape of tourism development. Whether or not this can be squared with deregulated global capitalism is another matter. A celebration of the small scale and alternative then can actually be seen as a logical extension of macro changes to the global political economy (Appadurai 1990) and as market responses to western patterns of consumer demand.

As this chapter has argued so far, the structure of the global political economy has had an enormous impact on the forms of tourism development at both a macro and a micro level. In chapter two I raised the issue of the aestheticisation of place, and the consequent spatial commodification that characterises the tourist system, and in the preceding sections I noted how such processes are not confined to the developed economies but are now played out on a global stage. Now these forms of commodification may also be viewed as the dominance of what Sklair terms the culture ideology of capitalism. He argues that this domination is so pervasive that if local practices challenge the global system, they are commodified, marginalised or destroyed (1994b: 178–9). Perhaps in certain instances this may be the case, yet at the conceptual level this formulation creates some problems. Such analyses of the political economy tend to view cultural forms as a reflection of economic forms in terms of a simple base–superstructure model, which is to say that economics determines culture. In a similar fashion Britton (1991) also argues that culture is something that has been hijacked and debased by the global spread of tourist commodification, the net results of which are neo-colonial relationships which are as much cultural as they are economic. Now, although both Sklair and Britton are correct in that the relation between economics and culture needs to be addressed, there are three important points to consider. First, is the universal nature of the claims, which assumes that host or receiving nations, cultures or societies can only ever be passive recipients, that they have neither internal dynamics nor agency (Böröcz 1996: 16). Secondly, this formulation also contains a moral agenda of cultural elitism in which the masses are deluded, but the critical analyst is not. While it cannot be denied that there is a connection between the ways in which both economic and cultural forms interact, the ways in which people adjust to global circumstances are more complex than this formulation allows for. Thirdly, this also assumes that cultures, especially those of the developing world, somehow existed in a pre-commodified or pristine authentic state which globalisation is threatening to debase or destroy, in which the representational space of the local becomes an 'arena of homogeneity and authenticity in a world of inauthentic and unrooted global influences' (Amin and Thrift 1994: 9). As Butcher points out, people in less developed countries 'do not recline in their uncomplicated, unsullied existence, at one with nature, but strive to free themselves from poverty and drudgery' (Butcher 1997: 36).

Local practices though are set in the context of the overall global political economy. One debate that this has given rise to, and will be discussed in more detail below, is whether or not such economic changes are leading to the emergence of an homogenous global culture. As Mittelman argues (1997: 232) such factors cannot be accepted as proof of the emergence of a universal global culture (see for example Boniface and Fowler 1993, and Go 1994). Jessop also cautions against seeing globalisation as a coherent causal mechanism, and argues it is better considered as the structural context within which the 'local, urban, cross–border, national and macro regional [are] . . . substantive sites of real economic activities' (Jessop 1999: 23). In this sense, and as the material presented on this chapter indicates, globalisation is neither as monolithic nor as universal as it may appear, it is not a 'one way' process (Tomlinson 1999: 26) and therefore we should not assume that its effects are either universal or inevitable.

Conclusion

As this chapter has shown, we can no longer think of tourism in simplistic terms as being either a blessing or a curse, nor in terms of providing an easy route to modernity, nor as an index to underdevelopment. In all the cases discussed in this chapter the development of tourism is seen as a way to diversify and expand economic activity, and to do so on a global stage. For many of the LDCs, and the transitional economies, the attraction of tourism lies in the fact that, unlike some forms of development, it does not require the same degree of investment, and also appears as a relatively easy way to generate foreign exchange. However, it is also clear that for many of the smaller nation states, an over-reliance on tourism can have its dangers, leaving them vulnerable to the operations of MNCs.

It would also be misleading to assume that such changes are themselves universal, or that even their effects are evenly distributed not only on a global basis, but also within the developed economies. There are of course significant differences. Although the developed economies are less reliant on tourism as a source of economic growth, tourism is nevertheless recognised as an important economic sector. The dynamics of globalisation are clearly leading to new forms of economic, cultural and political organisation, and the spaces of globalisation are less tied to the nation state, and as such we can say they are de-territorialised. Boundaries, both physical and conceptual, are less fixed than they have been, and the global flows of capitalism go hand-in-hand with the global flows of both people and cultures. It is within this context that we can also identify attempts to emphasise distinct characteristics of localities, but these are not competing with each other for domestic markets, but are now competing in a globalised market. As we have seen, tourism policies are being formulated as responses to structural changes in both the developed as much as the less developed economies. For example, the decline of the early resorts and the reinvention of urban spaces for consumption has been as mixed as the extension of tourism into the more distant long-haul destinations of the Third World. By focusing exclusively on the less developed regions of the world the importance of these factors in the developed economies may be overlooked. The case studies discussed here show that each has to be taken on its own particular merits, and that the role of the state as much as the relations between states and MNCs must be considered. In all cases we have also seen how, despite the rhetoric of free markets and the broader context of de-territorialisation, local and national policies, planning procedures and other political factors can play a crucial role in attempting to control the form and trajectory of economic globalisation.

The patterns and types of tourism development differ in significant ways. Although it is possible to identify global trends or a dominant paradigm of spatial practices, these patterns are, perhaps paradoxically, those of diversification and fragmentation. What distinguishes the more recent forms of tourism development from previous manifestations, driven by notions of modernisation, is that fact that it is difference, rather than similarity, which is striven for, and tourism arguably encourages the commodification of uniqueness. In this sense we can point here to the interelationship between the material and the symbolic in the ways that the local or the small scale is conceptualised as a counterweight to the apparent monolithic tendencies of the global market. Celebrating difference is once again a critique of modernity cast as a struggle between utopia and dystopia, but one that is played out in terms of global issues. Notions of community involvement and eco-friendly attitudes may induce a warm glow in the hearts of western tourists, and salve their consciences. Yet we need to stand back from simplistic moralising here, and ask whether such developments do benefit those on the ground, or are particular manifestations of western romanticism, a form of idealising other places and indeed other people, aimed at particular consumer niches. Underpinned by the notion that other cultures need preserving from the onslaught of a totalising modernity and that their authenticity is under threat, such forms of romanticising nature and the primitive may in fact simply consign the less developed economies to the status of an eco-or cultural theme park for the developed world.

Finally, this raises two important and interrelated themes. The first is the current, and largely uncritically accepted, orthodoxy within tourism analysis that the intrusion of commodification associated with the global political economy into 'other' cultures leads to their standardisation. Whether or not this results in increasing shallowness and inauthenticity has been a matter of some debate. However, this in itself cannot be adequately addressed without a more detailed examination of what is involved in commodification, and how this in turn affects patterns and forms of consumption. This will be dealt with in the next chapter.

Chapter 4

Tourism: Modernity and Consumption

Introduction

In the previous chapters I drew attention to the development of tourist spaces as arenas of consumption, and also argued that this needs to be seen in the global context of the spread of consumer capitalism. It can also be argued that tourism itself is an 'extension of the commodification of modern social life' (Watson and Kopachevsky 1994: 645). However, before this argument can be explored, it is necessary to examine, at least in outline, what commodification involves. The concept of commodity as generally employed within the social sciences has been largely derived from Marx (see for example Craib 1997, Callinicos 1999, Dodd 1994, Giddens 1971). Commodities are conceptualised as items that have not been produced for direct use, but rather for the monetary value that can be gained from them in the marketplace. The significance of commodities therefore lies in their exchange value, that is, the surplus or profit that can be extracted from them. However, commodities also have use value, which is to say they satisfy basic human needs. What distinguishes the capitalist systems from others is that exchange value is seen as the dominant element (Swingewood 1998: 156).

In chapter one I also mentioned that the condition of modernity rests on a division of labour which allegedly alienates or dispossesses individuals from the processes of production as 'human relations become reduced to the operations of the market' (Giddens 1971: 12). In other words, relations between people become concealed or distorted as relations between objects, or commodities, resulting in forms of 'commodity fetishism' (Craib 1997: 92–3) As Callinicos writes:

> The social relations between producers are mediated by the exchange of their products on the market: it is this real feature of a commodity economy which facilitates the perception of capitalism as a natural phenomena outside human control (Callinicos 1999: 95).

The important point to take from this is the way in which commodities are seen as a form of falsification. 'Humanity becomes increasingly dominated by a world of things', the means by which the true state of affairs is concealed (Swingewood 1998: 157). It is also possible in this formulation to identify elements of nostalgia, for the days when labour was not alienated, and utopianism, a look forward to the days when the alienation of labour will no longer occur.

The concepts of commodification and alienation have proved to be of great significance in many sociological and anthropological analyses, and tourism is no exception, whether or not it has been explicitly derived from Marx. For example MacCannell, while criticising what he terms Marx's 'antagonism' towards seeing commodities as no more than a form of 'fetishism' (1976: 20), still holds to the notion of alienation as the motivating force behind tourism. As Watson and Kopachevsky note, such formulations can only result in an 'overgeneralized view that the modern tourist is a metaphor for the shallowness and inauthenticity that are endemic in . . . modern life' (1994: 645).

To see the processes of commodification as being, by definition, alienating is to privilege exchange value, to see the 'desire for goods as a fetish' (Lunt and Livingstone 1992: 10), as being in itself something inherently false and undesirable if not morally reprehensible (see also Appadurai 1986, Douglas and Isherwood 1978). In its more extreme manifestations, such as the critical theory of the Frankfurt School, the masses are viewed as being brainwashed (Classen and Howes 1996, Merriman 1991, Swingewood 1977). Such formulations also rely on an initial split between the economic and the broader cultural context in which it is located. To view the processes of commodification in this way either ignores the cultural values inherent in commodity production and consumption, or views them as being of secondary importance. Because of this there was a general tendency, certainly within sociology, but less so in anthropology, to concentrate on issues of production rather than issues of consumption.

In more recent years however this trend has been reversed. Conceptualisations of the nature of commodities have broadened away from a focus on the production and consumption of material goods to encompass non-material or symbolic element, which in turn relates to the ways in which such factors are now becoming more important in practical as well as theoretical ways. In the previous chapters for example, I drew attention to the ways in which the more intangible qualities of places are being utilised in terms of the creation of tourist spaces. The contemporary importance of commodities therefore lies as much in their sign value as in their use or exchange value, as in Lefebvre's words: 'One consumes signs as well as objects' (1996: 115) perhaps even to the extent that Miller can state 'Consumption has become the vanguard of history' (1995a: 1).

Production – consumption

The focus of attention on consumption, as with the production of space, cuts across disciplinary boundaries (Bocock 1992a, b, 1993, Howes 1996, Miller 1995a, 1995b) and is therefore tied into various arguments concerned with both globalisation and postmodernism. For the moment, however, I wish to concentrate on the relation between production and consumption in terms of the differences between Fordism and post-Fordism (Allen, 1992, Miles 1998, Slater 1997). As Allen points out, the concept of Fordism can be associated with modernity in that it exemplifies progress, control, rationality and a 'new type of worker, a different kind of life-style, and a specific form of state and civil society' (Allen 1992: 230). As such, the concept is used to describe both the techniques of mass production and standardisation as well as patterns of mass consumption. Drawing on the work of Sayer (1989) Allen outlines four different but interrelated meanings of the term. First, as a labour process involving mass production; secondly, as a lead growth sector in the economy or, in other words, the dominance of Fordism within the overall economy; thirdly, as exerting an influence such as the organisation of work beyond the confine of industrial production and into other sectors of the economy; and lastly, as a mode of regulation. This latter point is worth more detailed consideration.

To conceptualise Fordism as a mode of regulation means considering wider aspects of the political economy, in particular, the ways in which government policy acts in order to secure a balance between mass production and mass consumption. For example, the ways in which both the labour force and industrialists are partly self-regulating. Both profits and wages need to be controlled in some form or another to fuel both production and consumption within the boundaries of the nation state. The principles of Fordism are also associated with all forms of centralisation and hierarchy, characteristics that mark it as being part of modernity. Arguably, such principles permeated beyond the boundaries of manufacturing which according to Murray has 'given rise to an economic culture which extends beyond the complex assembly industries' (1989: 41).

Drawing on a variety of examples, Thompson also shows how similar modes of regulation have been extended into the sphere of culture and leisure activity which, at a state level, was tied into the overall provision of welfare and statutory paid holidays (1997: 21). Under Fordist modes of production and consumption, consumers were aggregated into mass markets, and the products differentiated from each other. In terms of tourism, it could be argued that the 'traditional' two weeks at the seaside was the standardised mass product, with the resorts seeking to differentiate themselves from each other. As Slater goes on to argue, consumer taste could then be mapped onto patterns of social structure such as class (1997: 190–1). As I have already mentioned, this can be seen by the ways in which resorts were classified according to the dimensions of class and the patterns of consumption associated with these socio-spatial divisions, even if the distinction between mass and non-mass was perhaps not quite so straightforward. In short, and at the risk overgeneralisation, Fordism can be viewed as the mass production of standardised products for mass consumption in relatively homogeneous markets.

In terms of production processes, post-Fordism means smaller runs of more customised goods. Due to changes in technology, in particular computer-controlled design and manufacturing, the time-scale involved in the turnover rate and the time-lag between design and production was considerably shortened. As a consequence, this meant that the production costs for smaller more customised batches of commodities were no longer more expensive per unit than those produced under the Fordist system (Slater 1997: 189). The increasing flow and globalisation of information also resulted in a decentralisation and globalisation of production that is no longer as tied to particular localities, as it once was. Both post-Fordist production techniques and de-territorialisation go hand-in-hand with a more mobile and transnational workforce.

As the spatial and economic organisation of production changed, so too did patterns of consumption. The logical outcome of post-Fordism is niche marketing in which the mass markets of Fordism are disaggregated into segments or niches or lifestyle segments (Abercrombie 1991). These are not defined by socio-demographics nor class, but rather by the 'cultural meanings which link a range of goods into a coherent image' (Slater 1997: 191). In terms of tourism, this has resulted in the emergence of more flexible patterns of both marketing and holidaymaking, short-break weekend holidays, and the development of 'specialist' holidays, such as forms of eco-tourism. This has shifted the emphasis away from mass markets, resulting in what perhaps inevitably has been described as new or postmodern tourism. (Ioannides and Debbage 1997, Poon, 1993, Urry, 1990b).

This breaking down of established categories has resulted in tourism becoming indistinguishable from other forms of activity, such as shopping and sport, for example. C. M. Hall summarises the argument succinctly 'what is now tourism and what now is culture are relatively unclear' (1994: 187). It may appear therefore that, with the old boundaries having being dissolved, we find ourselves in a situation where the satisfaction of consumer needs is governed by an apparently limitless splitting of markets into ever smaller segments and niches. This pattern, in which tourism ceases to be a discrete activity in itself, is perhaps leading to what Urry has proclaimed as the 'end of tourism' (1995: 150). This apparent dissolving of categories has also been addressed in terms of 'de-differentiation' (Featherstone 1991). What this is referring to are the ways in which the established pattern of hierarchies are being challenged and reordered, resulting in heterogeneity rather than homogeneity (Miles and Paddison 1998). The term 'de-differentiation' is perhaps a little misleading in itself as it could be taken to imply that all distinctions are dissolving, leaving some kind of undifferentiated free for all.

Earlier I suggested that meanings have to be maintained and constantly worked at, and whereas values and boundaries may well fall into disuse and disappear, they are also being replaced by new sets of values, new sets of boundaries. The arguments that surround post-Fordist argument are then very similar to the debates that surround both postmodernism and globalisation. In some respects, the reordering to which they both refer can be viewed as the extension of commodity relations into the sphere of the social and non-material, and the expansion of commodity relations on a global scale. Featherstone for example, points out that this expansion of commodification through Fordism and rational 'scientific' management can be analysed as the 'triumph of exchange value', that is, all aspects of culture can become transformed into commodities (Featherstone 1991: 14). Yet we also have to consider the sign or symbolic value of commodities. The nature of commodities cannot be reduced to production for exchange value alone, but is also grounded in social contexts from which they derive their symbolic value. The argument advanced concerning the production of tourist space, that is, it is as much material as symbolic, provides one instance of a general process of commodification. Boundaries, both conceptual as much as material, are never as fixed as they may appear, to think otherwise is to be blind to history. There is no doubt that the processes of commodification have indeed spread into spheres of life that once were *relatively* non-commodified, but as Savage et al. point out, 'the discovery of "post-modernism" is largely a belated recognition by academics of forms of behaviour (especially various forms of commercialised consumption) which have actually been in existence for some time' (Savage et al 1992: 128).

This point is also underlined by Benson who comments that within historical studies, the consumer society is seen to have emerged at any time from the seventeenth century to the 1980s (1994: 2, see also Brewer and Porter 1994, Carrier 1995, du Gay and McFall, 1999). However, showing first cause does not negate other explanations, nor actually proves anything in itself. The roots of consumerism may well be deeper than first thought, or its significance may well have been anticipated by both Veblen and Simmel a century ago (Dodd 1994: 108–9, Miles 1998: 18–20). Yet claims that such a reordering is therefore evidence of an epochal shift from one mode to another, as with postmodernism, must be treated with caution.

As Slater (1997: 201) also warns, explanations couched in these general terms do tend to be somewhat universalistic, as if we have entered into a new phase or mode of regulation which applies across the board. To do so would imply that, for example, the principles of Fordism had applied to all economic activity. As an example against this form of overgeneralisation, Ionnadies and Debbage point out that the travel industry exhibits facets that are as much pre-Fordist as Fordist and post-Fordist (1997). In a similar fashion, Bouquet and Winter's (1987) study of bed- and-breakfast provision among farming households in Devon, UK, shows how this form of work was incorporated into the domestic division of labour within households, which arguably is pre-Fordist rather than anything else. Although some aspects of the tourist system may indeed display Fordist and even post-Fordist characteristics, such as package holidays in terms of the former, and specialist holidays in terms of the latter, this cannot be generalised. Arguably though, the importance of Fordism and post- Fordism may well lie not in their universal application to all forms of production and consumption, but rather in their being viewed as a set of ideals, or as a dominant mode of organisation or regulation (Allen 1992).

Marketing and niches

One of the outcomes of accepting the principles of post-Fordism is the move from mass markets into smaller, better defined niches. In terms of tourism, I have already drawn attention to the relative decline of mass tourism, and the consequent rise of more specialised holidays and short breaks. Yet we also have to accept that such changes are not only indicative of changes in consumption preferences, but are also in part a consequence of different marketing techniques. In theory, a market can be segmented in any number of ways (Olivier, 1995, Piercy, 1997, Weinstein 1994) on the assumption that consumer preferences can be predicted through the presence or absence of factors such as socio-economic position, gender, age, household and family structure, housing tenure or other 'lifestyle indicators'. Put together two or three of these variables and you have 'cluster segments' (Poon 1993: 247) that is, a mix of attributes seen to be causally linked to presumed consumer or lifestyle preferences. A recent UK policy document (Department for Culture, Media and Sport 1999, DCMS) shows how this new orthodoxy has been embraced at a national level. The British Tourist Council (restructured from the British Tourist Authority in 1999) a semi-autonomous agency charged with implementing national policy in the UK, aims to develop what is termed 'relationship marketing' (DCMS 1999: 38). This involves building visitor profiles according to factors such as age, employment, area of residence and so on, in order to develop ways of targeting 'precisely defined sets of consumers' (DCMS 1999: 39).

The document also draws attention to the changing nature of tourism consumption and visitor profiles, and identifies six broad trends. First, tourists will be not only more affluent, but also more cautious with their money. Secondly, they are more likely to be single travellers. Thirdly, there will be an increase in the number of shorter breaks and fourthly, tourists will have less time, and therefore will seek to maximise their experiences while minimising the effort required to find them. Fifthly, they will be seeking more individually tailored travel rather than packages, and finally, although they will be older, they will be less sedentary (DCMS 1999: 22).

The significance of this approach, which sees niche marketing as a response to apparently fragmenting markets, shows how the principles of a post-Fordist political economy are shaping the policy and . future direction of tourism, not only within the UK, but also elsewhere. For example Faulkner (1998) shows how similar issues were tackled in much the same way in Australia, while Mazanec et al. (1988) record the use of 'eurostyle' segmentation in Austria, and Morgan (1998) cites Spanish tourism policy as another example. The global spread of tourism and the development of new tourism spaces have resulted in intense competition between destinations, which in turn requires increasing differentiation within the market. Countries, as much as the places within them, need a 'specific character' (Lanfant 1995: 32) or brand which acts as a 'signal and a reference for the product's identity' (Kapferer 1997: 59) and is designed to appeal to viable market segments or a cluster of markets (Go 1997: 25). Segmentation therefore relies on the generation, or recognition of difference, and its purpose is to achieve 'greater efficiency in the supply of products to meet identified demand' (Middleton 1988: 67). In turn, this may only be achieved through the development of centralised gathering and analysis of market data (Cornford 1999). This generation of difference, while appearing on the surface to be admirably postmodern, may actually only be the application of an instrumental modern rationality by the producers.

Control or choice?

It may appear, therefore, that patterns of consumption, while appearing to offer some notions of choice and hence individual control, may actually be no more than the working out of broader structural trends within society. On the other hand, there are also forms of analysis that see consumption – and hence tourism – as simply being a matter of free choice, the 'epitome of freedom and personal choice characteristic of Western individualism' (Graburn 1983: 13). As Miles cautions, there is no straightforward way of determining which is the 'correct' approach (1998: 33). Yet choices are always constrained. As Dellaert et al. note, tourist decision making involves 'complex and multifaceted decisions' which may involve three types of constraints which are beyond the control of individuals. First, those imposed by law or by institutions which include factors such as the opening hours of shops, bars, clubs banks, and so on. Secondly, 'coupling constraints' that is, those faced by household members, friends and colleagues, and thirdly, capacity constraints which include the availability of travel options, accommodation provision, and of course, financial resources (Dellaert et al. 1998: 315).

At best perhaps it is possible to argue that consumption is part determined, but this also involves macro structural elements such as the consequences of globalisation, and the management of the political economy as much as micro social or individual factors such as financial affluence balanced against time impoverishment. In some ways this formulation recapitulates another well-trodden theme in the social sciences, that of the tensions between structure and agency, or if you prefer, between society and the individual (Giddens 1991). What cannot be denied, however, is that many of our leisure and holiday experiences are, to a greater or lesser extent, controlled. Hannigan, for example, observes that:

> What is significant is not so much the role of consumption in helping to assert status and identity but the fact that consumption is frequently occurring within the context of programmed leisure experiences (Hannigan 1998: 70).

Again, there is perhaps nothing especially new about this. Arguably, all package tours have, as part of their appeal, the notion that everything is predictable and controlled. The unexpected, and potentially dangerous, is excluded. Similarly, the kinds of experience offered by the holiday camps as described in chapter two were also predictable to the extent that all activities were scheduled and programmed. Packaging in this way can therefore be seen as the application of rationality in both production and consumption. All itineraries are methods of anticipating and controlling, of mapping out in space and time where and when. Chance, if not entirely eliminated, is at least diminished. By developing highly organised schedules, as in coach tours for example, tourists can cover more ground and see more sights than would otherwise be possible if they travelled individually. Producers – that is, tour organisers, can thus utilise economies of scale of both space and time, while the consumers can in turn maximise their leisure time by purchasing organisational expertise. In this sense, the logic of commodification which applies to production also applies to consumption as, in effect, tourists are eliminating risk and uncertainty by 'subcontracting' their travel arrangements to tour operators and travel agents.

One of the current debates within the sociology of consumption which focuses on this controlled aspect of consumption is that offered by Ritzer (1993) who coined the rather clumsy term 'McDonaldization' to argue that, despite the appearance of choice that consumption seems to offer, it is in fact becoming more globalised and standardised. Drawing on Weber's concept of rationality (Craib, 1997, R.C. Wood, 1998) Ritzer argues that this ubiquitous and global fast-food chain can be seen as nothing more than the spread of a rationalising modernity, of applying Fordist principles to the mass production of food. A later formulation of this, served up as 'McDisneyization' by Ritzer and Liska (1997) argues that this state of affairs can also be applied to tourism. In contrast to Urry's (1990b) claim, and also argued throughout this book, that tourism is demarcated from the mundane, Ritzer and Liska argue that many people appear to want vacations that are highly predictable, highly efficient, highly calculable, and highly controlled (1997: 99–100). There is no doubt that certain forms of package tourism are of precisely this kind, and have been on offer for quite some time, indeed, since the early days of tourism. But so too, are forms of tourism that deliberately seek out new experiences and new places. Just to reiterate a point I made earlier, we are in fact dealing with tourisms rather than tourism as single category.

Yet even seemingly uncontrolled and hedonistic forms of tourism contain elements of control. A recent study by Andrews of package tourists described as 'British... white, heterosexual, and "working class"' (1999: 4) in the Spanish resorts of Palmanova and Magaluf records how the pattern of consumption by the tourists is highly controlled by the company representatives. This often involves bar crawls and drinking games which are not only forms of social coercion, and thus express group solidarity, but also often means of infantilising the tourists. This turns them, at least temporarily, into a state of childlike dependence and having freedom from responsibility (see also Carr 1999 and Josiam et al. 1998). As Rojek aptly comments 'Only adults have leisure: children merely play' (1985: 174). Tourist consumption of this kind clearly is a form of escape from the mundane which is marked out not only in terms of consumption patterns, but also in time and space. The idle childlike pleasures of unstructured time are sanctioned through the appropriation of space, or rather, the ability to consume time within a specified place set aside for that purpose. (Urry 1990a: 24)

Selänniemi provides an interesting example concerning the consumption of time. His research with Finnish tourists on Rhodes utilised individual time diaries among other techniques to discover how time was actually spent. What he found was that the tourists slept late, spent a great deal on time on the beach, and at night, often stayed up partying until the early hours of the following morning (Selänniemi 1994: 36). In some ways this should not come as a startling find in itself. These are clearly people involved in the conspicuous consumption of time freed from the constraints of routine wage earning. Rhodes, he adds, was chosen because it was considered both safe and familiar, but was in many ways interchangeable with other resorts in 'the south'. These sun, sea and sand tourists were predominantly under the age of 35, and travelled once a year or less (1994: 35). The use of time in this way as idle unstructured leisure is the antithesis of the routinisation of the workplace, and is a form of consumption most associated with mass tourism. Yet Selänniemi also notes the contrast between these tourists, and those Finns who travelled to Athens. This particular group he found were older, better educated and travelled more frequently and, although the same basic motivation was evident, simply to 'get away' Athens was chosen because of its cultural and historic distinctiveness (1994: 35–6). This form of leisure consumption uses time in a more structured way, as a means of acquiring some form of cultural knowledge. In both these cases, the patterns of time use and the chosen location appear to reflect social distinctions and distinct market segments. Yet these can also be cut across by other considerations. One factor that may well be of crucial importance, but is under-researched, is the role of gender in holiday decision-making. There are a number of studies which address the use of leisure space in relation to gender (Aitchison 1999, Henderson 1994a, 1994b, Kinnaird and Hall 1994). Whether or not there are significant differences between women and men in terms of holiday patterns and choices, which cannot be accounted for by other factors, such as socio-economic status or age for example, remains to be determined (Carr 1999).

Overall though, and despite evidence that indicates increasing fragmentation in the tourist market, it is still dominated by family holidays. The study by Thornton et al. which was carried out in Cornwall, UK, also utilised time diaries and shows how children are an important factor in decision-making among families on holiday. Also, the patterns of family structure are also a key factor influencing holiday type and choice. Those families with children spent less time travelling, and more time on activities centred on swimming pools and beaches. Those without children, on the other hand, spent more time travelling between sights (Thornton et al. 1997: 291), but the influence of children grew less, as they grew older. As in the case of the Finns in Rhodes, reliability and predictability or 'product loyalty', that is, repeat visits using the same accommodation and at the same time each year, were also important factors (1997: 294). Patterns of consumption here are replicating social divisions, and also show that in certain forms of tourism the elimination of risk and uncertainty is a key factor in determining both holiday type and destination choice. People chose to go to places precisely because they are predictable, controlled and safe.

Yet people will not always follow the same pattern of consumption. As Thornton's study shows, family obligations are often the key consideration, but these can vary. This can be more clearly seen in relation to what is known as the visiting friends and relatives (VFR) category. Seaton and Palmer show these people as 'overwhelmingly young, single, or married/single with children under 15 ... most likely to be in the upper income/occupational groups' (Seaton and Palmer 1997: 354). Now visiting of this kind may well be a matter of fulfilling family and social obligations, yet what these examples show is that choices over leisure consumption are not simply matters of personal choice. They are also cut across by a variety of factors which may include a sense of obligation to family and kin as much as the desire to spend time in the pursuit of leisure.

Another factor which has recently received attention in the tourism literature is that of sexual orientation, arguably the emergence of the 'pink pound' or the 'gay consumer' during the 1990s (Pritchard and Morgan 1997, Pritchard et al. 1998) indicating the arrival of a new market segment. As Hughes points out, a number of tour operators in the UK offer overseas holidays specifically aimed at gay men (1997: 3) Pritchard et al. write that although gay tourism is being described as an emerging and profitable segment, it remains largely unknown (1998: 273). What is important here are the ways in which certain places are often, but not exclusively, identified as gay and lesbian resorts. In the UK these are Blackpool, Brighton, London, and Manchester, in Holland Amsterdam, in Spain Ibiza and Grand Canaria, in Greece Mykonos, and in the USA, Miami, New York and San Francisco (Hughes 1997: 3). It is not only holiday destinations that are regarded in this way. Hughes argues that the development of 'gay space', most usually a 'spatially discrete concentration of pubs and clubs but also cafés, shops, residences and public space' (1997: 4) allows gay identity to be validated and affirmed. This space however is a 'leisure arena' into which only gays with the appropriate spending power can buy into. Hughes argues that because of the stigmatisation that can still be attached to same-sex relationships, many people in this situation find they are constrained to using such gay space for the security that this provides. Such gay spaces are forms of spatial recontextualisation and commodification, and serve to indicate the importance of the symbolic nature of space in providing not only a focus for identity, but also a focus for tourist leisure activity (Skeggs 1999).

Yet we should not assume that sexuality in itself predetermines consumption patterns. In a survey of over 500 gay men in the UK, Clift and Forrest report that although some of their respondents travelled in search of sexual liaisons, and some gay men take holidays in places that are regarded as gay destinations. Overall they 'show no essential differences in their general patterns of travel when compared to UK heterosexual tourists, and to global patterns of tourism overall' (Clift and Forrest 1999: 621–2). What is different about these tourists is the fact that they tend to have greater amounts of disposable income than heterosexual couples with children, and therefore take more frequent holidays (Clift and Forrest 1999). Choosing holiday destinations, which have a reputation as gay spaces, may only be a way of seeking some sort of security, of eliminating potentially risky and dangerous places.

Perceptions of risk of one form or another are clearly factors that shape patterns of tourist consumption. For example Carter's (1998) study conducted in a Glasgow travel clinic, where people would receive inoculations before travelling abroad, notes how the constructions of places as being risky involved a mixture of received wisdom about other destinations, derived from both traveller's tales and guidebooks. The 'further' the cultural as well as physical distance, the greater the perception of risk.

As the above cases indicate, the elimination of risk and issues of safety and security appear to be prime factors in the choice of destinations regardless of, or in addition to, other considerations. If people choose holidays that are controlled, predictable and so on, it is because this in itself creates a feeling of security and eliminates uncertainty (Giddens 1991). By transferring responsibility, so to speak, into the hands of tour operators or of holiday company reps, tourists free themselves from the constraints to which they are normally subject, it is not that their choices are limited, rather it is a case of freely giving responsibility to someone else.

Of course, not all forms of tourism follow this pattern. At the other end of the scale from the highly controlled and organised mass package holidays, or those associated with factors such as sexual orientation, family responsibilities or obligations of friendship are what is known as 'alternative' or 'real' holidays. Often, these are consciously marketed as being non-packaged, and non-standardised. Those who chose such an option are, in Cohen's (1988a) terminology, 'existential' tourists or 'travellers' who seem to wish to escape from the kinds of programmed, controlled leisure of the masses, and would probably reject the term 'tourist' in relation to their own activities. Yet this rejection can in itself be seen as a means of asserting some form of collective identity. Munt offers an interesting analysis of this segment: 'As "Tours to Remember" warns, if you are looking for "two weeks in the eastern equivalent of Benidorm", look elsewhere!' (1994: 115). Munt argues that the development of this form of tourism, which consciously sells itself as being 'alternative' or 'other' can be seen as attempts by certain social groups, such as those described by Savage et al. to distinguish themselves from the masses through their patterns of consumption. Another study of 'alternative' tourism is offered by Macleod who notes that in this particular case in the Canary Islands, the tourists were predominantly German, and also that they 'might be classified as those working within the liberal professions, members of the 'chattering classes' (Macleod 1997: 132). Unlike the kind of 'alternative' tourists described by Munt, these were not people embarking on planned trips, but rather, were individual backpackers. Macleod also reports that there were:

> no universal markers for these tourists, no shared symbols of identity, no single common language or physical boundary; however, they do appear to share a desire for freedom of thought and movement, a need to escape constraints (Macleod 1997: 135).

What they do appear to share however, is the conscious rejection of such visible symbols which, in itself, can be construed as a marker of identity. As Macleod also reports, the term 'alternative' was one used by the tourists themselves, as an 'oppositional category' (1997: 144 n2). These people appear to share, I would suggest, a romanticised rejection of modernity, and in some ways their antecedents can be traced back to the hippies of the late 1960s and the 'new age' travellers and ravers of the 1980s and 1990s (see also Bender, 1993: 271–6).

In a recent paper Elsrud (1999) suggests that backpacking travellers, mainly young and single, may in some senses, invert that whole notion of security in travel described by Ritzer and deliberately indulge in risk-taking behaviour. She argues that 'acts of risk taking can be used as tools for, and symbols of, distinction between the traveller 'self' and the 'self' of others' (Elsrud 1999: 1). Elsrud suggests that what these people are engaged in is a form of identity construction which revolves around personalised narratives of adventure and risk-taking. What is occurring in these cases is that the consumption of space and time is being worked at (see also Elsrud 1998), in other words consumption may involve active and purposeful interpretation and re-interpretation over and above the purchasing of goods and services. In a similar manner the holiday-makers described by Andrews and Selänniemi also work at their transitory leisure identities through the conspicuous consumption of space and time. Yet this is not simply an individual matter, forms of consumption are as much about establishing social differences as satisfying individual needs (Bourdieu 1984).

Although the consumption of tourist space involves deriving meanings from the environment and the activities pursued within it, as Cohen has pointed out, tourist destinations are the 'realization of the tourist's motivations' (1995: 13). Tourists also bring with them their own social and cultural perceptions (Clifford 1997) so that places are never viewed through a neutral lens. Accounting for tourist space at both the levels of production and consumption therefore requires some way of accounting for the values and preconceptions that tourists bring with them, as well as the values and preconceptions that the producers of tourist space create or impose.

The consuming gaze?

There can be little doubt that the visual component of tourism, sightseeing, is a major element in tourist consumption. In 1976 MacCannell wrote: '*sightseeing is a ritual performed to the differentiations of society*' (1976: 13), a formulation which was later developed in Urry's metaphor of the 'tourist gaze' (1990a, 1992) and, more recently, into a concern with the sensual (Urry 1999). What these approaches have in common is the emphasis they place on the visual aspects of sightseeing as a fundamental and defining characteristic of tourism, as that which marks it as a distinct form of social activity. What they also share is the idea that the marking of places or sites as distinct, as being apart from the day-to-day routines of daily life means that in Urry's words the signs collected by tourists have to be 'out of the ordinary' (1990b: 11). Despite the criticism by Abrams (1997) which asserts that Urry's formulation overemphasises the visual, I would still argue that the gaze (Urry) or the semiotic of attraction (see also MacCannell 1992) are key elements in the tourist system. The demarcation of places or sites as distinct and different is both a necessary and defining characteristic of tourism, yet I also have doubts that this is the entire story.

Apart from the differentiation of spaces as distinct, as objects to be looked at, Urry defines three other salient aspects of this gaze. First, professionals often self-consciously produce them – these are the imagined worlds of popular discourses of travel and otherness.

Secondly, they are 'authorised by different discourses' (Urry 1990b: 135) and thirdly, there is a further distinction between the romantic and the collective gaze. The first aspect is the least contentious of the three, and there is plenty of evidence to support this claim. After all, those involved in the production of the tourist system must, by necessity, draw on themes that are recognisable at a commonsense level. The second point is more problematic, and requires some explanation. At one level it means that the images and objects of the tourist gaze are derived from a wide variety of traditions or genres concerning the nature and function of tourism. These can include, for example, the grand tour, holidaying for health as in sea bathing, or the unbridled hedonism of sun, sea and sex. Such genres do not spring into autonomous existence, but instead are the result of historical processes, which in turn can be seen to link into particular social formations, they are in effect, symbolic constructions.

On another level, however, it amounts to saying forms of discourse, or genres of writing, speech, images and the environment, have a semi-autonomous existence as cultural products and are privileged over individual actions, as if discourses themselves constitute the world (Callinicos 1999: 275). In this sense, Urry suggests that the ways in which people gaze at sites is in part determined by the existence of narratives that frame expectations, that prescribe what should and should not be gazed at. They are in short, forms of authority in the Foucauldian or deconstructionist sense (Delanty 1997: 105–7). It would be foolish to deny that narratives, discourses or genres shape our expectations. As an example, we can see that ideas and images of a prelapsarian paradise continue to provide the basic material for many tour brochures that create an exotic other (Dann 1996, Selwyn 1993). But not *all* social reality is simply socially constructed through discourse or by symbolic means. Despite Luhmann (and indeed others), who asserts that society is a 'self observing and self describing system' (1999: 149), people are not simply subject to gazes or discourses, but to actual material processes and practices of the tourist system which is realised in particular social formations in particular localities. To adopt an approach that privileges the gaze in this way tends towards an idealisation of both the symbolic realm and tourist consumption in which meanings are detached from the material circumstances out of which they are constructed. The central issue is one of representation, image is seen to be more important than anything else because the tourist gaze is conceptualised as being evidence of the shift from modernity to postmodernity (Luhmann 1999: 85).

Although the idea that symbolic realms are both culturally and historically contingent is accurate, indeed, they could not be otherwise, Urry's formulation of the gaze implies that we all decode the same messages, the gaze is 'universalised' (Urry 1990b: 135). What the tourist seeks, he argues, is a set of prescribed images, which are then collected through the medium of photography. Not only does the gaze sanction what can be looked at, it also becomes the whole reason for tourism itself as 'photography gives shape to travel [which is]...a strategy for the accumulation of photographs' (1990b: 139). Although Urry acknowledges that tourism in some way recapitulates social divisions (1990b: 141) the gaze nevertheless presupposes an ideal category of *the* tourist who can only respond to a set of prescribed meanings encoded in discourses and images. In chapter two I drew attention to the problems of assuming that readings could be derived from the environment in a simple one-to-one fashion without accounting for the ways in which this may be mediated by a variety of social factors. In other words, the gaze cannot adequately account for multiple, different, conflicting interpretations, apart from that offered by the ironic detachment of the postmodern subject. This hapless individual is apparently doomed to flit aimlessly from simulation to simulation, aware that 'Everything is a copy, or a text upon a text, where what is fake seems more real than the real'. (Urry 1990b: 85) This indeed is a seaside funfair hall of mirrors. The possibility that different readings may not only exist, but may also actually conflict with or reinforce each other in complex ways, although mentioned, is largely glossed over (see for example Edensor 1998, Picard 1996).

The third aspect I mentioned above, the existence of two dominant gazes is also problematic. The romantic gaze is equated with solitude and privacy. In other words it is elitist, and also requires a particular form of social knowledge (Urry 1990b: 86). The collective tourist gaze, by contrast, requires the presence of other tourists, or people like oneself (1990b: 46) and is equated with mass tourism. The problem here is the split of a complex phenomenon into another either/or binary distinction. As Frow points out, the romantic and collective are not necessarily exclusive. Indeed to talk of collectivity in this sense 'establishes a false universality' (Frow 1997: 96). Now whereas in the past it could be argued that as tourism was a pre-

dominantly western phenomenon, one exported as it were to the rest
of the world, then these gazes may have some form of historically
contingent universality. However, in terms of the global system, this
no longer holds true. As I mentioned in the previous chapter, the
newly industrialised countries of Asia are themselves becoming net
'exporters' of tourists. There is no evidence or reason to suppose
that, for example, the 'gaze' of other cultures is intrinsically the same
as that anywhere else. There is more than enough ethnographic
evidence to make a convincing case otherwise (Fardon 1995, Martinez 1998, Miller 1995a, 1995c, Sahlins 1985). Even if we allow for the
fact that there are different gazes situated in different cultures, the
interesting question, then, is what is the basis on which they are
formed, and in a globalised world, how do they interact?

However, the criticisms I have advanced here are not sufficient
reason to reject the whole idea as such and certainly both Urry and
MacCannell are correct in drawing attention to the visual elements of
tourism which are clearly key components. It cannot be denied that
places are commodified for forms of tourist consumption which
involve a visual component, they are indeed made into sights or
sites, and also, it is their visual distinctiveness that sets them apart.
Neither can it be denied that discourses of travel and otherness play a
role in the motivation of tourists, and hence patterns of consumption. However, the notion of the gaze is problematic in a number of
respects, not the least being the status that is accorded to one aspect
of the tourist system at the expense of others. The utility of the gaze
rests, I would argue, in its use as a general concept of some aspects of
tourist consumption, it is not an organising principle as such, a point
also made by Böröcz who comments that although the gaze is an
'unremovable part of consumption' (1996: 11) it is only one part.

Narratives of place and consumption

Earlier I mentioned that tourist consumption was often something
that needs to be 'worked at' beyond the point of purchase. The same
point is also made by Urry (1990a: 25) in terms of the use of
photographs, which may be thought of as the means by which people
commodify their own experiences. A photographic record provides
the material witness so to speak, that one has seen the sights, been
there and done that. In this sense, they are goods to be worked at

beyond the immediate point of commodification, functioning in much the same way as other forms of souvenirs and mementoes (Bruner 1995) perhaps to the extent of being used, like other goods, as personalised extensions of the self (Belk 1995). On a similar note, Miles argues that the notion of McDonaldization overemphasises the controlling aspect of contemporary society, and underestimates the ability that consumers have to interpret and negotiate or indeed to create their own particular meaning (Miles 1998: 63). If we allow for this, then, it is possible to say that the gaze is not the end point of consumption, but one element in the creation of personal narratives that order and shape experience. As MacCannell astutely observed, 'The commodity has become a means to an end. The end is an immense accumulation of reflexive experiences which synthesize fiction and reality into a vast symbolism, a modern world' (MacCannell 1976: 23).

Now it could be argued that the production of images through photography is not actually a form of commodification in the strict sense of the word, as these are not goods produced for their exchange value. However, this is a rather restricted and limiting conception of commodities. Kopytoff (1986) for example, argues that commodities are not fixed in the sense that they can enter into or leave the cycle of production and exchange. As an example, in the previous chapter I pointed to the de-commodification of redundant industrial spaces and their recommodification as consumption spaces, as spaces that have been worked at to provide a new range of meanings (Zukin 1995). Kopytoff also adds that the biographies, or histories, of material goods, especially in terms of culture contact, can reveal that their significance 'is not the fact that they are adopted, but the way they are culturally redefined and put to use' (Kopytoff 1986: 67).

He also argues that in complex societies, 'public' commodification coexists with other schemes of valuation such as those held by individuals, social categories and groups (Kopytoff 1986: 79–80). In terms of the gaze, it could be argued that what Urry identifies are forms of public commodification and consumption, as is the revaluation of urban spaces. Much the same point is made by Lunt and Livingstone who, drawing on the framework provided by both Kopytoff (1986) and Appadurai (1986), argue that the social lives of commodities 'can be understood as a series of narratives' (Lunt and Livingstone 1992: 14). Also drawing on the same analytical framework, Long and Villareal (1999) show how a commodity can go through a series of transformations of meaning as it progresses along the commodity chain from production to consumption. These examples serve to underline the point that the symbolic nature of commodities is not fixed but is open to a variety of valuations and interpretations which do not exist as free-floating entities, but are derived from material practices.

In terms of tourism, it is possible to argue that commodification can be conceptualised as occurring on two interrelated levels, first, in terms of the images and preconceptions presented by tour operators in brochures, and through other forms of media, that is, representations of space. Secondly, as being derived from the representational spaces of lived experience, which are organised into more or less coherent narratives at a personalised level. To conceptualise aspects of the tourist system in this way is a move away from the notion of the consumer as simply being a passive recipient at the end of a commodity chain, to being an active agent capable of reflexively organising experiences into forms of self-identity (Giddens 1991).

The fact that experiences are mediated through forms of commodification, or expressed through the possession of commodities does not diminish them. In fact, this process can be seen as a means to render abstract personal experiences into material forms capable of being recognised as such by others. In this sense, the symbolic representations of space are appropriated and incorporated as forms of personal knowledge derived from the representational spaces of others. The backpackers described above by Elsrud are a case in point. What is occurring here, she argues, is that the experiences of travel are worked at beyond the actual event, they become narratives to be traded and exchanged between other backpackers. They provide another way in which the consumption of experiences of tourists, whether in visual (photographs), physical (souvenirs), or narrative form (stories) are used to position the individual. 'Through retelling an act' she adds, 'through postcards, photo-shows or article writing, the traveller may carry out more identity work' (Elsrud 1999: 13). As she indicates, what is occurring here are forms of social distinction, of social segmentation as the backpackers are defining their identities in terms of experiences which distinguish them from other categories of tourists, while at the same time confirming membership of some other form of social group. In this sense it is possible to say that, through their actions, they are accruing some form of symbolic capital:

> Many of the interviewed travellers also believe their actions will work favourably when applying for jobs or when making new friends. It will make them an 'exciting person' or 'self reliant', 'powerful' and 'strong' (Elsrud 1999: 13).

By the same token, gays and lesbians, by becoming consumers of certain spaces enact forms of social differentiation, just as much as the hedonistic tourists in Palmanova and Magaluf. From these examples we can see that forms of tourist consumption involve a large number of variables, and from that we can also infer they involve very different motivations. What these examples also indicate, however, is how patterns of tourism consumption can also be mapped in terms of the social position of those involved. This cannot be carried out in any simple deterministic way, through applying categories such as 'class' or 'socio-economic status' but rather as a combination of factors including lifestyle, age, income, group and individual identity. Although differences may be expressed through the spatial location of holiday choice, or the kind of holiday chosen, broad patterns of tourist consumption can be identified. The fact that such similarities exist at all can be taken as evidence that tourism consumption is a social rather than an individual matter. Even the individualisation of experiences and their creation as narratives of the self takes place in a context that is mediated by the material as much as symbolic means. Earlier I drew attention to a projected trend in tourism that implied that tourists in the near future will be financially rich but time impoverished. The implication of this for the development of tourism is that tourists will be more active in seeking what could be termed quality of experience, that the conspicuous consumption of time and space in itself will not be sufficient, and that what is done may be of greater importance. In other words, people may well have to work harder at consuming their leisure.

Conclusion

At the start of this chapter I outlined some of the broad issues relating to the changing nature of production and consumption.

What is significant, is the general trend away from mass production and how consumption can be seen as a consequence of accepting the principles of post-Fordism as standard orthodoxy. Tourism may in some ways appear to be fragmenting, yet it still shows that forms of social cohesion are of central importance. This may involve an apparent rejection of modernity and an assertion of individual difference, or 'subcontracting' the organisational aspects to travel agents or adult responsibility to others. It is clear that the processes of tourist commodification involve more than simply the exchange value of commodities or more than the consumption of a range of goods and services in the strict material sense. What is being consumed here, or rather, produced by the tourists to be consumed later, to be 'worked at' past the point of origin, is an amalgam of received cultural categories. In turn, these include expectations, desires and wants, ideas of what is important to view and record, to maintain and discard. The tourist, armed with a still or video camera, is rendering their experiences into a socially recognisable form, a personalised memento or commodity through which cultural capital can be accrued. The gaze is important, but this is only one element, it is not the end point, nor the sole underlying causal factor. Tourism also involves forms of experiential practices other than simply looking.

These, in turn, are a combination of individual forms of knowledge and experience derived from the places visited, as much as from the preconceptions and culturally defined forms of knowledge that tourists arrive with. In this sense people are not passive consumers but active agents in the construction of the symbolic economy. Consumption then can be seen not as an end point but as a means of creating and positioning the individual in relation to others. It is the symbolic values that are ascribed to, and derived from, places and their development as coherent and personalised narratives of consumption that are of significance. Yet this process does not take place in a vacuum in terms of both social values and constraints as much as material constraints. As I have argued in this chapter, there is also a substantial element of order and control within the tourist system that either consciously strives to channel and direct tourist consumption, or results from people willingly giving over responsibility to others. In the preceding chapters I also noted how many analysts have tended to see the process of commodification as inherently false and even alienating. As I have argued in this chapter, there is much more to it than that. Tourists are not simply driven in simply determined causal ways, they are not passive. Yet this still needs further discussion, particularly in relation to the ways in which many criticisms of tourist commodification have been cast in terms of a loss of authenticity.

Chapter 5

Authenticity and Heritage

Introduction

In chapter one I argued against essentialist and reductionist analyses of tourism, and I also noted that the interrelated concepts of authenticity and heritage have been a dominant theme within the analysis of tourism. In chapter three I also pointed out that many of the criticisms of tourist development tended to assume that modernity was a universal and essentially negative phenomenon which, through the processes of commodification, destroyed or modified the authenticity of other cultures and places. Usually, the problem of 'cultural contamination' or the 'staging' of authenticity is simply uncritically accepted as a given or a necessary state of affairs, as if, as Kuper writes 'The rest of the world is apparently condemned to repeat the cultural drama that had its premiere in the metropolis' (1999: 232). In this chapter I will argue that the notion of authenticity within tourism analysis is predicated on a false dichotomy between the non-modern, viewed as the authentic, and the modern, viewed as the inauthentic. If this dichotomy is accepted as false, it therefore follows that it is a fundamental error to assume that there is a universal category of authenticity composed of innate, essential cultural attributes (Frow 1997). Authenticity, therefore, needs to be seen as a category that is created and recreated in contingent circumstances, sometimes serving to uphold political or ideological positions as much as catering for the tourism market.

Authenticity, alienation and the 'exotic other'

The idea of tourism as a search for authenticity to counteract the alienation and loss of modernity immediately begs the question of what precisely the authentic is, and where it can be found. In itself, this is far from being a subject of recent concern (May 1996: 716) and within the tourism literature, a concern with authenticity has been one of the more consistent themes since the emergence of the genre (Cohen 1988a). In many ways such concerns are not unique to tourism and can be seen as a reiteration of the long and well-worn theme concerning the corrosive nature of modernity on traditional life, which is found not only within the social sciences, but also in popular discourse (Lowenthal 1985). In turn, this is largely derived from Marxist notions of alienated labour (Craib 1997: 88–91, Lyon 1999) which, more recently, has been filtered through the Frankfurt School of critical theory (Britton 1982; MacCannell 1992)

As I mentioned in chapter one, such approaches have relied heavily on MacCannell's initial analysis (1976) and have been reworked in a number of versions since (MacCannell 1992). Tourism is seen as a metaphysical search for completeness, for the authenticity of 'primal' social and cultural relations, a pilgrim's progress of the alienated. If this basic assumption is accepted, then it logically follows that all that modernism brings with it will *by definition* be false, alienating, unreal and inauthentic. Therefore all attempts to recover authentic ways of life and being are simply compensatory mechanisms enacted as individual responses to some unfulfilled need which is both structurally determined and inherently irresolvable. In this way, the contemporary and traditional are regarded as possessing essential and mutually exclusive characteristics. Modernity is dystopia and tourism the search for utopia.

There is no doubt that certain cultures or, more precisely, destinations are portrayed as 'exotic' and are often described within promotional literature as being places set apart from modernity where the tourist can encounter the untamed other in its natural, authentic habitat (Dann 1996, MacCannell 1992, Selwyn 1993). At one level, to view other cultures as the remnants of the pre-industrial age amounts to little more than a misplaced romanticisation of traditional life (Crick 1989). Modernity is viewed as both the antithesis and rampant destroyer of the authentic. The tourism literature is replete with dire warnings of cultural collapse or contamination that will inevitably occur with the arrival of tourism. No sooner is 'paradise' discovered than it is apparently overrun by the barbarian hordes of alienated moderns (Turner and Ashe 1975) or is contaminated by acculturation. Even to invoke the term authenticity presupposes some state of inauthenticity against which it can be measured and compared, even if only in an impressionistic or superficial manner.

It is of course not just people that are the problem, but the entire structure of modernity. As Finlayson argues, there is a conflict between the 'developmental tendencies of mass society and the 'traditional' culture it supplants' (1999: 148). In particular, this conflict can apply to the processes of commodification of both cultures and people to serve the needs of the tourist system. Such arguments propose that aspects of the lives of others such as rituals are decontextualised and thus rendered inauthentic and, following from that, indigenous crafts and artefacts become degraded if they are produced not for internal use but for external tourist consumption. In short, culture cannot be bought and sold without negative effects (Bleasdale and Tapsell 1999, Henrici 1999).

Now it seems to me that, on the surface, such a scenario has both an obvious appeal and some explanatory power, which probably explains why it has been so commonly accepted as a given state of affairs. If we accept the premise, then it appears to explain the whole tourist system in terms of a rather simple and easy-to-grasp cause–effect model which goes as follows. The division of labour within modern capitalist societies causes alienation, and a consequent loss of authentic social relations and authentic material culture. This, in turn, creates a need to find the Holy Grail of authentic otherness. However, due to the all-pervasive nature of modernity, many of the authentic elements of cultures have either been irretrievably lost, or are in danger of becoming lost. It follows, therefore, that a concern with authenticity is, on the one hand, a critique of modernity while, on the other, a call to action to protect what is left from any further loss. The problem here lies in presuming that authenticity is first, an essential characteristic of the non-modern and, second, a key principle in the organisation of tourism per se, as Urry writes 'it would be incorrect to suggest that a search for authenticity is the basis for the organisation of tourism' (Urry 1990b: 11).

There are, therefore, a number of problems with this scenario. The notion of a loss of meaning for both the 'natives' and the tourists is problematic. The former are either criticised for commodifying and selling their heritage, or for being the passive victims of modernity, while the latter are either being deluded by the 'natives' or are deluding themselves if they think that what they get is the real thing. Both positions run the risk of falling into a patronising elitism which views other cultures as possessing essential authentic attributes which need to be preserved simply for the gaze of the tourists, which also assumes that such cultures are locked in the past and 'going nowhere' (Butcher 1997: 29).

At another level, to accept alienation as the prime motivation behind individual choice presupposes another universal category, that of 'the tourist'. This idea, as mentioned in chapter one, has been challenged by Cohen (1988a) who argues that alienation may be a motivating factor for some groups of tourists, but not for others. In order to solve this problem, Cohen proposes a typology that seeks to differentiate between different kinds of tourists, and different forms of tourism that can be represented in table 5.1.

Table 5.1 Typology of authenticity

Tourist type	Alienation	Authenticity	Holiday type
Existential	high	central	elitist, independent
Experiential			
Recreational			
Diversionary	low	unimportant	mass package

Source: adapted from Cohen (1988a)

It can be seen that this typology does not dispose of the twin concepts of alienation and authenticity, rather it sees them as part of a continuum. This ranges from the highly alienated existential tourists, who deliberately seek the authentic other – and who often regard themselves as travellers rather than tourists – to the non-alienated diversionary tourists for whom authenticity is not important. As I noted in chapter three, there is certainly evidence to suggest that some tourists are motivated to seek out the 'real' and 'authentic' but whether or not this is for personal or existential fulfilment, or for the purposes of accruing some form of cultural or social capital, is open to debate.

Wang's (1999) recent and comprehensive review of authenticity in tourism builds on these distinctions. He argues that there are three broad definitional approaches to the problem of authenticity: the objective, the constructive and the existential. The first, objective definition of authenticity is applied in situations where the provenance of an artefact needs to be established as in, for example, museums. For purposes of historical research, for example, the provenance of an artefact needs to be established beyond doubt. At a base level, this implies some form of individuality and uniqueness, an essence, which cannot be replicated without loss. As Wang observes, confusion often arises when this type of definition is applied to other situations, such as whole cultures, or the tourist system, as if it is the only measure of authenticity (1999: 353).

The second form of authenticity is what Wang terms constructive, that is, authenticity defined in terms of 'beliefs, perspectives, powers' (1999: 351). In other words, authenticity is a matter of negotiation, or ascribed meanings. It is either therefore specific to a particular culture, or to some subsection or social grouping, which is not to say that such claims to authenticity are therefore false or mistaken. What is important here is not whether the object or indeed ritual or culture in question fits any measure of external objective criteria in terms of its provenance, but rather the socially constructed consensus that it has some form of symbolic value. This formulation is similar to the concept of 'emergent authenticity' proposed by Cohen (1988a) and that of the 'invention of tradition' (Hobsbawm and Ranger 1983). What they amount to saying is that traditions or indeed artefacts may come to be seen as the embodiment of cultural authenticity over a period of time. The search for origins or first causes of an artefact or ritual as proof of its authentic nature is therefore the application of the museum definition of authenticity to situations where it is simply not appropriate.

The third form that Wang identifies is that of existential authenticity, which relates to experiences at an individual level, a formulation that is very close to Cohen's. Both challenge the idea that there is one category of the tourist, and argue that motivations cannot simply be explained by the hidden hand of an abstract system, that people are not passive dupes. However, the value of these approaches is that they allow for the fact that some people may well feel alienated and see tourism as a way to compensate for this perceived lack, but this cannot be applied as a universal category.

Wang's article devotes a great deal of attention to this latter category, which he seems to rate as the more important. As the examples discussed in the last chapter indicate the meanings of commodities are not fixed, but open to reinterpretation at both an individual and social level. In certain circumstances, people may work at their identities through the construction of personalised narratives of the self mediated through commodity forms. If there is a danger in this approach, it is that of elevating individual perceptions and individual forms of consumption, and relegating the social and material elements from which they are constructed. Authenticity, I would argue, is a constructed value or set of values, but cannot be accounted for without considering the social and material contexts in which it is located.

Tradition and heritage

Tradition is a term used to justify all manner of social practices and institutions on the commonsense basis that, having survived for a number of years, they therefore possess some intrinsic value for the culture in which they are located. In short, they are the embodiment of authentic ways of life. Indeed, the whole concept of modernism itself, as a distinctive form of social, cultural and political organisation, is predicated on a contrast with what are perceived as more traditional ways of life (Handler 1988, Macdonald 1997b).

There are a number of aspects that need to be considered under the headings of tradition and authenticity, bearing in mind that they often overlap in a variety of ways. First, there is culture in its broadest sense such as language, literature, music and the arts, and of course, history. Secondly, there exists national borders and tracts of land regarded as sacred homelands, patterns of agricultural production and particular forms of social and political organisation, which we can refer to as national culture. Thirdly there are particular forms of material culture which are seen to embody the essential qualities of difference, of distinctiveness: styles of clothing, domestic architecture, certain forms of art, to which we would also need to add the production of indigenous crafts and souvenirs. Fourthly, there are the day-to-day means of coping with the routines of existence: patterns of work and domestic arrangements, distinctive cuisines, forms of religion, rituals, ceremonies and traditions of all kinds. It needs to be borne in mind that a full list would really have to include every aspect of human activity and material production. The important point, however, is that each or any of these has the potential to be taken as the authentic embodiment of national, regional and local culture. It is through such systems of classifying both people and objects that identities are both created and sustained.

Now it could be argued that only those traditions which actually have some resonance with people's needs and identities are those that survive, yet in popular discourses it often seems to be ignored that all traditions must have started at some point in time (Cannadine 1989, Hobsbawm and Ranger 1983). However, it is not sufficient to say that, therefore, all traditions are invented, for the interesting questions here are invented by whom, where, and what for? Further, simply to reveal the origins of traditions, or even to accept that they are not perhaps as 'timeless' as they are often portrayed, does not explain the power they may exert, nor the attachment people may have to them. To reveal the origins of a particular tradition does not therefore diminish the role that such traditions, whenever they were first created, may have in the lives of individuals or groups.

Whereas the term tradition usually refers to ways of life, heritage typically refers to material culture, although this is no longer a hard and fast distinction (see below). Originally heritage was applied to aspects of the built environment which were considered to be of architectural or historical importance (Department of the Environment 1975). Concerns about the natural and built environment, as much as culture in its widest sense, have resulted in both national and global legislation to preserve and conserve the authentic heritage. This is not only for the purposes of tourism (Herbert 1995, Swarbrooke, 1995, Zeppel and Hall 1992 for example) but also for the more politically expedient purpose of creating and sustaining a sense of nation and place through symbolic means (Gillis 1994, Lowenthal 1993; A.D. Smith 1991).

The discovery or creation of heritage grew out of concerns in the developed economies that modernity was sweeping all before it, and was originally applied to the preservation of the historic fabric of towns and cities (Ashworth, 1994, Hunter 1981, Lowenthal 1985). Although this can be dated back to the nineteenth century, it was only during the 1970s and 1980s that the vogue for nostalgia moved from being an elite preoccupation to one that was more populist (Lowenthal 1994: 43). In turn, this was reflected in changing fashions such as interior decor, the revaluation of domestic architecture and the processes of gentrification which occurred within urban areas across the developed world, resulting in the revaluation and aestheticisation of space as discussed in chapter two.

Changes in popular taste were matched by changes to the national legislation, and the importance of the state in defining heritage can be seen by the enactment of conservation laws. In the UK, a succession of Acts of Parliament set out to both define and protect the heritage for future generations. Considerable powers were also granted to local authorities, in particular the power to list buildings that were deemed to be of significance. The criteria for inclusion on this list was based initially on a form of museum definition of authenticity. It was the singularity or uniqueness of individual buildings of particular architectural merit that was the main consideration. During the 1970s, as gentrification gathered pace, this was then extended to encompass particular townscapes and collections of buildings. In addition, the industrial heritage of late Victorian Britain was also added, and more recently, buildings in the modernist style have also come to be seen as worthy of inclusion. What we see here then is a broadening of the classificatory scheme. What was being conserved was considered as the authentic embodiment of the nation.

Similar patterns of development can be see in other advanced industrial economies. In the USA, the Register of Historic Places was established with the passing of the 1966 National Historic Preservation Act and now has 68,000 properties listed (US Department of the Interior, National Park Service, 1999a). Once more, we can see that a broadening of the classifications as the 1980 amendment to this act added both 'intangible' elements as well as 'ethnic and folk cultural traditions' (Parker and King, 1995) – further evidence of a shift away from the initial concerns with material elements of the built environment to broader issues concerned with cultural history.

The natural environment, too, was also subject to legislation through the creation of national parks for example, which were not confined to the developed world (Elliott 1997: 220). Such measures also have a political component, as both practical and symbolic legitimacy for the nation stems from the existence of borders, the demarcation of a homeland as the repository of shared history. In turn, this is considered to be authentic, natural and 'sacred' (A.D. Smith 1991: 9). Particular tracts of land are deemed significant either because historic events of national importance occurred there, or as the embodiment of some more abstract ideals (Jackson and Penrose

1993, Lowenthal 1993). Macdonald, for example, points to the ways
that the highlands of Scotland 'furnished so many of the visible
symbols of Scottishness' (1997b: 5) while Jones (1993) writes about
similar processes in identifying the cultural landscape of Norway. In
this way the physical landscape acts as a metaphorical evocation of
the authentic nation (see also Cosgrove and Daniels 1988).

Imagined pasts, imagined places

As I have shown, the category of heritage has been expanded beyond
notions concerning the original provenance of objects to include less
tangible aspects of culture and the natural environment. As well as
the obvious physical manifestations of heritage then, we also need to
consider the metaphorical and imaginary components of places, as
tourism relies to a great extent on the commodification of ideals as
much as the physical environment. Short for example, examines the
relationship between landscape and metaphor in literature and the
arts and demonstrates how these are linked to political ideologies so
that, for example, the Western as a genre of film-making 'embodies
general myths of wilderness and countryside and, in particular, US
ideologies of nation building' (Short 1991: 178). By way of contrast,
he also shows how successive styles in Australian landscape painting
reveal a shift in perceptions from a romantic and Eurocentric notion
of landscape to one in which Aboriginal paintings are being viewed as
an authentic manifestation of a distinctly Australian culture, although
the production of such works of art is not without controversy (see
below). Further examples of this form of commodification can be
seen in Japan, where the heritage of Holland, Britain and Turkey have
been successfully imported in the forms of cultural theme parks for
Japanese domestic consumption (McGuigan 1996). In a similar vein
Pretes (1995) draws our attention to the development of Santa Claus
tourism and the arguments over which country could claim to be the
'authentic' homeland of this ubiquitous seasonal commodifier.

The creation of such imaginary places, or spatial narratives, is one
of the standard tools in tourism, and can depend as much on the
ubiquitous influence of film and television as much as print. The
British Tourist Authority for example publishes a film map which
matches films to the locations in which they were shot (BTA 2000).
Another form of development which owes much to the imaginary

can be found in the numerous heritage centres, where theme park technology meets history. The Jorvik Centre in York, the first of its kind in the UK, prides itself on its authenticity and detail, even down to the simulated smells, while the Robin Hood Centre in Nottingham presents a series of tableaux based on the legendary tales of the folk hero. Another variant on this theme is that of re-enactment, one example being that of the Plimoth Plantation site in the USA, where people in period costume play out the roles of early seventeenth century settlers (Plimoth-on-Web 1999, Tramposch, 1994). In these cases we can see the realm of the imaginary being commodified as heritage for the purposes of tourism. Places are seeking to distinguish themselves from each other through generating narratives of an imagined past, presented as definitive, essential characteristics. These narratives of place come closest to supporting Urry's notion of the tourist gaze, and are further evidence of the ways in which forms of cultural symbolism are now firmly incorporated into the tourist economy.

The politics of heritage

The idea of the national heritage can encompass notions of landscape and, indeed, notions of race (Schama 1995, Wright 1995). By labelling an object, building or site as part of the heritage, it is elevated above the mundane into a symbol of a nation, or people. For example, it has become somewhat commonplace, but nonetheless true, to assert that nations are imaginary constructs (Anderson 1983) partly defined and maintained through symbolic means such as flags, anthems, rituals and traditions (Hobsbawm and Ranger 1983). The idea of the nation is also inextricably bound with the idea of place at a variety of spatial scales, and the existence of a definable heritage. Claims that a distinct culture has existed in an area in the past is in some respects to lay claim to a particular history and, as Hall makes clear, arguments concerning the nature of heritage are as much about history as politics. He goes on to say that 'the cultural and heritage resources of any country should not be seen as existing solely to serve the needs of the tourism industry' (Hall 1994: 186).

Although heritage is a significant factor in the cultural economy of tourism, it can serve other purposes too, or perhaps even several purposes at once. The city of York, UK, has for many years pursued urban policies which seek to conserve the historic fabric of the city. Although at one level concerned with the national importance of many of its buildings, at another level such policies are also the means by which the city is commodified for the purposes of tourism (Meethan 1996a, 1997). Similar instances can be found in almost all urban areas in both the developed and developing world (Chang 1997, Judd and Fainstein, 1999). The concerns of authenticity and heritage are therefore played out on more than one level. Both Browne (1994) and Graham (1994) focus on the development of heritage in Ireland. Graham argues that the possession of a heritage is a necessary component of the nation state, and as such, is specific to both time and place (Graham 1994: 135). He also notes that the incorporation of the Irish Republic into the European Union (EU) has resulted in a new form of heritage which reflects this change in political alignments, while Ulster asserts its own particular identity through a different kind of heritage. Of course such links between heritage, politics and indeed the transnational economy of the EU are also important in terms of tourism. Graham also points out that a Bord Fáilte (Irish Tourist Board) survey of 1988 revealed that the most popular activity for overseas tourists was visiting heritage sites (1988: 152). Browne's analysis also draws attention to the conscious government strategy initiated in 1988 to double overseas visitors, and the role of EU structural funding committed between 1994 and 1999 to help develop the tourist industry (Browne 1994: 24). Macdonald (1997a) also points out that the development of a heritage centre on the Scottish Island of Skye was as much to do with creating a sense of regional and local identity as it was about tourism, while Worden (1997) records that in South Africa, government policies are designed to foster a new post-apartheid sense of nationhood through encouraging internal as well as external tourism, and that using the heritage of the anti–apartheid struggle is one way of achieving this aim.

Although heritage can appear to be about the rendering of abstract ideals into visible forms, it can also be open to conflicting interpretations. In chapter two I noted how space can be subject to a variety of interpretations, or 'readings' concerning its symbolic significance. Consider the Taj Mahal, one of the best known buildings and most famous tourist attractions in the world. Edensor (1998) notes that there are many different interpretations of just what the Taj represents, some of which are charged with political and religious overtones as both Hindus and Muslims have different, if not competing claims over the site. In turn, these are very different from the interpretations that tourists will place on the site. Another example of the relationship between place, heritage and politics is Lewandowski's (1984) study of architecture and urban planning in postcolonial Madras. She records that when the Tamil nationalist party took control of the state of Madras in 1967 they not only changed its name to Tamil Nadu, but also made conscious attempts to create a specific Tamil heritage through the renaming of streets and roads, the championing of Tamil writers, and the encouragement of Tamil forms of architecture in public buildings. She also points out that such processes can be found in other regions and states of India, where forms of planning and architecture were less tied to European models and style, and becoming indigenised. In this case we clearly see conscious attempts to impose or create some form of political and cultural cohesion though the manipulation of the spaces of representation. Another attempt to create, or more precisely control, distinctive forms of architecture directly as a result of tourism is provided by Williams and Papamichael's study of the town of Paláiá Epidhvaros (1995) whose local economy was heavily dependent on tourism. In 1984 a Presidential Decree was enacted which required conformity to a specified kind of domestic architecture, and created zoning restrictions in the town, in part to provide an appropriate setting for the nearby archaeological sites. These restrictions caused resentment among the population for a number of reasons. First, it was imposed by outside interests. Secondly, the proposals ran counter to the established patterns of land use for building purposes, and finally, what was regarded as 'traditional' was not only vague, but also did not conform to what might be regarded as 'authentic' local architecture. From these examples, which are not so unique, we can see the clear linkage between the construction of heritage as an expression of national identity and the political and cultural economy.

There is more to heritage and authenticity than either the need to conserve, or the need to commodify the past for tourist consumption. Heritage can also serve a didactic purpose in educating or fostering a sense of nationhood (Handler 1988), or a more locally based sense of belonging (Bohlin 1998) for consumption by both 'insiders' and 'outsiders', as well as simply providing some form of diversion or entertainment. The increasing commodification of heritage does not diminish this fact, nor does it render heritage inauthentic, rather it indicates that the production and consumption of heritage is closely tied to the broader issues of politics, the economy and other forms of cultural distinction, and can serve more than one purpose. It is also clear that one of the purposes of heritage, inasmuch as it is consciously planned, is to act as a bulwark against modernity, heritage is a means of differentiating cultures in terms of both space and time, and as such stresses heterogeneity as opposed to homogeneity.

Global heritage

Notions of authenticity and its manifestation as heritage then are closely connected to idea of the nation state, and perhaps to competing claims from different social or religious groupings as much as to the development of local and regional economies or a sense of distinctiveness. Yet like so many aspects of contemporary life, heritage is also a global concern. In 1972 UNESCO adopted a resolution involving 150 member states to define sites, both natural, cultural and mixed, deemed to be of international significance (Herrmann 1989, UNESCO 1999a) and hence worth preserving. Enacted in 1975 (Hewison 1989) the list had, by 1993, grown to include 378 sites of which 276 were cultural, 87 natural, and 15 mixed (Eidsvik 1993: 45). By 1997, this list had doubled to 552 sites (UNESCO, 1999b: 111.1, 7) and by December 1998, the total reached 582 of which 445 were cultural, 117 natural and 20 mixed (UNESCO 1999a). These include places such as the Grand Canyon, USA, Angkor Wat, Cambodia, Durham Cathedral and Stonehenge, UK, Auschwitz, Poland, Taj Mahal, India, and Robben Island, South Africa, all of which, if not actually top tourist attractions, have the capability of being so. The listing of sites as being of global significance confers status and entry to the elite group of nations whose cultural authenticity cannot then be doubted.

Despite this rather rapid growth of designated sites, UNESCO recognises that firstly, there is a bias towards what they term 'the monumental vision and the aesthetic notion of an artistic master-piece' (UNESCO 1999b: 111.11, 18) within which both Africa and South East Asia are under-represented. In other words, the value system by which places are assessed has been dominated by western aesthetics which in turn have tended to emphasise the museum definition of authenticity. Partly in response to this situation, recent developments include a concern with the preservation of the more 'intangible' heritage such as languages and music (UNESCO 1999b) or even 'living cultures' (von Droste 1995: 22) which, as we have seen, is a global trend. For inclusion on the world heritage list, sites must meet 'the test of authenticity in design, material, workmanship or setting and in the case of cultural landscapes their distinctive character or components' (von Droste 1995: 22). The purpose of this definition is to avoid the inclusion of copies or reconstructions, unless these are done 'without conjecture' (1995). As we have seen, defining authenticity is not an easy task, and as von Droste acknowledges heritage must be considered as an 'open, flexible concept which has to be applied on case by case basis' (1995: 23). One of those that von Droste uses as an example concerns the vernacular architecture of the Haida, an indigenous people of the Canadian Pacific coast. One site was deemed worthy of world heritage status, despite the fact that over time the wooden structures had deteriorated and subsequently been renovated to the extent that the 'original' was outweighed by the restored. What is of interest here is that fact that the Haida themselves, as von Droste notes, have a concept of authenticity that is different from the dominant Eurocentric view, emphasising 'culture and tradition more than the material aspects' (von Droste 1995: 23).

Although the aims of UNESCO are to preserve the global heritage, sites are only designated at the request of participating national governments (UNESCO 1999a). In effect this means that both the natural and built environment, and other forms of defining and retrieving the past such as archaeology are not free from political influences (Kristiansen 1989). Indeed it can be argued that the nation state in part defines itself through the creation and maintenance of some form of cultural distinction in which traditions and heritage are key components. In turn, it is these forms of distinction and uniqueness of both places and cultures that become incorporated into the tourist system as commodities. Tourism therefore is implicated in the creation and sustaining of national identities for both domestic and overseas visitors. It is also clear that there is an uneasy relationship between the need to conserve, to manage tourist numbers, and the drive for commodification of people and places which is an integral part of the tourist system. Whether or not this is a development to be welcomed or decried has been the subject of a long-running debate.

More than entertaining nostalgia?

There is little doubt that the popularity of the past, its consequent
commodification and spread across a wide range of cultural activities
contained elements that were obviously anti–modernist, or at least
were deemed worthy of protection. It is worth noting that the
rediscovery and popularising of the past occurred at the same time
that postmodernist styles of cultural production, in particular architecture, were engaged with dismantling the perceived monolithic
status of modernity, and were creating pastiches and parodies of
past stylistic forms.

   In terms of the political climate, the rise of heritage also coincided
with the emergence of the neo-liberal economic orthodoxy discussed
in the previous chapters. To many analysts, at least in the UK, such
populist nostalgia, combined with economic recession was clearly an
indicator of a significant shift in the political and cultural economy.
Heritage became to be viewed in some quarters as an indicator of
decline, most notably perhaps by Hewison (1989) and Wright (1985).
Wright argues that the commodification of history abstracts and
redeploys it within the public realm where 'National Heritage is the
backward glance...a sense that history is foreclosed' (Wright 1985:
70) while for Hewison, the commodification of culture is inherently
negative, resulting in a 'depthless' world of heritage (Hewison 1991:
176).

   Such positions were not without criticism, the historian Raphael
Samuel for example provides a spirited and witty rejection of what
he terms the 'heritage baiters'. Noting that while heritage has
proved to be popular with the general public, it has come under
sustained intellectual criticism from both the left and the right,
and also acts as one of the 'principal whipping boys of Cultural
Studies' (1994: 259–61). These 'heritage baiters' he goes on to
say, view heritage as a distorted, commodified and vulgar appropriation of history, which is being attacked because it 'lacks
authenticity. It is a simulation pretending to be the real thing' (Samuel
1994: 266). As far as Samuel is concerned, this is as much a matter
of elitism and snobbery as anything else, and to a great extent
relies on what he terms the 'perceived opposition between "education" and "entertainment" and the unspoken and unargued for
assumption that pleasure is almost by definition mindless' (Samuel
1994: 271).

As he also argues, many of the criticisms of heritage have tended to come from people who may be – or perhaps would like to be considered as – cultural custodians and arbiters. Indeed the criticisms could also be seen as attempts to wrest control of cultural arbitration away from the perceived distortions and vulgarity of commodification, and to place it back into the elitist world of academe. In a similar fashion, Parker (1998) argues that the whole notion of 'mass culture' in itself implies some form of elitism which can be both from the 'left' as much as from the 'right', or can just be critical for the sake of it. Game for example views heritage as 'not serious history', but rather that which 'is to be consumed as leisure' (Game 1991: 164) as if this in itself is both wrong and indeed, inauthentic. As Kuper comments, 'Every cultural product is judged ... by applying the simple test of the radical' (1999: 231).

Although I have a lot of sympathy with Samuel's analysis, and Kuper's tilt at cultural radicalism for the sake of it (and I write this as a self-confessed, but reformed, heritage baiter), there are some problems. Rather like those he takes to task, Samuel's analysis is as much polemical and conjectural, although I would argue that his criticism is in many respects accurate. Certainly the idea that entertainment, and by implication tourism, is always a passive and mindless activity does not stand up to serious scrutiny any more than assuming the meanings and values of commodities in general are fixed and passively accepted. As the previous sections have shown, heritage can serve more than one purpose, perhaps even at the same time.

Two recent examples, both travel itineraries from the USA, also show how heritage can be used not only as a source of tourism revenue but also as a means of recovering, or rediscovering, aspects of history that may otherwise have been neglected. The first is the 'Places Where Women Made History' itinerary, which lists 74 sites in New York and Massachusetts which are associated with women's history, designed as a strategy to 'revitalize communities by promoting public awareness of history and encouraging tourists'. The second itinerary focuses on the Civil Rights movement of the 1960s. For those unable to travel these itineraries literally, there is also an associated website which describes the significance of each site, with essays explaining their context and background (US Department of the Interior, National Park Service 1998, 1999b). What is interesting about these itineraries is the way in which they are 'recovering' aspects of history which had previously been ignored, or regarded as minority interests. This in turn leads into a series of questions concerning whose heritage is being preserved, recovered, or even invented. It also shows how certain forms of tourism are perhaps less to do with entertainment, and more to do with inculcating a sense of national or minority values, or pride in a particular aspect of ethnic or personal identity.

Heritage, therefore, is not a unified category of objects or places or, for that matter, even people. In Australia, for example, a distinction is made between indigenous heritage, historic heritage, and natural heritage, which together comprise the Register of the National Estate. Indigenous heritage is described in the following manner:

> Over many thousands of years, Aboriginal people have left signs of their occupation in Australia. The reminders of where people lived, where they ate or collected food, how they hunted, their art and their sacred sites. (Australian Heritage Commission (AHC) 1997, unpaginated)

By way of contrast, the historic environment 'refers to places associated with people since European settlement of Australia' (AHC 1997) while the natural heritage appears to be that remaining when the other two categories have been taken into account. There are several points of interest here, a significant example being the recognition that there are two different, if not mutually exclusive, definitions of heritage each of which is linked to very different interpretations of the land, its history and culture.

Heritage therefore encompasses a variety of definitions and interpretations, some of which may well be more openly contested than others. In each case though, heritage is also a means of defining the individuality and authenticity of places, cultures and people and, as such, is a socially constructed means of distinction.

The production of heritage is in some cases irreducibly associated with national, local, religious and ethnic politics and, in others, with more obvious commercial aims or even, in some cases, a mixture of both. In all cases though, heritage serves more than one function. It not only defines that which is seen as the embodiment of authenticity, both material and imagined, but it also creates the conditions in which symbolic value, having been identified, isolated and made tangible, can become the next commodity for sale on the tourist market. It also needs to be borne in mind that, so far, this chapter has been dealing with its production. Less attention

not worrying about the state of the culture, the spread of *kitsch* consumerism, or misrepresentation of their heritage' (Mellor 1991: 107). Whereas Light and Prentice found that heritage consumption was differentiated by socio-economic status, Mellor found that age differences were also an important factor. Older people often used the experience of visiting places to reminisce about their past lives. Mellor's conclusions are that rather than treat people as passive consumers, shaped by the symbolic environment, we need to treat them as active participants. Paraphrasing Marx, he writes that 'People make their own culture, albeit not in circumstances of their own choosing' (Mellor 1991: 114). As I pointed out in chapter three the evidence from other forms of consumer research underlines the point that people are not simply caught in a web of textual significations or signs and symbols over which they have no control. At an individual level they often negotiate the significance of heritage (Mellor 1991). As an example, Squires shows how the consumers of Beatrix Potter-inspired tourism in Cumbria, UK, although based on wider cultural perceptions of the countryside as a rural idyll, also involved the tourists negotiating their own particular version of the authentic 'in attempts to fulfil expectations about what Potter's home, the setting for her books, and the version of English country life within which these ideas are embedded, should be like' (Squires 1993: 115).

We can see here clear parallels with the creation of personal narratives discussed in the previous chapter. People here are working at, or working with, the symbolic components of heritage and not just accepting them. It is intriguing to speculate whether or not the people who travel the itineraries mentioned above, and others like them, engage in similar forms of negotiation. Arguments relating to the consumption of places and the intangible imagined aspects of heritage could also be extended to the consumption of objects. I have on my desk a small transparent plastic box which contains a piece of wood, approximately 15 mm square and 60 mm in length, mounted on a piece of blue felted card, on which is written 'Original Oak from H.M.S. Victory'. I have little doubt, seeing as it was purchased in Portsmouth Naval Museum, UK, that this object is an authentic part of that ship. There is also a possibility that it was even a material witness at the Battle of Trafalgar, a defining moment in English history and nation building. Of course, it only has that resonance of authenticity because its provenance is not in doubt. My motivation for buying it however was to use it as a prop in lectures, not because of its provenance per se. In this sense, I was negotiating the symbolic value of that particular object in terms of my own needs. The purchase of souvenirs can also involve some measure of negotiation between the buyer and seller in establishing the authenticity of objects. In her study of Pueblo and Navaho silversmiths in New Mexico, USA, Evans-Pritchard notes that the authenticity of particular artefacts produced for the tourist market is more in the eye of the beholder, rather than the producer:

> People buying Indian art are often very concerned with the traditionality and the "Indian – ness" of an art piece. They want a particular pot, jewellery design, storyteller doll, or whatever to illustrate a cultural story, to have symbolic meaning (Evans-Pritchard 1989: 95).

As far as the producers are concerned, the use of traditional shapes is for aesthetic, not narrative considerations. The fact that some of the traders 'respond to tourist's needs for cultural significance by telling them just what they want to hear' was a practice that was neither universal, nor approved by all (Evans-Pritchard 1989).

Similar forms of negotiation between buyers and sellers can be found elsewhere. I have witnessed occasions at craft fairs in this country where some potential purchasers of handmade items will ask the seller to explain its significance, or how it was made. On a similar note, Shenhav-Keller's (1995) analysis of the purchasing behaviour of tourists in Israel also draws attention to the negotiation of the object's authentic 'Israeliness' between the buyer and the seller. In both these cases, what is significant is that authenticity is being defined in terms of the provenance of objects. This in itself is not an objective but a subjective criterion. Certainly at this level we are dealing with a form of existential authenticity (Wang 1999) but one which is socially mediated through the production and consumption of material culture.

A common criticism of heritage commodification is directed towards the apparent degradation of artefacts for tourist consumption. Teague's study of Nepalese tourist art is of interest here. He writes that religious artefacts are now sold in Nepal for the tourist market as much as pilgrims, and now tend to be made on an 'assembly line basis' rather then individually. This results in a degree of 'reduction' in quality where the profit motive 'overrides the aesthetic standards of the producer culture, and the alien consumer becomes dominant' (Teague 1997: 185). Teague however argues that this process does not in fact detract from their authenticity, but rather represents a form of cultural syncretism where elements from 'outside' cultures are combined with the traditional to create new forms, hence they are 'authentic' (1997: 186).

Similar problems arise when dealing with Australian aboriginal art. For example the analysis by Short draws attention to the recent development of distinct aboriginal forms of painting which is both a 'source of pride and income for Aboriginal communities . . . Art is giving aborigines much needed respect' (Short 1991: 221). Although he also draws attention to criticisms of these developments, which see them as a loss of artistic 'integrity' (1991: 222), they can also be seen as the emergence of a new tradition of contemporary art, or to use Cohen's term, 'an emergent authenticity'.

It is also worth considering why arguments concerning the degradation of arts and crafts through tourism commodification are mainly applied to those of ethnic or third-world origin. Consider as a counterpoint, the number of postcards sold in art galleries around the world. For a nominal cost, the purchaser can have a copy – a simulacrum – of a work of art, while possession of the original would remain out of reach to all but the wealthiest. We can see the same processes of mass production and reduction in quality. The postcard or even the most expensive reproduction will never match the original and they are clearly, in the strict museum definition, inauthentic commodities. Yet this form of cultural reproduction for the mass tourist market has not, to my knowledge, been treated with the same kind of condemnation with its overtones of moral righteousness as the production of ethnic arts, and I can only agree with Howell who argues it is time to ditch the 'moralistic preoccupation with authenticity and single origins' (1995: 165). Perhaps behind this implicit moralising we can see a form of cultural imperialism at work. Other more exotic societies need to preserve their culture, not perhaps for their own benefit, but to cater for the demands for the authentic from the tourists of the developed economies, or to satisfy the moral preoccupations of the analysts. This also carries with it the implication that the benefits of modernism should not be extended to the exotic others, in case 'they' lose what 'we' want.

Conclusion

In this chapter, the notions of heritage and its correlate authenticity have been explored. The authentic/inauthentic couplet, I would argue, has had a pervasive and negative effect on the analysis of tourism at a number of levels. The first problem lies in it being treated as one part of a simple either/or binary distinction in which the authentic is opposed to its opposite, the inauthentic. Both are thus conceptualised as mutually exclusive categories, which presuppose the presence or absence of some essential, innate quality. Related to this problem of essentialism is the implicit assumption that there is only one way of interpreting other cultures in a true fashion or, in other words, as a combination of essential attributes and meanings.

What the material presented here shows are the problems inherent in applying universal – or Eurocentric – notions of the authentic. As noted, the concept of authentic heritage has not only become localised, but also globalised in both its spread, and broadened in its conception to the extent that it is questionable whether it can any longer serve a useful purpose as an analytical category. As I have argued in this chapter, to look for single origins, to be overly concerned about issues of provenance and authenticity is to miss the point. This is not to say therefore that heritage is unimportant, it clearly is, but in different ways to different people. It is clearly not a unified or universal category that can be measured against external objective criteria in all situations. The questions of importance then are to whom is the authentic of interest and to what uses it is put? Some of the examples cited in this chapter have drawn attention to the macro and micro politics involved in creating heritage, as well as the possibility that claims to authenticity and heritage, while closely related to the processes of tourism commodification, can serve more than one purpose at the same time. These are not necessarily driven by the needs of the tourist system. The examples also show that, as with other forms of consumption, it may well be the work that is carried out beyond the point of purchase or gazing that is important.

Both authenticity and heritage can be seen as critiques of modernity as representing perhaps a desire to return to an imaginary past where things were reputedly less complex. There is little doubt that for certain forms of tourism, such as those described by Cohen, the search for the authentic other is a key component. However, such forms of existential tourism are a minority pursuit, and cannot be applied to tourism per se.

It may also be tempting therefore to see the processes of tourism development in certain parts of the world as a form of cultural colonialism, a symptom or even cause of the relentless spread of commodification. But behind this is the equally mistaken assumption that people are simply passive consumers or even cultural dupes, in particular that 'the masses' are easily fooled into accepting contrivance as the 'real thing'. Such a position is both arrogant and patronising and, as the evidence presented in this chapter shows, quite erroneous. What we are dealing with cannot simply be accounted for in terms of a simple cause–effect model of cultural dominance and exploitation, even allowing for the possibility that this may occur in certain circumstances.

If, however, we can get away from the unthinking application of the museum definition of authenticity, a different set of issues presents itself. I have argued that notions of heritage can be connected to the political processes involved in creating a national, regional, local or ethnic identity, and how, in turn, this becomes the commodity to be traded in the global tourist market. This latter factor itself should be sufficient to call into question the whole notion of authenticity as it clearly signals that the production of heritage, whether in the form of intangibles, material goods or ritual performances can only ever be the result of contingent circumstances. As Sahlins has noted, each reproduction of a cultural system is a dialogue between received categories, the past; and contingent circumstances, the present; in which meanings are always 'at risk' (Sahlins 1985: 144). Each addition, each interpretation reorganises and redirects what is there, and this may also involve economic, political, religious and ethnic factors over and above those considered to be merely forms of tourist consumption.

One final point on which to conclude. It is one of the curiosities of tourism analysis that the idea of suspending disbelief, of accepting fiction *as if* it were fact when we are confronted by a book, a play or a film, which we know is only a representation of reality, tends to become deferred when dealing with the creation of tourist sites and tourist behaviour. Cohen is one of the few who has drawn attention to this, arguing that the willingness to accept 'contrived' tourist attractions is 'culturally sanctioned by the post-modern ethos' which is one of 'playfulness' (Cohen 1996: 22). A concern with inauthenticity can be seen as a major theme within many attempts to analyse the postmodern or even global condition, but this in turn raises a number of issues that form the subject of the next chapter where the problem of culture will be examined.

Chapter 6

Whose Culture?

Introduction

The preceding chapters have raised questions concerning the inter-connections between culture and power and the political economy at both global and national levels. Within the current debate concerning the relationship between globalisation and culture two main trends can be seen. The first argues that one of the consequences of globalisation is the increasing homogenisation and westernisation of culture. The counter-argument is that globalisation is leading to the increasing differentiation of cultures and the reassertion of cultural identity at a localised level. While tourism in general must be analysed as a global phenomenon, its spatial component means that locality, or the speci-ficity of places and cultures, is not diminished but actually reinforced. Within much of the tourism literature, culture tends to be accepted as an unproblematic category, referring either to the social characteristics of people and place or specific kinds of tourist activities and sights.

As I argued above, the commodification of culture is a significant factor in contemporary life, and one that is increasingly bound up in the development of a global tourist system. In chapter three I also argued that there were clear links between the political economy and culture, and that many tourism policies can be seen as attempts to control the trajectory and flow of the global political economy. I also noted that one of the features of contemporary consumption is the apparent dissolving of the boundaries between high and low culture and the aestheticisation of everyday life, which involves, among other things, the consumption of space as culture.

In this chapter I will argue that tourism studies have, in the main, not adequately conceptualised culture, tending to view it simply as

114

'given', or to see it in rather simplistic terms of national or regional differences which exist between discrete population groups, often simply defined through the possession of a shared history or heritage. The processes of globalisation that are evident today mean that the idea of cultures as being internally homogeneous and geographically bounded needs to be rethought. It will be argued that while tourism is globalised in terms of the movement of people and capital, it is also leading to the reassertion of more localised forms of culture, and the emergence of new 'hybrid' forms created for both domestic purposes as much as tourist consumption.

Drawing on sociological and anthropological theory, this chapter will distinguish between the problems of defining culture as an analytical category within a global system and defining culture for purposes of the tourist industry. It will be argued that cultures are best conceptualised as dynamic systems containing both material/ symbolic elements which cut across accepted notions of boundedness, and which also have the capacity to be made and remade for consumption within a global market.

Culture

Culture is a term that, although being pervasive, is difficult to pin down with a precise definition. This fact alone could be seen as a valid reason for simply ignoring it, as many do. On the other hand, it could also indicate that what we are dealing with is a category that obviously has some salience in people's lives. The fact that it is open to many interpretations indicates that rather than attempting to uncover its essence, we should rather focus on the ways and contexts in which it is used. In this chapter I will isolate some of the dominant ways in which culture has been conceptualised.

In a commonsense fashion, culture is often conceptualised as the high arts, literature, music, theatre and so on, and as such carries with it implications of social exclusivity and superior knowledge. In this sense, culture is concerned with the development of an aesthetic sensibility that enables the individual to appreciate the differences between good and bad art, to make value judgements on the basis of their superior knowledge of the accepted canons of good taste. The acquisition of these skills then is something to be worked at, it requires both time, effort and some form of education, either formal or informal, to accumulate the specialised knowledge necessary for aesthetic appreciation. As Bourdieu puts it, 'A work of art has meaning and interest only for someone who possesses the cultural competence, that is the code, into which it is encoded' (1984: 2). The museum definition of authenticity, as I noted in the previous chapter, also applies to the high arts. The merits of a work of art are judged in terms of its unquestionable provenance as the work of a single autonomous individual. The value of a work of high art is also often seen as possessing qualities that will stand the test of time. To use current phraseology, we could say that the high arts are a grand, totalising narrative of aesthetics.

Mass, popular or low culture is by definition the inverse of high culture. Mass culture is neither elitist, nor does it require the development of a highly refined aesthetic sensibility. Neither for that matter is it so concerned with the autonomy of the producer, or with the authenticity of the finished product. Indeed to call it mass in the first place undercuts the notion of the single autonomous work of art, mass culture is culture mediated by mass production and mass consumption, it provides commodified, unsophisticated, throwaway instant gratification. As Bocock points out, as with high culture, mass or popular culture also carries with it notions of social divisions (1992b: 231). Again, we can draw parallels here with the issues discussed in the previous chapter in relation to heritage. This high/low distinction should not disguise the fact that to think of culture in this way, of either type or all shades in between, also implies some form of leisure activity. Culture is differentiated from the world of work. It is for example, watching a play, a television programme, listening to music, reading a book, attending a sports event or visiting a museum and so on. Culture, like tourism, can therefore be seen as the consumption of non-working time. As Martinez points out, popular culture is not only mass, it is also 'culture consumed, and consumed in various ways by different people' (1998: 6).

Popular culture is often seen in terms of serving to perpetuate a false ideology, as a means of obscuring social relations and so concealing the true state of the world from the poor deluded masses. As Miller notes, this is founded on the suspicion that is often attached to the notion of culture as consumption, in that it implies a loss of authenticity through commodification (1995a: 4). Also, as in the case of heritage, museum definitions of provenance can be used to mark an object or other form of cultural production as unique and, as such, outside the processes of commodification. As Frow makes clear: 'We tend to assume an equivalence between the commodity and mass production... [but] 'Singular' objects, even if they have not been industrially produced, can still be commodities' (Frow 1997: 62). A further element is that to formulate culture in terms of mass can only result in what Parker terms a 'prescriptive elitism' (1998: 3). To use the term culture then, in terms of this high/low distinction is to be both descriptive – it tells us what culture consists of – and prescriptive – it tells us what is allowed, and what is not. It follows, therefore, that value judgements such as 'high' and 'low' are far from being universal categories, but rather are to be assessed in terms of the particular context in which they are located. The distinction between high and low culture, I would argue, is part of the differentiation inherent in modernity.

There is another way of viewing culture, which sees it in a more anthropological, holistic way, as comprising of the sum of both material and symbolic production. Martinez, for example, argues that in this sense, what we should examine are the relationships between the production of material goods and the symbolic meanings that these may carry (1998: 3–4). Culture is then conceptualised as a mode of communication, as a symbolic system by which and through which people create and recreate shared values, a formulation which has much in common with that employed within cultural studies (Bocock 1992b, du Gay 1997, Storey 1999, Tomlinson, 1999). However, this is not to argue that therefore cultures are simply written into existence, or can be read as if they are only texts. There are also economic and political dimensions to consider. Culture, in the sense that it is used here is seen as a set of practices, based on forms of knowledge, which encapsulate common values and act as general guiding principles. It is through these forms of knowledge that distinctions are created and maintained, so that, for example, one culture is marked off as different from another. But there are a number of twists to the argument, which concern the apparent dissolving of the boundaries and hierarchies of taste, the popularisation of aesthetics and the effects of globalisation and, of course, the spectre of postmodernism.

Global culture?

The basic tenets of postmodernism were outlined in chapter two, and in the previous chapter I drew attention to the issue of authenticity and the ways in which a concern with the authentic other could be viewed as a critique of modernity, as a way perhaps of conjuring up a presumed unchanging essence in an uncertain world. One of the claims of postmodernism is that, in terms of cultural production, the high/low distinction is no longer as hard and fast as it once was. It could be argued that what we have is the emergence of postmodern cultural forms which, by rejecting the grand narratives of elite aesthetics and incorporating elements from other cultures, have redefined the parameters of culture per se (Jameson 1991, McGuigan 1996, 1999).

As I have argued in the preceding chapters, the processes of modernity are characterised by differentiation. In terms of the development of tourism, this can be seen in the development of specific tourism places that were marked as distinct from the places of work in both temporal and spatial terms. As the previous chapters have argued, such distinctions are no longer so easy to maintain, leading some to suggest that we are now seeing a process of de-differentiation (Featherstone 1991, Urry 1990b) a 'flattening of hierarchies' (McGuigan 1996: 36) or a 'blurring of the boundaries' (Robinson 1999: 5). Perhaps this even signals the end of modernity itself, and the emergence of the brave new world which appears to be a rather flat, blurry and uncertain state of 'ephemerality, fragmentation and discontinuity' (Harvey 1989: 44). Now I have doubts that all this is cause for a celebration of diversity and eclecticism. However, these claims do need to be examined.

There are a number of important questions to be raised here, first, concerning the relationship between culture and the economy, and secondly, concerning the ways in which culture is bounded. In chapter two I outlined the idea of the cultural economy (du Gay 1997 Zukin 1995). I pointed out the increasing interconnections between the political economy, the aestheticisation of place, and the role of culture in this process. In short, culture has become more businesslike, while at the same time, more goods are deliberately produced as 'cultural', that is, designed with a specific set of meanings and associations (du Gay 1997: 5–6). Space too is now often associated with the existence of discrete subgroupings, such as the gay spaces mentioned earlier, or with forms of ethnic identity or heritage. If we follow the logic of this through, the implication is that culture is commodified in a way analogous to the logic of the post-

Fordist political economy. Does this then mean that, like the political economy, it is footloose, globalised and de-territorialised?

We can begin to unravel this if we consider why cultures were ever thought of as being self-contained or bounded in the first place. According to Friedman, this is because culture itself is a product of modernity as it 'consists of transforming difference into essence' (1995: 79). In other words, distinctions are attributed to demarcated populations, most notably those of the nation state, itself a product of modernity (Hannerz, 1996). Again, the material presented in the previous chapter showed how ideas of the nation as the people are represented through the creation and use of symbolic forms. Welsch makes a similar point, adding that notions of single, bounded cultures are based on three basic propositions: that cultures are homogenous, they are ethnically bound, and delimited vis-à-vis other cultures (Welsch 1999: 194–5). He goes on to argue that these three conditions are no longer tenable. First, modern societies are now more multicultural than they have been in the past, and more internally differentiated in terms of gender and socio-economic status. Also, to assume that cultures are ethnically bound, that is, associated with particular ideas of race, assumes there is little contact between different cultures which in turn also implies exclusivity and purity (Welsch 1999: 195).

Now at first sight, tourism may appear to be a prime mechanism by which cultural influences are diffused and assimilated as it involves the large-scale movement of people from place to place, often involving the crossing of national boundaries. It also involves people consuming narratives of place, which encapsulate certain cultural values, regardless of whether or not these are populist or elitist. Even at a superficial level then, tourism involves some form of 'culture contact'. One way of approaching these issues is through the notion of travelling cultures, initially formulated by Clifford (1992) and subsequently developed by Rojek and Urry (1997). They write that: 'cultures travel as well as people . . . what is involved in the movement of cultures is the migration of objects and peoples' (1997: 11). In itself, this is hardly surprising, and is little more than a contemporary repackaging of diffusionism (Hannerz, 1996; Howell, 1995; Kuper, 1999; Nash 1996). Anthropologists, archaeologists and historians, for example, have long wrestled with the problems of accounting for the ways in which cultural influences, both material and non-material, have been adapted, absorbed, and transformed between cultures and places. What can initially be foreign, exotic and imported can rapidly become indiginised and accepted as an integral and natural part of a culture. The humble potato, whose 'authentic' home is South America, is one such transplant (Salaman 1985). Even if this idea of travelling cultures is not an especially novel conceptualisation, it is still useful, in that it reminds us of the complexities of global local relationships. We can no longer assume that cultures are as spatially bounded or territorially coherent as they may at first appear. In short, there is no *simple* correlation between place and culture. (Albrow, et al, 1997, Appadurai 1990, Hannerz 1996, Lovell 1998, Miller 1995a,b, Tomlinson 1999).

Tomlinson argues that simply inverting the way in which culture has been conceptualised, from being an essential quality of people and places to one that views cultures as nomadic and rootless, does not solve the problem (see also Friedman, 1999b). It is not a case of replacing 'roots' with 'routes' but seeing both as coexistent, and both as being subject to change through the processes of globalisation (1999: 29). People and indeed material objects are more mobile and transient than they have been in the past, and there is little doubt also that tourism plays a significant role in this movement. At the same time, the local becomes the arena in which globalisation is played out. The idea of travelling cultures as Tomlinson (1999) writes, is perhaps better conceptualised as de-territorialisation, that is, the loss of the assumed natural relationship between culture and the geographical and social territories in which it is located.

The points to be drawn from all this, despite the smoke and mirrors of postmodernism, is fairly straightforward. We cannot conceptualise cultures as if they were integrated and self-contained wholes. The central problem here lies in treating cultures as possessing innate essential attributes, whereas they are better conceptualised in terms of processes of symbolisation that involve systemic elements as much as the individual (Featherstone and Lash 1999; Hannerz 1996). Culture is not simply some external force that we respond to, rather it is something that we are actively engaged in creating and sustaining. As Hannerz sums it up, culture is 'fitted to new circumstances' (1996: 51). Nor for that matter, can we conceptualise the nation state as a bounded unified entity as the container, so to speak, of specific ways of life or cultures, as if what occurs beyond their boundaries is simply what 'they' do 'over there' (Featherstone and Lash, 1999; Hannerz, 1992, 1996; Lovell, 1998; McMichael, 1996;

Robertson 1992; Welsch 1999). Robertson sums up this approach when he writes that a

> Commitment to the idea of the culturally cohesive society has blinded us to the various ways in which the world as a whole has been increasingly 'organized' around sets of shifting definitions of the global circumstance (Robertson 1992:114).

Tourism and culture: homogeneity or heterogeneity?

As I have argued in the previous chapters, both spatial and social relations are being redefined through the processes of globalisation. This has resulted in a world where the interconnections between politics and economics are such that we can no longer assume that the nation state delimits the boundaries of culture. Even at a more localised level, the increasing culture contact that is evident through tourism and other forms of translocational movement means that representational spaces or localised forms of knowledge are also less bounded than before. One of the arguments within the literature, and one which is of key significance in terms of tourism, is whether or not the changes brought about by globalisation are therefore leading to the eradication of cultural differences, and the replacement of cultural heterogeneity with a global culture characterised by homogeneity. In turn, this is part of a consistent undercurrent in much of the tourism literature and beyond which takes an a priori, dystopian view of the effects of modernity (Albrow et al. 1997, Tomlinson 1999) and equates globalisation with westernisation (Nederveen-Pieterse 1995: 47).

As I noted in chapter one, MacCannell viewed modernity as the force that disrupts 'real life', shifting people away from the 'stability of interpersonal relations' found in the 'primitive case where family structure *is* social structure' (MacCannell 1976: 91). Compare that to a more recent formulation by Elliott, who writes that due to tourism.

> There has been a movement away from traditions and religious and other values and vigorous local communities have disappeared; others have become more materialistic, hedonistic with weaker family networks and community support systems (Elliott 1997: 261).

Such sentiments are in part the result of conceptualising modernity as a process that tends towards sameness (Hannerz 1996: 51). According to Appadurai (1990) the argument for homogeneity is often cast in terms of commodification, seen to be the process through which cultures are reduced to inauthentic shadows for sale to the gullible masses. Once more, what we are dealing with here is a notion of cultures as being pristine and unspoilt until the intrusion of tourism commodification, at which point they are seemingly locked into a spiral of 'erosion' (Fennel 1999: 102). Now it may be tempting to see the internationalisation or globalisation of tourism as the inevitable spread of modernity, of similarity and homogeneity (Sharpley 1994) and on the surface, this may appear to have an obvious appeal. Yet such approaches are little more than implicit criticisms of mass culture and, quite often, it is the global MNCs that are taken to task, such as Disney and that perennial whipping boy, McDonalds.

In chapter four I criticised Ritzer's notion of McDonaldization for failing to account sufficiently for human agency in terms of choice. The McDonaldization thesis also supposes that forms of rationalisation are inevitably leading to global standardisation and homogeneity of cultural forms. R.C. Wood (1998) for instance, describes the schema outlined above as the 'four horsemen of the rationalisation apocalypse' (1998: 92). Parker criticises Ritzer's analysis as elitist in its preoccupations, and presupposing some notion of high or unspoilt culture. Parker argues that by identifying mass society as inherently negative, the McDonaldization thesis is more concerned with 'pointing to cultural decline than with theorising rationality' as the authentic past is contrasted with the shallow and inauthentic here and now (Parker 1998: 9). The assumed homogeneity of the McWorld rests on a conceptualisation of culture as being composed of essential and unchanging attributes which can only succumb to the onslaught of modernity and rationalisation, rather than adapting and changing.

Another way in which arguments concerning cultural homogeneity are often cast concerns the influence of the media and other forms of communication technology. Now it could be argued that global forms of media help create the demand for the exotic, the unfamiliar and the other. Broadcast, as well as print media, often seeks out what is different and other, whether in the form of travel programmes, travelogues and documentaries, guide books, travel supplements and travel writing. Yet, what often occurs is a conflation between culture and technology, that the spread of technology is seen as evidence of cultural change in itself (Boniface and Fowler 1993). Although it is clearly important, electronic and global media only form part of the process by which globalisation is experienced (Tomlinson 1999: 20–1). But even the introduction of new technology itself to other places can be seen as a threat to their authenticity and cultural cohesiveness. As Hughes-Freeland comments on the introduction of television to Bali:

> The arrival of television in Bali in 1977 may indeed seem a socio-cultural anomaly, if we persist in thinking of Bali as an unspoilt island paradise, and conceptualise cultures like this as insular totalities, until only recently out of history and out of contact (Hughes-Freeland 1998: 48).

Also, we should not ignore the fact that 'other' cultures, more precisely non-western ones, are quite capable of producing their own indigenised forms of broadcast media (Abu-Lughod 1995, Das 1995, Gore 1998). In turn, to see such media as being causative mechanisms assumes that broadcasting and other electronic information technologies will have the same effects in very different contexts which does not seem to tally with the evidence (Barker 1999).

Yet it is not only analysts who view modernity, whether in the forms of new technologies or tourism, as posing a threat to cultural cohesiveness. For example, Picard records how the development of tourism in Bali was viewed as a threat by some of the Balinese themselves that could lead to 'cultural pollution' if not correctly managed. Similarly, Howes (1996) discusses the ways in which the Hopi, an indigenous people of south-western USA, have reacted against what they perceive as the appropriation of their culture, and how they are seeking redress through the legal system. Conway (1993) and Wilson (1997) also point to the internal criticisms of tourism raised by people in the Caribbean and Goa respectively. What appears to be challenged here, or at stake, are particular forms of localised knowledge, which are in danger of being subsumed under globalised forms of commodification.

The important point in these cases is that what we are dealing with are internal conceptualisations of culture, not analytical ones. As Zukin notes, 'the rules of culture have changed' (1995: 263) and struggles that were once considered to be economic or political are now being fought over in terms of culture. If we are to analyse culture in relation to tourism then, it is necessary to contextualise such arguments and criticisms. Are they the result of internal dynamics in response to change, or are they inherent in the analytical framework that is used to analyse them? What is important, I would suggest, are not arguments concerning the essential qualities of cultures, whether a culture is 'really' this or 'really' that, but rather, the way these arguments and debates are utilised and deployed, and the ways that they draw from and influence localised forms of knowledge. In other words cultural change is as much about internal dynamics as much as external dynamics. As I noted above, culture contact is hardly new, and neither is the fact that cultures borrow and adapt from each other; nor for that matter, are internal arguments concerning what cultures should be. Of course, what is different now is the fact that the global interconnections between places and people are becoming more pronounced, and are impinging more on the daily lives of people. Robertson (1995) argues that the homogeneity heterogeneity argument needs to be transcended, as all it offers is a false either / or choice, and that increasing connections do not in themselves imply homogeneity, nor call it into being. Nor should we simply accept that the 'west', usually taken to be mass industrial society, is in itself culturally homogeneous either now, or in the past (Keily 1998, Nederveen-Pieterse 1995).

Perhaps one way to resolve this problem is to see the convergence of cultures as leading to new forms of creolisation or hybridisation (Hannerz 1996 Nederveen-Pieterse 1995, plus others). That requires a consideration of the ways in which cultural influences are adapted, borrowed and reinterpreted for more localised forms of consumption. Friedman (1999b), however, criticises the notion of hybridity as in itself it presupposes some notion of a 'pure' culture to begin with. Nederveen-Pieterse also adds that hybridisation is often seen as a matter of 'regret and loss – loss of purity, whole-ness, authenticity' (1995: 54–55). Friedman further argues that the notion of hybridity is by and large an ideological position used to justify the 'rootlessness' of metropolitan and cosmopolitan elites. Although such qualifications need to be borne in mind, they do not call into question the fact that cultural change and borrowings do occur, and are an integral part of globalisation (Chua 1998 Fardon 1995 Gurnah 1997 Howes 1996 Martinez 1998 Oakes 1993 Watson, 1997).

A few examples though will be sufficient to make the point. As I noted above, Ritzer's notion of McDonaldization assumes that rationalisation is tending to produce a globally undifferentiated mass. Yet, even in terms of the burger giants themselves, things are not as they may seem. The series of ethnographic studies undertaken in East Asia by Watson (1997) and his colleagues focuses on the ways in which the global system of McDonald's is adapted and consumed at a local level. Watson comments that although some aspects of routinisation have been effectively transplanted into East Asian cultures, others have not, leading him to remark that 'localization is not a unilinear process that ends the same everywhere' (Watson 1997: 37). Chua (1998) also points to the cultural mediation of consumption patterns in Singapore, which questions the whole notion of global homogeneity. Even the spread of the more visible signs and symbols of global capitalism is not always what it seems. Ohnuki-Tierney's ethnography of McDonald's in Japan reports that 'The Americana that is created... often bears little resemblance to the cultural system(s) prevailing in the United States' (1997: 180). In a similar vein, writing about the adaptation of foreign theme parks in Japan, McGuigan comments that 'Japanese culture is eclectic yet totalising and comfortable with hybridity' (1996: 130).

Similar examples can be found in other places and cultures. Linnekin records that 'In Hawaii, local people have become collectors of culture – but of their own culture in terms of stereotypical artifacts' (Linnekin 1997: 217) and further that the products originally designed for the tourist market have since been adapted for the local markets (1997: 219–20). Another example relating to material culture is that provided by Eckholm-Friedman and Friedman:

> Until recently, African cloth was made primarily in Holland and Germany. The production was targeted to specific regions and 'tribes'... and the cloth was not for sale in Europe... Now, for the cosmopolitan culture expert, this may become a matter of some amusement – the innocent tourist who buys genuine African cloth in the local market and returns home to find 'Made in Holland' printed on the edge (Eckholm-Friedman and Friedman 1995: 135).

They argue that this indicates a form of control over localised consumption through differentiation, and is not an example of a loss of authenticity through commodification. What these examples indicate is that the notion of cultural homogeneity, driven by the logic of globalisation, is simply not borne out by the evidence. Further, as Howell argues, flows of knowledge are not uni-directional or one-sided, and that the borrowing and adaptation of cultural knowledge occurs as much 'here' as it does elsewhere (1995: 165). The question that immediately follows then is what role does tourism play in this cultural give and take?

Before we go any further though, in terms of the production and consumption of tourist space, there is an apparent contradiction, at least on the surface. On the one hand both theoretical developments and empirical evidence point us in the direction of accepting that cultures are not bounded entities, are not composed of unchanging essential elements, and that they are more mobile than before. On the other hand, we have people attempting to define their place in this global system by asserting essential characteristics, often bound to place, as the basis for their unique cultural identities.

This apparent contradiction can be accounted for if we draw a necessary distinction between *commodifying* and *analysing* culture. In order to sell culture, complexity is commodified and reduced to a recognisable formula or narrative for the purposes of consumption. For this purpose, cultures are represented through the creation of essential differences which isolate specific characteristics of people and place and contextualise them as normative descriptions. In short, marketing culture requires commodified essences such as the creation of forms of heritage. I also cautioned against seeing such commodified forms as being inherently false, as if tourism is a con trick played on the gullible masses, and pointed out that many of the problems arising from authenticity are the result of confusing analytical categories with other forms of knowledge. Analysing culture requires an approach that can account for the processes of commodification, but which does not reduce culture to being merely the commodified form itself, and goes beyond simple descriptions of commodity formation. We therefore have to focus on the deployment and use of culture, and the ways in which commodification both interpenetrates cultures, and also acts as a means by which cultures are changed and maintained.

Another related point is that the evidence also indicates that the local, or indeed, national context is the arena in which the complexities of globalisation are mediated and forged into new cultural forms. But there is also a danger here of collapsing everything into one catch-all category and, in doing so, removing any heuristic purpose it may have. If everything is culture, then that's that, and what's left to say? Kuper, for example, is one who warns against the tendency to consider culture as a totality, 'unless we separate out the various processes that are lumped together under the heading of culture' he writes, 'and then look beyond the field of culture to other processes, we will not get very far in understanding any of it' (Kuper 1999: 247).

There are a number of levels then that need to be distinguished. First, the commonsense forms of knowledge which tend to see cultures as collections of distinct essential characteristics. Often, these are rooted in particular notions of place and identity, they are the spaces of representation and are employed as much by the host society as by the tourists who encounter them. Secondly, representations of culture used in an instrumental fashion by policymakers and tour operators as commodities for the tourist market. These can also be 'indigenised' by local people as a means of asserting a specific identity. Thirdly, conceptualisations of culture used for analytical purposes, which may be different from both commonsense and instrumental forms. If cultures in tourism or cultural tourism are to be approached in a coherent manner, then the process of distinguishing between these levels must be made evident. Policymakers, tour operators and the tourist industry as a whole may well think of culture as a collection of essential differences, perhaps as 'high' or 'low', and see these in instrumental terms as commodities for the market. For analytical purposes though, we need to take a step back from such categorisations, and not accept them at face value. Rather, we need to focus on the ways in which they are deployed and utilised. In chapters two and three I drew attention to the ways that the state can and does intervene in the global economy and can also mobilise culture for both internal and external purposes. In order to carry the argument forward in the following sections I will examine some case studies concerned with cultural tourism and the ways in which the national and local state intervenes in the production of cultural tourism.

What is cultural tourism?

Given that culture is difficult to define, and often presented in terms of an elite pursuing an essence at their leisure, it is hardly surprising that an array of tourist activities can come under the heading of cultural tourism. As an example, Borley writes that it is:

> that activity which enables people to explore or experience the different ways of life of other people, reflecting social customs, religious traditions and the intellectual ideas of a cultural heritage which may be unfamiliar (Borley 1994: 4).

There is an implicit notion of self-improvement in this statement. As I have already pointed out, one way of thinking about culture is to see it as distinct from work, as a form of leisure which also involves some notion of self-improvement, an idea deeply embedded in western culture (Rojek 1993: 110–16). Rather than the simple aimless pleasures of mass tourism, the cultural tourists are those who go about their leisure in a more serious frame of mind. To be a cultural tourist is to attempt, I would suggest, to go beyond idle leisure and to return enriched with knowledge of other places and other people even if this involves 'gazing' at, or collecting in some way, the commodified essences of otherness. In this way cultural tourism is clearly demarcated as a distinct form of tourism. As discussed in the previous chapter, it may also be seen as a means of acquiring cultural capital and acquiring knowledge that can then be worked at past the immediate point of consumption. Richard's (1996a, b) studies of European cultural tourism found that cultural tourists tended to have 'a high socio-economic status, high levels of educational attainment, adequate leisure time, and often having occupations related to the culture industries' (Richards 1996b: 55–6).

This profile fits with that discussed earlier in relation to consumption in general, and the consumption in particular of heritage, eco and other forms of alternative tourism. Cultural consumption, as much as other forms of consumption, may be seen as a means of creating and maintaining social distinctions (Bourdieu 1984). Yet the form of culture that Richards analyses is of the elite kind: it is museums, art exhibitions, architecture and the built heritage, and as such is also predominantly urban. In terms of its production, this form of cultural tourism is also linked in to national and local policies concerned with urban regeneration (Law 1993, Page 1995). As Robinson points out, the debates on cultural tourism have tended to be 'dogged by the dominant perspective of culture in the high-arts sense' (1999: 4). There are two questions that need addressing here.

First, is this simply a reflection of what tourists, policymakers and tour operators expect, and second, is it possible to consider cultural tourism as other than the high arts? Can it also refer to culture in the broader senses I outlined above, as comprising of discrete ways of life, or even mass culture?

Other people, other cultures

Zeppel's analysis of the portrayal of the Iban in Sarawak, Malaysia, is a case in point. She writes that Sarawak is promoted as an exotic destination with the Iban 'longhouse lifestyle' in particular (1997: 83). The Iban, the largest ethnic group in Sarawak, were previously notorious as headhunters during the nineteenth century. Skulls were displayed in the longhouses, where many still remain. Tours to the longhouses are marketed as adventures into an exotic realm of former headhunters, who are now however, more domesticated in a western sense (Zeppel 1997: 84–5). Authenticity is ascribed by the use of the term 'traditional' to describe the people and their culture:

> Tour guides direct tourist attention to the primary markers of Iban cultural authenticity, that is, the longhouse building, tattooed Iban men and fire blackened human trophy skulls. The reality is that tourists will also see Iban people in western clothing and sarongs, living under tin roofs, using outboard motors and chainsaws and other modern consumer items (Zeppel 1997: 91).

Bali provides a good case of the complexities involved in the give and take of globalisation and the commodification of culture, not least because of the ways in which it has always been regarded in European eyes as an exotic location (Picard 1993, 1996). Picard writes that ' "culture" is the focus of touristic promotion in Bali: tourism in Bali is "cultural" tourism' (1993: 71) while Hobart observes that what 'people in a particular part of Bali previously just did is coming increasingly to be constituted self consciously as "culture". In part a response to tourism, but also as a result of government policy' (Hobart 1995: 64). Rather than the homogeneity presupposed by the McDonaldization thesis, it is possible to see the logic of global capitalism resulting in further differentiation through the instrumental use of places, people and activities as commodities for the market.

One example of the relationship between cultural identity and tourism as economic development is provided by Pedersen who describes the Gaelic tourism of Scotland as designed to enable 'visitors and local people to interface actively with the modern Gaelic speaking community in Scotland' (1995: 289). In this case, we have an example of the commodification of culture and place as a form of economic development, but one aimed at particular markets. As he writes: 'If the market penetration and income generation are to be maximised, the product must above all be based on demonstrable quality' (Pedersen 1995: 292). Whatever cultural tourism is, in the eyes of both operators, policymakers and many analysts, it is generally not mass tourism. Indeed we can see this as further differentiation, as a form of niche marketing which is considered to be more upmarket than its poor popular relative. Such a linkage between the commodification of cultures and niche marketing is also noted by Richards (1996a, 1996b) and Robinson (1999). Indeed it is feasible to see the development of cultural tourism as the logical continuation of product differentiation associated with post-Fordism, as in the case of the African cloth (Eckholm-Friedman and Friedman 1995). The extent of these developments can clearly be seen when we examine a variety of cultural policies initiated at international, national and local levels.

The politics of cultural tourism

One ambitious attempt to link culture to tourism and the development of a transnational sense of identity can be seen in the workings of the Council of Europe (CoE). This organisation, established in 1949, and not to be confused with the European Union (EU), has two main aims, 'defending and extending a plurality of cultural identities, and ... above and beyond these diversities, revaluing Europe's common heritage by approaching it in a dynamic and forward-looking way' (CoE 1999a, unpaginated). Stevenson (1995) describes the creation of European silk and textile itineraries, initiated by the CoE in 1987. This involved academics, museum, heritage and tourism officials from Italy, France, Turkey, Spain, Greece, Portugal, Holland, Belgium and the UK. The purpose was to develop itineraries for both tourism and for the purposes of education (see also Mangion and Tamen, 1998).

In a more recent development linked to the CoE, Therond (1999) argues that the architectural heritage of early twentieth-century mass tourism itself should also be viewed as part of the pan-European cultural heritage. It would indeed be ironic if the legacy of the late nineteenth century was itself to be commodified as an itinerary for the cultural tourists of the twenty-first century. There are also some interesting parallels here with the itineraries mentioned in the previous chapter, such as using tourism for didactic purposes to inculcate some form of shared history and knowledge. In terms of the CoE there is a more obvious, or at least more openly stated, political slant in that the declared aim of the CoE is to foster a sense of pan-European identity, one that is based on the recognition of diversity and that actively discourages homogeneity (Council of Europe 1999a, b, c).

At a national level, recent policy developments in the UK are of interest. In commonsense terms the realm of culture has tended to be seen as separate from the realm of the political, despite the fact that, for many years, successive governments subsidised the high arts. Casey et al. (1996) provide a comprehensive overview of the economic importance of culture in the UK. They found that the idea of the cultural industries gained currency throughout the 1980s, a time when, as McGuigan (1996) notes, there was a shift from state to market regulation (Mort, 1989, Slater, 1997). The scope of the culture industry was progressively widened from a concern with the 'high' arts to one that included media, sport, recreation and leisure (Casey et al. 1996: 4). In many respects this parallels the broadening of the scope of heritage, both nationally and globally, as discussed in the previous chapter.

Despite government interest in the strategic economic value of tourism, and the sudden burgeoning of heritage attractions throughout the 1980s and early 90s in the UK (Elliott 1997: 30) there were no attempts to plan or coordinate strategy at a central level, developments being largely but not exclusively left to the operation of markets. By the mid 1990s, however, a fall in overseas market share coupled with the lack of a national strategy was being noted by the British Tourist Authority (BTA) 'the industry is poorly organised to market itself' (BTA 1996: 5). In order to respond to the decline in overseas visitors and the highly competitive nature of the global market, although heritage was still regarded as a 'core value' (1996: 5), the report also drew attention to the need to 'Invest in new customer segments [and]... develop the powerful brand image of Britain' (1996: 11).

Following the election of the Labour government in May 1997, the Department of National Heritage was renamed and relaunched as the Department for Culture, Media and Sport (DCMS) and described itself as 'a department of the future... It is about creativity, innovation and excitement' (DNH 1997), and this future is to be the development of the 'creative economy... those goods and services in the cultural sector' (DNH 1997). This was followed by the official 'rebranding' of Britain by the BTA:

> The arts are an integral part of tourism and feature prominently in tourist board activities. 'Style and Design', the... current campaign to position Britain as a stylish, up-beat and contemporary destination – symbolised by BTA's new tourism marque – is the latest in a long line of projects to improve links between the arts and tourism and raise Britain's cultural profile world wide (BTA 1997b, unpaginated).

Such developments were partly an attempt by the new government to project a forward-looking national identity, which became somewhat disparagingly known as 'Cool Britannia'. Culture and national identities are firmly and unequivocally to be remade in the service of economic interests, to be achieved by a consensus between public and private sectors. In turn this supports the claims by Mort (1989) and Slater (1997) concerning the realignment of economics, culture and consumption. Even the Foreign Secretary was to announce: 'This does matter: it matters for business, it matters for tourism, it matters for Britain's place in the world' (Foreign and Commonwealth Office 1998 unpaginated).

What is of interest in these developments are firstly, the centralisation of tourism policy, and secondly, the linkage between such centralisation and the overall commodification of national culture for commercial purposes. In part, this is also a broader political strategy in which the current administration desires to be seen as new, dynamic and progressive, to be for the future, and not about the past.

The linking of overseas marketing for both manufactured goods and tourism through the extension of partnership agreements at a national and ministerial level also shows the extent to which tourism is no longer regarded as an optional extra, rather, it has been legitimised as an integral part of the UK economy. For example, the creative industries have been targeted as areas of future economic growth in their own right, as well as providing the basis for future tourism strategies. The most recent policy document, as the latest national policy document from the Department for Culture, Media and Sport states, tourism has the potential to 'encourage local culture and diversity' (DCMS 1999: 8). In short, the document from the DCMS shows that tourism is no longer being considered as an ancillary or second-rate industry, but rather as an integral part of the national political economy. Culture has been unequivocally given over to the marketplace, but the marketplace is also a means by which 'cultures' can be maintained. It is not only local and national identities that are being remade for the purposes of economic regeneration. Indeed the example of the UK may be seen as an attempt to carry out, at a national scale, what had already been achieved at a more localised level.

The use of cultural policies as an element of urban regeneration is not new, but is, as I explained in chapter two, part of the revaluation of urban space which occurred across the developed world during the 1980s. Bianchini and Parkinson (1993), for example, draw attention to a number of cases in Europe where culture is being used instrumentally to serve two purposes. First, to inculcate some notion of civic pride or identity, and secondly, to serve the needs of the leisure industry for both residents of specific localities and tourists alike. Similar developments are also found in the USA (Judd and Fainstein 1999, Zukin 1995). In all these examples, what we see are municipalities instituting policies at the subnational local level, even if this leads to the development of international connections. As Bianchini notes, in these cases we are not dealing with culture as the high arts, rather, as something that is broader and more inclusive, often involving deliberate attempts to incorporate disadvantaged urban minorities (Bianchini 1993: 199–200).

Two examples both connected with popular music – or mass culture – illustrate these points. The cities of Liverpool, UK (S. Cohen 1997) and New Orleans, USA (Atkinson 1997) have long been associated with popular music, the Beatles and Jazz respectively. As such, the unique heritage of these places has been commodified for the purposes of tourism. In her study of the pop music industry in Liverpool, Cohen found that the musical heritage of that city was a means of asserting difference, of associating it with 'particular images and values' (Cohen 1997: 78). However, there were significant differences in the ways in which local people and tourists conceptualised these images and values. Many Scousers (an indigenous term used to define natives of that city) tended to view the Beatles as deserters, and those in the city's music industry also viewed this heritage as a something of a drawback. To those concerned with the tourism industry, the Beatles still remained a way of projecting the city onto the global stage. As one tourism official put it: 'The Beatles are to Liverpool what the Pope is to Rome and Shakespeare to Stratford. If you can milk it then you should' (Cohen 1997: 82). As Cohen comments, such different and at times opposing valuations of this unique legacy mean that the Beatles – or more precisely the projected representations of them – are symbols which are contested, and this contestation concerns the nominal ownership of representations. To many in Liverpool the heritage of the Beatles is theirs, it is part of their localised knowledge, and part of the representational space of that city. Atkinson's study of New Orleans draws similar conclusions. She notes the city has long been associated with music, and played a pivotal role in the development of jazz. Since the 1980s, the economic fortunes of the city declined, and tourism began to attract attention from policymakers, becoming the primary income generator (Atkinson 1997: 92), resulting in conflicts concerning who should own these representations of the city (1997: 98).

One significant aspect of both these cases is the relationships that were established between these two cities. As Atkinson points out, they have much in common: they are declining port cities of similar size, with historical trade links and tend to be regarded as rather peripheral, both economically and culturally in relation to their nation states. In the late 1980s both had become 'Sister Cities' or 'Friendship Linked', a relationship less formal than 'twinning' but one which still involved a degree of cooperation (Atkinson 1997: 103–5). A related point of interest is the way in which the national boundaries are being circumvented by localities which have something in common. In turn, what these cases, and indeed many others, raise are questions concerning the ownership of culture: by whom is it being commodified, and for what? In Liverpool and New Orleans, we can see cities attempting not only to diversify their economies through tourism, but also to improve their 'image' by instituting a variety of policy measures, under the broad rubric of culture, in order to sell their uniqueness. Globalisation has resulted in the spread and adoption of broadly similar economic policies and also global definitions of international heritage. It should come as no surprise then to find that the processes of cultural commodification, for the sake of tourism, are also being played out on the global stage, and are not the prerogative of the developed economies of the West.

As this chapter has shown, similar examples can be found in other parts of the world too. The process of cultural commodification, like capitalism itself, is now played out on the global stage and in some cases is irreducibly associated with the dynamic interplay between politics and markets, or attempts to harness the markets for political ends. What we see emerging is what Wilk describes as 'structures of common difference', similarity across cultures is a matter of form, not content (1995: 118), and the form is the logic of the post-Fordist political economy and its associated strategies of segmentation.

Conclusion: culture and commodification

As I have been arguing, culture needs to conceptualised as a dynamic process of creating and sustaining symbolic meanings, which cannot be reduced to a set of essences linked to either people or place, although within the tourist system, cultures are presented as such. I also pointed out that culture is a lived experience, and that to divide activities and commodities into categories of high and low, or elite and mass is to perpetuate a rather lop-sided and western concept of culture. The idea of cultures as being both mobile and place bound is, I would suggest, fundamental to the whole notion of cultural globalisation. For example, in the previous chapter, I discussed the ways in which heritage could be seen as a means to recover or invent some notion of cultural cohesiveness bound to specific localities. The boundedness of culture in this sense is still obviously important at a number of levels. Despite the premature obituaries for the nation state, it has not withered away. As the case studies outlined above show, national and local governments in the developed and the developing world are enacting interventionist policies in order to direct the form and patterns of cultural development. Such developments are, however, uneven in both their spread and effects.

One of the important, distinguishing features of tourism is the fact that it is socially and spatially marked as distinct and different. Places from nation states to localities are attempting to commodify and present themselves as different, as possessing singular qualities of space and culture, as being composed of essences. The production and consumption of narratives of space created through heritage not only provide the means by which a sense of national or local identity can be constructed, they are also one of the means by which commodities are produced for the global tourist system.

So, although we appear to be in an era characterised by the dissolving of old certainties, we can also see that places are still trying and indeed are driven by the necessity to differentiate themselves from each other in terms of both the tourist market as much as for internal, or local cultural imperatives. If we are seeing the emergence of de-differentiated cultural forms, or a blurring of the boundaries between high and low culture, this does not mean that places and cultures are tending towards similarity, or homogeneity, in fact, it indicates the reverse. De-differentiation for example, or even the postmodern condition, simply do not unwind or unravel the processes of modernity. Rather they signal a different kind of differentiation, one that is more complex and that cuts across old divisions such as high and low culture, the authentic and the inauthentic, the exotic and the familiar, work and leisure and so on. Also, as I noted in chapter one, simply to state that the boundaries are blurred or things are de-differentiated, or whatever, does not actually solve anything, and may only be a way to dodge a set of complex issues. I would argue therefore that de-differentiation is best considered as a more complex form of differentiation, one that is no longer played out to the old rules or indeed in terms of the nation state, but on a global stage.

Within this chapter, I have also argued that there is a pressing need in tourism analysis to tackle the problem of culture in a more informed manner. There are clearly links between the political economy and culture, and hence between the use of culture for tourism purposes. Yet culture is too often seen as a consequence of economics, and too little attention has been devoted to an examination of the interplay between them, and the ways in which cultures may be driven by their own internal imperatives as much as by any outside influences. Also, I have argued that globalisation does not in itself lead to cultural homogeneity, rather it seems to be generating more differences than similarities.

I also argued that it is necessary to distinguish not only between descriptive and normative models of culture, but also to focus on the ways that culture is used in an instrumental fashion, as much as the ways it is used in the formation of localised identities. One way of assessing such claims is to look beyond the obvious processes of commodification produced solely for the purposes of tourism, and the attempts to harness the cultural economy on terms of policy directives. The focus then should be on the ways in which commodification impinges on the cultural norms of host societies in terms of locality and identity, and the ways in which the patterns of daily life, the practices of representation and knowledge are both affected by, and adapted to, the development of tourism.

Chapter 7

Whose Place? Tourism, People and Change

Introduction

The theme of cultural impacts is well documented, yet exhibits a tendency to fall into a rather sterile debate concerning the presumed negative effects of tourist commodification upon the host society. While not denying that tourism can have negative effects, I also argued that such analyses tend to be premised on the assumption that cultures, in particular those considered to be exotic, are first, closed systems, and secondly, tend to be viewed as the passive victims of modernity. The idea of travelling cultures discussed in chapter six, even if it overstates its case, nonetheless draws attention to the increasing flows of both people and objects that are an important element of globalisation.

I also argued that what marks tourism off from other forms of consumption is the commodification of space as distinct places. In turn, this is viewed as a dynamic process through which particular interests are maintained and legitimised. Within this framework struggles over both the material and symbolic construction of space are conceptualised as struggles to objectify meanings, to impose or appropriate a particular order. I will pick up this theme by examining the interplay between hosts and guests in terms of mutually reinforcing elements which each bring to the symbolic economy of tourism, and from which each constructs models of identity which are not only rooted in tradition, but also incorporate change. Analysing identity is a complex issue but, for the purposes of this chapter, I will restrict my approach to a set of defined issues which relate to the problems of cultural commodification discussed in the previous chapters and how these processes are mediated at a localised level.

Place and identity

In the previous chapters I described the concept of de-territorialisation as a component of globalisation, but I also cautioned against the idea of seeing cultures as if they were somehow being reconstituted as free-floating entities. Although, as I have argued, cultures are concerned with creating and communicating symbols, they nevertheless also have a material basis. The importance of place, and the ways in which it is lived in and lived through, is not diminished by globalisation (Lovell 1998) but, arguably, may even be reinforced by it. On the surface these opposing tensions, greater integration at an economic level, and greater differentiation at a more localised level may appear to be paradoxical, but only superficially. Although one characteristic of globalisation is the mass migration of people (Held et al. 1999), and not just for purposes of leisure, most people still experience their day-to-day lives in one location. The importance of globalisation then is in 'the transformation of localities themselves' (Tomlinson 1999: 29) that is, the ways in which the forces that tend towards globalisation are realised in specific socio-spatial forms. To apply Lefebvre's analytical framework, what we are dealing with here are representational spaces, that is, space as directly lived and experienced which draws on, and is also informed by, particular forms of localised or indigenous social knowledge. In turn, this is communicated through a set of associated images and symbolic forms as much as forms of social practice (Bourdieu 1977, 1991).

To belong to a place is to know the significance of such symbolic forms, the collective meaning of particular places which may encapsulate some notion of collectivity, perhaps as a form of localised history that ascribes significance to particular sites, such as shrines, monuments, buildings or workplaces, the raw materials, so to speak, out of which heritage is forged. Forms of indigenous, localised knowledge also contain normative elements, such as prescribing the correct ways of acting in certain places and at certain times, what is appropriate, and what is not. It is through the possession of these forms of knowledge that, among other things, distinctions between insiders and outsiders are made. Take for example, the idea of 'home'. The values and meanings that are attached to this notion vary between different places and in different cultures. At some base level though the idea of home generally evokes a set of beliefs and associated symbols which embody notions of attachment to a particular place, particular forms of family and kinship, perhaps religious or political affiliations and perhaps even a particular time. The idea of home may also relate to wider forms of social cohesion beyond the ties of family and kinship to encompass an ethnic or religious group, a region or even a nation. As Lovell points out, 'home' may also be seen as a place of return after displacement or even death (1998: 3) for those who may count themselves as dispossessed. Either willing migrants or refugees, they may invoke some notion of homecoming as a focus for their collective identity.

Attachments to both people and place in this localised sense may well be important, but this should not be romanticised into some notion of spatially bounded and distinct 'communities' which, by virtue of being labelled as such, exhibit a cosy form of tradition and solidarity which 'we' have somehow lost (Crow and Allan 1994, Macdonald 1997b, Taylor and Davis 1997). To think of communities as homogeneous entities is to assume that everyone in a specific locality will have the same wants, needs and expectations, and while some people may have a clear sense of attachment, others may not. In the previous chapter I noted that one of the presumed defining features of a culture was that of being ethnically bound, and therefore delimited in respect to other cultures (Welsch 1999). Local forms of identity legitimise claims to a form of commonality and shared experiences by contrasting these with other places and other people. They are as much about exclusion as inclusion, in much the same way that notions of ethnicity are conceptualised.

As Lanfant points out, to evoke forms of identity in relation to tourism is to make a claim for the preservation of, and respect for, other cultures (1995: 31). She adds that this is, in part, an appeal to local populations to preserve what they have, that which makes them distinct. Furthermore, ethnicity is often assumed to be a form of belonging that is the antithesis of the majority (Tonkin et al. 1989). In other words, to define an identity on the basis of ethnicity is in many cases, to presume a minority status, and in terms of tourism, to consider other cultures as exhibiting non-modern traits, as if an ethnic identity is a form of 'elemental attachment' (Hitchcock 1999: 19) which is often seen as indivisible, if not 'natural'. For example MacCannell argues that reconstructed ethnicity, that is forms of ethnicity produced as a result of tourist commodification is 'false' and 'alienating' (1992: 168–9). As J. Scott argues, the problem of identity in tourism analyses has often proceeded on the basis that it is equivalent to an 'inner core of "culture" which resists or gives way to externally induced changes' (1995: 386). The problem here is that such formulations assume that identity and ethnicity are somehow given, fixed and essential. Yet as Hitchcock argues, it is better to consider ethnicity as a process, a 'matrix of significance that is relative and contingent' (1999: 19). In short, as consisting of contested, not essential, categories. If this is accepted, we cannot consider such forms of identity and knowledge as invariant, primordial or unchanging, in spite of the clichés with which they are often surrounded.

Localised forms of knowledge, and claims to identity based on some notion of attachment to place and people, are produced through constant processes of interaction which can have both an internal as much as an external dynamic (Sahlins 1985). Jamison (1999) for example shows how localised forms of ethnic identity can produce both conflict and uneasy alliances between opposing factions depending on whether or not the perceived threat is internal or external, while Waldren draws attention to the ways in which political ideologies can create different and conflicting representations of space, time and identity (1998: 135–6) which, in turn, can revolve around wider issues of national and ethnic identity which may need to be maintained against other conflicting claims. The processes of globalisation are key elements here, and Appadurai's observation on this point is worth quoting:

> for the people of Irian Jaya, Indonesianization may be more worrisome than Americanization, as Japanization may be for Koreans, Indianization for the Sri Lankans, Vietnamization for the Cambodians, Russianization for the people of Soviet Armenia and the Baltic Republics ... for polities of smaller scale, there is always a fear of cultural absorption by polities of a larger scale (Appadurai 1990: 295).

We also need to bear in mind that the community or the ethnic group may be seen as the last bastion of tradition to be maintained in the face of modernity's onslaught, or perceived threats to the political and cultural life of social groups. The rosy glow of romanticism that surrounds the non-modern and primitive should not blind us to the possibility that tradition and even ethnicity may also be seen as forms of stifling conformity from which modernity frees us. Taking all these factors into account it is possible to state that the representational spaces of lived experience, localised forms of social knowledge are mutli-vocal. They present, to paraphrase Lefebvre (1991), an horizon of possible meanings, a resource that is both physical as much as symbolic, out of which identities can be constructed (Hitchcock 1999, Lovell 1998). Given that tourism requires the commodification of space, culture and people in the form of distinctive localities and ways of life, then this immediately raises the question as to how tourism impinges on, and affects, such forms of knowledge, and whether or not it therefore constitutes a threat to identity, or acts as another resource through which identities are created.

As tourists cross borders in the literal sense, they also cross cultural barriers. The notion of 'travelling cultures' discussed above also serves to remind us that tourists bring with them not only a set of perceptions and expectations about their destination, but also their own cultural preferences and forms of behaviour, their own forms of indigenous knowledge. Such cross-border and transnational movements are by their nature temporary, and contacts between hosts and guests are transitory. Tourists as transient visitors may remain outsiders, as anonymous to their hosts, as the hosts are anonymous to their guests. Each party will view the other as a generalised type, as the opportunities to develop any form of social interaction above and beyond the superficial level are generally limited, and may not even be desired or encouraged. It is at this level of representational lived space that we can locate the dynamics of contestation, which are fought out as much in the symbolic realm as the material. In turn, this raises the question of whose interests are being served, those of the hosts, or those of the guests? The main issue that needs addressing here then are the ways in which such factors are related to forms of tourism, and how tourism in turn interacts with the forms of representational space and with forms of knowledge concerning belonging and identity.

Tourism impacts

As I have noted throughout this book, one consistent theme in the tourism literature is the idea that tourism commodification leads to a loss or corruption of cultural distinctiveness (de Kadt 1979, Fennel 1999, Mathieson and Wall 1982, Pearce 1989). The changes attributed to tourism at a local level are often assessed in terms of 'impacts', which generally proceed on the basis of input–output or cause–effect modelling. In turn, these tend to be subdivided into the economic and the socio-cultural. The former refers to the capacity of tourism to provide employment, while the latter tends to focus on the effects of such changes in terms of patterns of behaviour and material culture. In this section, I will examine some of the main themes that touch on these latter concerns. Within socio-cultural assessments there is sometimes a further subdivision in which the social is split from the cultural, with the latter tending to refer to rituals and material products or material culture (Shaw and Williams 1994: 83–93). Assessments such as these, which are more often applied to LDCs than the advanced industrial economies, tend to assume that the processes of cultural change can be easily measured and compared on a scale or by some form of index. Now there are certainly aspects of tourism that arguably can be approached in this way, for example, the idea of carrying capacity, a concept employed to define acceptable threshold limits to the physical growth of tourism (Glasson et al. 1995, Murphy 1998).

Although most often concerned with the physical effects of wear and tear on the environment and therefore related to issues of sustainability, the idea of carrying capacity is sometimes carried over into the realm of socio-cultural impacts where overcrowding is seen as a form of 'social pollution' (V.L. Smith 1994: 211). Now there is no doubt that overcrowding can cause problems, and may lead to the local populace feeling overwhelmed by the sheer number of tourists, leading to the feeling that 'their' place is being given over to cater for the needs of tourists rather than the residents (Meethan 1996a). Clearly, there are a number of important issues here concerning control over the development and form of tourism. The physical capacity of places is not unlimited, and therefore needs to be subject to forms of control, yet there are a number of problems when ideas such as this are simply carried over from the physical problems of tourism management into the realm of cultural contact.

According to Vellas and Bécherel, contacts between hosts and guests can result in friction 'because of differences in lifestyle and culture' (1995: 323) They also consider that this problem of insider/ outsider relationships is one that can be controlled if not avoided through the careful management and manipulation of tourism development. This can be achieved by either locating tourists away from the host culture, or by attracting an upmarket clientele in the hope that fewer numbers means less cultural degradation (1995: 324). There may well be a case that certain forms of tourism may be less inimical to local cultures than others, and smaller numbers of tourists more easily controlled. Behind this assumption though, the idea that 'upmarket' tourists, that is, those with a lot of spending power, will be more sympathetic to others simply for that reason is highly questionable. As some have argued, greater disparities in wealth between the hosts and guests may actually exacerbate differences (Van Den Berghe 1994).

Some attempts to account for these socio-cultural changes or impacts attributed to the intrusion of tourism have employed the standard concept of 'demonstration effects' which assumes that host populations will simply mimic the behaviour and values of the guests. (Cooper et al. 1998, Youell 1998). The following definition is from Pearce:

> Emulating the visitors, the residents may adopt new styles of clothing, begin eating and drinking the imported food and beverages favoured by the tourist, or aspire to obtain the ... material goods so casually displayed by him (Pearce 1989: 223).

Although Pearce acknowledges that this can be a two-way process, in that tourists may well return with newly acquired tastes. Demonstration effects, or indeed other forms of tourism impacts are far too often taken at face value as evidence of cultural change caused by external factors. Burns and Holden state that 'The demonstration effect is almost unavoidable' (1995: 126) and, while acknowledging that there is more to culture change than a simple outside imposition, still regard tourism as a vector for the introduction of 'outside ideologies and foreign ways of life' (Burns and Holden 1995: 126). In a similar fashion, Fennel writes that 'Alien commodities are rarely desired prior to their introduction to the host community' (1999: 101) while Sharpley also regards tourism as the means by which 'alien values' are introduced to host cultures (1994: 204). It is hardly surprising that commodities are not desired until they are seen, but more worrying is the implicit assumption here signalled by the terms 'alien', 'outside' and 'foreign' that suggests other cultures are not only self-contained isolated entities, but are also somehow contaminated by contact with what is invariably seen as the West, or the developed world. Yet as Classen and Howes convincingly demonstrate in their book on cross-cultural consumption: "When non-Western people consume Western goods... they do not necessarily swallow them whole, symbolic values and all, but rather "season" them according to their own tastes and customs' (1996: 181–2).

A further problem with the notion of alien intrusions is the implied notion that 'other' people should not aspire to the same expectations of material wealth that people in the tourist generating countries take for granted. In some ways this is a result of concept-ualising other people as if they possess or embody an 'essence of culture' which, as the last chapter has argued, is a form of misplaced romantic utopianism.

In order to pursue this line of argument, I will use two illustrative cases both concerned with some changes attributed to modernity within 'other' cultures, which come to very different conclusions. The first is that offered by Bleasdale and Tapsell's study of tourism in Tunisia. They write that:

> In terms of the demonstration effect, the impact of tourism is obvious, but so far appears only to have penetrated the sector of the population, which has direct contact with the tourists, mainly younger men... Dress mode is frequently western with jeans and the black leather jacket being a preferred style of clothing (Bleasdale and Tapsell 1999: 190).

There are I feel a number of problems here. Tourism is seen as the single and external causative factor of change, and consequently, other possible external influences such as the media, both print and electronic, are discounted. Both Weaver (1998: 53) and Velas and Bécherell (1995: 323–4) also argue that the global spread of television is more likely to produce such effects, but here we have the simple substitute of one single causal mechanism for another. To return to the above example, the possibility that jeans and black leather jacket could be an indigenised or regional variation of a style is not con-sidered. The authors, it would seem, have not enquired into the local context and significance of such dress. It cannot be ignored that people in non-western cultures, as much as anywhere else 'are actively employing consumer goods to forge their own unique cultural identities' (Classen and Howes 1996: 179, see also Barber and Waterman 1995, Gurnah 1997).

The second example is provided by Harrison's (1992b) study of tourism and modernity in Swaziland. Harrison notes that 'foreign' influences were viewed by many elder Swazis as having a corrupting influence on the young, in particular, discothèques, drinking and the wearing of trousers by young women. This latter factor led to friction between the younger women and the more traditional male elements of Swazi society. As he comments:

> In defying (male) authority in such matters, women lay themselves open to several linked accusations. First, they are usurping male roles. Secondly, they are emulating tourists, and thirdly, they are engaging in 'immoral' behaviour (Harrison 1992b: 155–6).

As he comments, although modernity is clearly a problem to many Swazis, tourism alone cannot account for this. Swaziland is not isolated from the rest of the world, and there is also plenty of access to forms of media that detail European and North American fashion trends. A perspective, he argues, that sees such trends as a threat implies that ' "traditional" patterns of behaviour are both static and morally preferable, a viewpoint which, to say the least, is somewhat contentious if not downright patronising' (Harrison 1992b: 156).

One of the interesting points to take from this is the way in which certain traditional elements of Swazi society are placing the blame for change on the external intrusions of tourism. On one level, this may appear as evidence to support the notion that tourism impacts erode other cultures and ways of life, yet to accept this as evidence would be confusing localised explanations of social phenomena with analytical explanations. The examples I have given here are clearly evidence of contestation, and are by no means unique. However, to assess cultural impacts on the basis of some form of simple causation or cost–benefit analysis assumes the host culture is a 'static object inertly subjected to exogenous factors of change' (Picard 1993: 72).

Such approaches need to be challenged and disposed of. The processes of globalisation and the increasing cross-cultural commodification and consumption that this entails, mean that notions of the demonstration effect are at best outmoded and, at worst, reveal a patronising attitude predicated on mistaken assumptions concerning the relationship between culture and identity. What these two examples also show are clear gender divisions, which may be more to do with the internal dynamics of the societies in question.

Gender and work

Assessing the impacts of tourism, as I pointed out in chapter three, is often seen in terms of the economic prosperity against which success and failure are measured. I also mentioned that one of the problems in assessing such claims was the fact that the tourism sector is not easily disaggregated from other forms of work. Employment in tourism is often seasonal, part time, and can also involve migrant workers in the informal unregulated sector of the economy. One way of approaching this is to examine the changing patterns of work and labour market segregation in relation to gender. As I pointed out earlier, globalisation has affected not only the spatial but also the gendered division of labour (Massey 1994). This is a fundamental categorisation that occurs in all societies, although in different forms. Given that tourism is in some locations, a relatively new form of occupation that appears to cut across established patterns of work, we may expect to see changes in gender relations and tourism employment. Sinclair (1997) records a number of cases where employment in tourism relates closely to the domestic duties of women. Yet as she argues, tourism also offers the possibility that traditional gender roles and the division of labour may be renegotiated:

> changes in 'material' variables such as wage rates, or in perceptions of appropriate types of labour, can alter both labour demand and supply and the mutually supportive relationship between gender definitions and labour force divisions (Sinclair 1997: 10).

Wilkinson and Prativi's (1995) study of an Indonesian village is an interesting case in point. The local economy had tended to be dominated by fishing, small-scale agriculture and local retailing. In more recent years, tourism has come to play a more significant role, but this developed in an ad hoc and unplanned fashion. As a consequence, most of the tourism work, which largely catered for domestic visitors, comprised of informal rented accommodation. Generally these were owned and operated by extended families and therefore easier for women to enter in to. Yet there were other aspects of tourism work, such as acting as guides, which were regarded as being unsuitable, as they involved extended contact with outsiders, especially foreigners. This gendered division of labour was complicated by other factors such as ethnicity and socio-economic position, and the division between inside and outside entrepreneurs.

The most significant changes in gender roles as a result of tourism development tended to be seen mostly in the lower income groups, and money from these activities tended to be seen as a supplement to the overall family income. As they write, although such changes may seem small or even insignificant, they actually reveal an important shift in both the conceptualisations of gender relations and the social practices that are informed by them. However, this also needs to be seen in the context of other factors which contribute to the overall dynamics of the village such as 'modern telecommunications, international movies, improved health care, computers and the growing national economy' (Wilkinson and Prativi 1995: 297) In other words what we are dealing with here are not single causative factors, but a combination of both internal and external dynamics.

Similar issues are also identified by Garcia-Ramon et al. (1995) who examined the role of women in relation to farm tourism in Catalonia and Galicia, Spain. In response to both government and EU legislation, traditional farmers were encouraged to diversify their activities away from agricultural production and into new forms of farm tourism. By broadening the economic diversity of these regions, rural areas would be less likely to sink into a spiral of decline. Where such measures were adopted, the role of women tended to follow the prescribed and traditional pattern of food preparation and general household chores. Bouquet (1987) also records similar developments in farm tourism in Devon, UK. The money earned from these activities tended to be reinvested in the family business, and although it could account for up to one third of total income, could only be a supplement. What these women valued the most from such developments was first, the recognition that their 'ordinary' household work, when put to use as an income generator was valued more highly in itself. Secondly, they were also able to contribute to the maintenance of the farm without having to leave home. Thirdly, many of the women also welcomed the opportunity to have contact with people outside their usual, and sometimes isolated, routine existence.

What they also draw attention to is the way in which the introduction of guests into these households was often initially seen as a breach of privacy. Zarkia's (1996) ethnography of tourism on the Greek island of Skyros also records how economic gain outweighed considerations of domestic space as private:

> Those who rent part of their own house do not seem to mind this invasion of their privacy. It does not bother them to live in one room in order to rent the other to a stranger. 'It is only for two months'... for the time being, income is more important than privacy (Zarkia 1996: 155).

She also notes how tourism has affected other aspects of the local culture. Before the advent of tourism, the younger Skyrians tended to adopt more urban, modernist styles for their home interiors. The houses for rent to the tourists by contrast, are often furnished in 'traditional' style, even if the 'authenticity' of it is, by museum standards, somewhat contrived (see also Garcia-Ramon 1995: 272). However, unlike other cases where the taking of photographs can be regarded as an intrusion (Laxson 1991) on Skyros this appears to be rather different:

> What has remained intact is the passion of the Skyrian woman to exhibit her household. Women, when asked, actually open their houses to strangers with pride and exhibit their treasures. They usually like to be photographed, asking for the picture to be sent afterwards. They insist on arranging the house before the picture is taken and they like to be in the photograph (Zarkia 1996: 162).

Both these examples involve the provision of services within the home, and as such, may be seen as ways in which the boundaries between hospitality as a form of social obligation, and hospitality as a commodified form are changed through tourism. In other words the home–work–leisure divide is reconfigured, but the gendered division of labour within households is not greatly changed.

Scott's work (1995, 1997) on gender and tourism in northern Cyprus by contrast, looks at the role of women migrants, in particular those from Russia and Rumania who tend to work as nightclub hostesses, croupiers or waitresses. These migrants are generally viewed as being prostitutes, and are also required to obtain a visa and undergo an HIV test before being granted work permits. Although not all are involved in prostitution, some clearly are, despite the illegal nature of the activity. These women are subject to strict forms of surveillance by their employers, and in general only stay for a few months. Scott argues that such forms of control, or boundary maintenance, conform to a general view that they pose a series of threats to 'health, public morality, and the family' (Scott 1995: 392).

She also draws attention to the ways in which forms of tourism work were seen as being suitable or not suitable for Cypriot women. In general, those that involved regular and prolonged contact with tourists were seen as potentially dangerous. In turn, such perceptions of danger were due to traditional ideas dominated by patriarchal concerns of honour and shame, and were often utilised by men as arguments why women should not enter into the labour market. As a result, many women were employed in the tourism sector in roles that replicated their domestic duties, often in family-run businesses. Even so, as she comments, increasing participation in the labour force was due to 'a relaxation in traditional restrictions in response to changes in the social and economic environment, but continues to be circumscribed in ways which reflect boundary concerns' (Scott 1995: 401).

What these examples show is the clear need to contextualise adequately claims regarding the impacts of tourism, which may be in response to internal pressures as much as to external ones. In all cases we can see the growing role of global influences and small, but significant, changes to the patterns and practices of gendered work. We can also see that there is a tendency, despite cultural differences, to regard the income derived from women's employment as supplementary to other forms of earned income, so that gendered divisions of work in tourism seem to be reflecting the dominant pattern of flexible service-sector employment.

The final example used here also draws attention to perhaps the most obvious and contentious forms of commodification associated with tourism, that of prostitution or sex tourism (Hall 1992, Kruhse Mount-Burton 1995, Muroi and Sasaki 1997). Mass tourism has often been associated with unbridled hedonism and consequently is sometimes viewed as presaging a moral collapse (Harrison 1992a). For example, Cohen's (1982) study of prostitution in Bangkok found that, although tourism cannot be held accountable for prostitution, its impact was considerable. Due to the rise in tourist numbers, which began as a spin-off from the Vietnam War, the number of prostitutes rose. As the tourists were a new clientele the nature of prostitution also began to change. Yet, as Cohen discovered, those who catered for them were a relatively small number of the total. Now issues such as these are fraught with both conceptual and moral difficulties about which it is difficult to remain neutral (Richter 1998). There is little doubt that, in some cases, sexual exploitation of people by tourists occurs, and may even be a prime motivation for travel to places where forms of behaviour are less regulated than 'at home'. However, this is not a necessary consequence of tourism, not all prostitution is associated with tourism and nor is it limited to men's exploitation of women (Crick 1992). Indeed it seems to be driven more by economic necessity than anything else (Talle 1998).

All the examples discussed so far are concerned, in one way or another, with maintaining boundaries, of drawing the line between what is deemed suitable behaviour, and what is not (J. Scott 1995). In this sense we could say that such boundaries are forms of localised knowledge that comprise of normative prescriptive elements. These are not fixed but, like the earlier examples concerning consumption and identity showed, are forms of practice that have to be worked at. They are subject to a continuous process of negotiation and renegotiation which involves the global movement of people and tourists on the one hand, and the dynamics of localities on the other. In turn, these may be internally divided by the prevailing gendered division of labour which in turn may also involve ethnic and social economic divisions as much as ideas concerning tradition, modernity and change.

Creating and maintaining boundaries

One of the ways of dealing with some of the complexities involved in changing localities is to focus on the ways that places, and roles are equally defined and bounded. Most studies concerned with the impacts of tourism in relation to specific localities have tended to focus on small-scale localities, whether these are in the developed economies (Fees 1996, Lindknud 1998) or less developed economies as noted above. There have been comparatively few studies of the effects of tourism on local cultures and ways of life in urbanised areas (Atkinson 1997, S. Cohen 1997). In part this can be attributed to the problems of disentangling tourism from other forms of activity and patterns of consumer behaviour, the less localised and more diffuse patterns of social interaction that occur in urban locations, and the problems of defining discrete local boundaries.

The main problem that is most often associated with the development of urban tourism, apart from carrying capacity and overcrowding, are the ways in which the development of new consumption spaces creates symbolic boundaries between insiders and outsiders. In the smaller urban tourist centres, the historic cities for example, the local populace often express concern that their space is being given over to cater for the interests of outsiders (Ashworth and Tunbridge 1990: 116–7, Meethan 1996a). In its more extreme manifestations, usually in the larger urban areas, this gives rise to what Judd (1999) terms the 'tourist' bubble which consists of a standard set of facilities such as a convention centre, themed mall, sports facilities, and a restored historical area; forms of development which are increasingly to be found in the urbanised Asia–Pacific rim (Hannigan 1998: 177–186).

Rather like resort enclave developments, tourist spaces in the city are constructed around a series of implicit and explicit boundaries which in turn are often the result of policies designed to encourage economic diversification through niche marketing (Holcomb 1999, Zukin 1995). We could see developments such as these as forms of urban segregation, for by redefining city space, and by developing specific places to attract outside visitors, the functions of the city change from being that of serving the needs of its inhabitants to being that of serving the leisure needs of others. Yet we should not forget that the urban has always been segregated in terms of its functions in one form or another, and in some cases, is also associated with particular ethnic groups (Zukin 1995). Although there is a substantial body of evidence which points to the use of space in this way, the demarcation of borders, the limitations placed on the use of space and so on, it must also be borne in mind that boundaries can be as much symbolic as physical, if not a combination of the two. We can see this in the case of Jerusalem for example. Shachar and Shoval (1999) record that the development of distinct religious spaces within this city is the cumulative result of many years of religious and political conflict. In recent years the holy places of the Jewish, Muslim and Christian faiths, which are in turn subdivided in a number of ways, have also become tourist spaces that are both spatially and symbolically distinct. Each of these spaces they write 'is controlled by the institution of a particular religion, and each has a strong local political character that identifies it as a sort of enclave or mini city'. (Shachar and Shoval 1999: 210). The case of Jerusalem may be an extreme example, but as I have been arguing, the material order of space is also a social order, and some social groups will seek to define themselves in both spatial and symbolic terms, or alternatively, may well find themselves marginalised by such processes.

Mediating the boundaries

One of the elements in creating a sense of belonging or attachment to place is the distinction between insiders and outsiders, and the ways in which localities, in providing the focus for collective forms of identity, are bounded in various ways. Tourists are transient and, despite my reservations concerning demonstration effects, it cannot be denied that relations between tourists and hosts are often unequal especially when dealing with more peripheral or remote destinations and cultures (Boissevain 1996; Elliott 1997, Hitchcock 1999, Reisinger 1995, Van Den Berghe 1994). Even so, we cannot assume that people are simply the passive victims of outside processes. I have argued that, overall, the effects of tourism on host populations have tended to be viewed in dystopian terms. But if tourist–host contacts are not always negative, in what ways may they be considered positive? Perhaps one of the more contentious claims made on behalf of tourism is that it promotes greater understanding between cultures and societies (Var and Ap 1998). As Wahab claims, 'The movement of tourists . . . makes it easier to bring about social homogeneity' although with the qualification that even 'heterogeneous traditions . . . may bring about a cultural shock which might lead to social problems' (Wahab 1997: 131). However, as I outlined above, the idea that globalisation and increased contact leads inexorably to homogeneity is simply not proven, and the evidence strongly suggests that there is, in fact, counter-movement towards heterogeneity. Simply to see increased contact as necessarily leading to greater understanding may well be a laudable aim, and in certain circumstances may occur, but increased contact can also simply reinforce stereotypical attitudes of both hosts and guests rather than diminish them.

Hitchcock provides a comprehensive list of the ways in which both domestic and non-domestic tourists in a number of different cultures and circumstances are pejoratively categorised as 'others' and outsiders (1999: 25–7). Herzfeld records how in Rethymnos, Crete, the locals regarded the Finns as 'straightforward and easy', the Germans were noted for their 'insistence on bargaining' and the British for their 'rowdiness' while those on package tours were regarded as being docile 'little sheep' (Herzfeld 1995: 128) while Shackley (1999: 109) records how some elderly Lo-Ba people in the Himalayas blamed tourists for the drought that afflicted their region. Nor are such attitudes restricted to non-nationals. Martinez records how domestic tourists to a Japanese village on the Shima peninsula were regarded as both 'dangerous and dirty' (1996: 171) and Gilligan (1987) notes the antipathy faced by domestic tourists in Cornwall who were, and still are, derogatively termed 'emmets' or worse. There are, of course, also instances of resistance to tourism at the level of local interactions. Tourism is not something that is passively consumed by either hosts or guests. As Hitchcock observes, 'Ridicule reinforces boundaries as an inverse expression of identity' (1999: 27). Boissevain (1996) also points to the ways in which passive forms of resistance can be manifested. Localised forms of knowledge and identity distinguish between insiders and outsiders whether or not tourism is present. Arguably though, the transitory nature of tourist–host contact may exacerbate such perceptions, and hence create or reinforce such stereotypes.

For example, there are numerous recorded instances of tourists transgressing the boundaries between public space and private space. Boissevain, for example, shows how tourists in Malta often strayed into the private space of the Maltese residents, and cites other cases from Sardinia, Austria and the Lofoten Islands, Norway (1994: 50). Laxson (1991) also records instances of tourists visiting native American pueblos in New Mexico, USA, intruding into the homes of the residents. Now, given that boundaries as defined through localised forms of knowledge are often implicit, it should come as no surprise that misunderstandings can and do occur, but this does not excuse them. What is happening in these cases, I would suggest, are conflicts of expectations of both hosts and guests, which may involve differences in terms of what constitutes public and private. Such differences have often been conceptualised in terms of 'front' and 'back', the former referring to both the spaces in which social roles and relations are acted out, and the latter to spaces considered private or off-limits. As E. Cohen (1995) argues, such distinctions can be applied to tourism in relation to the deliberate staging of events for tourist purposes, which then allows the host community to preserve some distance between themselves and the tourists. As an example, he cites the case of an Amish community where the local populace were able to effectively stage a 'front' for the tourists, which enabled them to preserve their own sense of identity (E. Cohen 1995: 17). Yet division between front and back, public and private, is not always so cut and dried, and the role of tour guides and other cultural intermediaries may be significant here.

Such people often act as cultural brokers, 'buffering the visitor from the unfamiliar' (Harron and Weiler 1992: 87). In other words, they act as intermediaries and interpreters not just of language, but also of localised forms of knowledge, of what it is about places that makes them distinct, how one should behave in certain circumstances and so on. The role of guides, especially in situations where the language barrier is a problem, can be very significant, and also contentious. Van Den Berghe and Keyes, for example, state that 'The middleman becomes...an active agent in modifying the situation in which and from which he lives' (1984: 347). In some respects this is a simple statement of fact, people are not the passive receivers or carriers of culture but are continuously engaged in the processes of modifying their situations, albeit within limitations. However, the role of guides may also involve the promulgation of narratives, which present a sanctioned version of events (Dahles 1996). Yet we should not be surprised by this. Insider knowledge is not total, as it must be borne in mind that all narratives of place are partial and selective, whether or not they are generated by or reflect the interest of insiders as much as outsiders. We also have to consider the importance of others who mediate such contacts such as tour operators, tour companies, and even national governments (Philp and Mercer 1998, Picard 1996).

There is no reason to suppose, given the multivocal nature of place, that any one reading is absolute and correct. However, there are occasions when the promulgation of a sanctioned version of events for tourist consumption is linked into wider political and social struggles over the significance of place. One example that clearly illustrates this is a study of Israeli and Palestinian tour guides by Bowman. He notes that under Israeli law, a licensed tour guide must accompany any tour group that makes use of commercial transport. Although these are trained by the state, the interpretations they provide are also based on their own religious and political background (Bowman 1992: 123). Building on Eric Cohen's (1985) distinction between pathfinders, that is, guides who lead tourists through unfamiliar territory, and mentors, those who are more concerned to integrate the meanings and significance of place into a coherent narrative, Bowman notes that the strategies of tour guides are a significant factor in integrating the prior expectations of tourists into interpretative frameworks which are, in part, negotiated processes involving local interests, as much as the regulation of the tourist industry itself. Now, although this involves elements of what may be termed the tourist gaze, of controlling representational space, the important point is that this is realised as a set of practical accomplishments. Another area of activity where we point to the practical nature of action is that of ritual performances.

Acting it out: ritual, place and tourism

In chapter six I showed that the idea of heritage also extends beyond the material world of landscapes, building monuments and objects to incorporate less tangible aspects such as the spoken language and music, to which perhaps we also need to add ritual performances. My intention here is not to provide a comprehensive analysis of either ritual or performance, but rather to look at the ways in which contacts between tourists and host populations have affected some of the ritualised aspects of peoples lives. In brief, we can see calendrical rituals such as Christmas, Easter, Yom Kippur and Ramadan as ways of marking the passage of time. Others, such as marriage, are used to denote changes from one status to another, and both forms can also be seen as ways of distinguishing certain activities from the mundane (Hughes-Freeland 1998).

Rituals can also be associated with place, and may be forms of commemoration, linking both space and history. Also, some spaces may be set apart specifically for ritual purposes such as worship. Yet there are also a number of rituals that involve, to a greater or lesser degree, some form of public performance. Yet we should not simply equate ritual with the exotic or the other (Gusfield and Michalowicz 1984). Ritual forms are just as often found in modern secular societies, and are often linked to forms of tourism commodification. These, we could say, constitute shared sentiments of belonging and identity, they utilise localised forms of knowledge (Boissevain 1992). As such, they can be considered as ways in which distinctions between insiders and outsiders are reinforced. Outsiders may not be able to 'read' what is occurring in the same way that insiders are able to do. For example, Laxson (1991) examined the interrelationship between tourists and those performing pueblo ceremonials in New Mexico, USA. The rituals described by Laxson are primarily performed for religious reasons, and the idea of secrecy is an important element. A correct understanding of the events is only possible through a full and grounded understanding of particular forms of knowledge and, for this reason, some rituals need to be conducted away from the intrusion of outsiders.

Laxson's case study also reveals some of the ways in which the performers and inhabitants of the pueblos negotiate aspects of their performances, in particular at the Gallup Inter-Tribal Ceremonial. This annual event has been held in Gallup, New Mexico since the 1920s and was specifically created in order to encourage tourism. She notes that during this pageant, the Pueblo villagers contribute to the expectations of the audience by performing dances wearing costumes and face paint that originated from the culture of the Plains Indians. In some cases, this resulted in tourists becoming confused between what was 'authentic' and what was not (Laxson 1991: 378). Similarly, Picard (1996) records that most tourists in Bali do not have access to many of the ritual performances of Balinese dance organised for internal consumption, and also that many performances are now staged entirely for tourist consumption rather than ritual purposes.

As Boissevain (1996) argues, such control is one way that people are able to maintain both physical and social distance from the more obvious intrusions of tourism. There are certainly numerous instances of this occurring, yet at another level, the notions of front and back are drawn from western notions of drama in which action is regarded as trickery and deceit, and hence inauthentic (Hughes-Freeland 1998: 13). In both cases discussed above, access to the forms of indigenous knowledge which endow the rituals with meaning are kept for internal consumption, while others have been created as commodified forms. In both Bali and New Mexico, outsiders will be allowed access to some ritual performances but not others. Rituals then, like places, can also be polyvalent (Boissevain 1992, Davies 1998, Gusfield and Michalowicz 1984). In these cases they can be 'read' by both insiders and outsiders. It does not matter if the tourist receives or 'decodes' a different meaning to that of the insiders. The significance of a ritual may lie not so much in the mysteries it elucidates, but the fact that these mysteries are for insiders only. By the same token we should also be wary of assuming that 'sacredness' means the same thing to all concerned in all circumstances. Coleman and Elsner's (1998) study of Walsingham, a site of pilgrimage in Norfolk, UK, notes that the sacredness of the site can be subject to a number of overlapping interpretations which can encompass simple sightseeing as much as more serious spiritual matters.

In all the cases outlined here, it is clear that the presence of tourists has had effects that may be considered negative to a greater or lesser degree. However, this is not quite the same as stating that the tourist commodification of rituals therefore renders them inauthentic, or that those rituals and ceremonies devised for the tourist markets are therefore inauthentic pseudo-events. Picard writes that in Bali, attempts to distinguish between culture for the tourists and culture for the Balinese failed, because tourism itself became 'an integral part of a process of cultural invention' (Picard 1996: 199) or to paraphrase Hitchcock (1999: 28) the analyst's staged authenticity is the activist's cultural revival.

It is also worth considering some examples of rituals and performances that have not been adversely affected by their commodification, or perhaps, even rely on it. One interesting case of this phenomena is the annual Notting Hill Carnival in London (A. Cohen 1982, Sampath, 1997) where a particular Trinidadian style of festival was imported to the UK and underwent a series of metamorphoses, including one particularly bad year when it degenerated into a running street fight between the police and black youths. Despite this, the carnival ended up not only as the largest street festival in Europe, and hence in itself a major tourist attraction, but also as a focus of identity for British citizens of Caribbean origin or descent. The carnival is by and large a voluntary affair involving a great deal of both time and money in the design of floats and the lavish costumes worn by those who take part in the carnival parade. Similarly, the West Indian–American Day Carnival parade in New York provides a focus for creating a pan-Caribbean identity among immigrants to the USA (Zukin 1995: 20) and the Eisteddfod also acts to display forms of Welsh culture and identity (Davies, 1998). The success of such festivals and carnivals casts doubt on the perceived detrimental effects of commodification as such. Sampath notes how the Trinidadian Carnival, from which the Notting Hill variant sprang, has been able to incorporate the global aspects of tourism into its performances without sacrificing its more local cultural significance (1997: 167) and even the original carnival, from which this variant sprung is now seen as a means to attract tourists (Nettleford 1993).

How then are we to treat ritual performances that are invented or created solely for the purposes of tourism? The Festival of the Pacific Arts, described by Zeppel, is an interesting case. This was originally conceived as a way for the indigenous people of the Pacific Ocean region to celebrate their indigenous heritage (1992: 70), perhaps in the same ways that the Caribbean carnivals and the Eisteddfod originally did. Started in 1972, by the late 1980s, it had in itself become a major tourist attraction. Commenting on the fifth festival, she writes that 'While dance styles were largely based on traditional forms, the attire worn by performers ranged form traditional costumes to modified traditional items... and also contemporary clothing' (Zeppel 1992: 73). As she also notes, the festival itself fulfilled several purposes, not only was it an assertion of cultural identity and difference, it was also a way of presenting cultures as commodities for the tourist industry, as well as becoming a cultural institution in its own right (Zeppel 1992).

Similar examples can be found elsewhere. During the 1970s the city of York rediscovered its Viking past which was commodified in a number of ways (Meethan 1996a). One of these was the annual Viking Festival held during the month of February, the slackest time of the tourist season. This involves the staging of events such as longboat races on the river, a Viking craft fair, including stalls demonstrating crafts and selling Viking food and drink. The highlight of these festivities is a torchlight procession through the city by Viking warriors, and the burning of a (fake) longboat on the river. This festival is but one of a seemingly growing number of performances and rituals which are in themselves part of wider local policies designed to animate the new urban spaces of consumption. Other examples would also have to include seasonal events such as arts and cultural festivals such as those held in Edinburgh and Brighton (Meethan 1996b).

Some public rituals have also resisted, or seem unlikely to become incorporated into the tourist system. Although the development of the global tourist system may imply that nothing is seemingly immune from commodification, there are examples where this has not occurred. Consider, for example, the annual round of Orange Lodge marches held in Ulster and in particular, the Apprentice Boy's parade in Londonderry. This commemorates the victory of one section of the population over another, and continues to generate significant and deep-seated tensions between the two factions of the population. As it is constituted at the moment, it is politically charged and sectarian. Although a display of communal solidarity for one section of the population who view it as an assertion of their culture, it is also seen as a negative display of triumphalism by another sector of the population. It is inclusive as much as exclusive. In short, tourism commodification is not as inevitable as may be supposed.

Conclusion

The examples presented in this chapter show that the processes of tourism commodification are realised in a variety of ways, and can impinge on local ways of life in a number of respects. However, as I have also argued, globalisation, and the consequent cultural give and take that this involves, cannot be seen simply as a unilinear process of westernisation. There is no doubt that the introduction and development of tourism reconfigures social relations and local practices at a number of levels. For example, we have to account for the ways that commodities and forms of behaviour can become indiginised, or the ways that rituals are recontextualised in order to account for such change. However, the main thrust of my argument has been directed against models which attempt to assess such changes in simple cause–effect terms. In some respects, the ghost of modernisation theory still continues to haunt tourism analysis, especially so when dealing with places and cultures considered as more exotic. The problem here lies in the fact that many analysts have tended to uncritically accept or borrow theoretical positions, perhaps in the spirit of eclecticism mentioned in the opening chapter, without subjecting them to critical scrutiny. This, I feel, is most clearly seen in the uncritical assumptions concerning demonstration effects, and indeed in other forms of impact analysis without assessing their utility in what is a rapidly changing world. Now, it may seem unduly harsh to accuse some tourism analysts of perpetuating outmoded theories, but as I stated in the opening chapter, it is time to abandon simple eclecticism and consider what is worth keeping and what is not. The problem of cultural change and localised impacts is one area where a more informed approach is required.

My criticisms of how the problems of culture contact have in some instances been analysed, should not be taken as implying that culture contacts are unproblematic, as clearly they are not. The main thrust of my criticism is aimed at the rather simplistic way in which the problems tend to have been both framed and analysed which, in turn, is based on two related factors. First, that tourism is considered as *the* external cause of change and secondly, conceptualisations of 'culture' view it as a set of unchanging essential characteristics lacking any internal dynamism. If both these factors are uncritically accepted, then demonstration effects, acculturation, social pollution and alien intrusions can be observed and measured and indexed, for there is some invariant characteristic against which to measure them. Such claims are largely unwarranted, as they imply a unilinear process whereby cultures are not only fixed, but have no choice other than to fall back on tradition – and deny modernity – or simply adopt and mimic western values and embrace modernity.

Another problem here is the arbitrary and artificial divide often made between economic impacts and cultural impacts. Perhaps, in developmental terms, this is hardly surprising given that the dominant mode of assessing success or failure is on the basis of balance sheets. Yet the examples used here indicate that these two realms are often not easily divisible, and may themselves be cut across by forms of social division and classification such as gender, insiders and outsiders, ethnicity and socio-economic status. It is these divisions that comprise the spaces of representation, that is, localised or indigenous forms of knowledge. Yet tourists also bring with them their own outsider knowledge. Clashes between the two can result in misunderstandings, and may only serve to reinforce stereotypes rather than mitigate them. But these forms of knowledge should not be seen as existing in some idealised and reified form as 'discourses' or 'texts' which the analyst subjects to a 'critical reading'. They are, I would suggest, better conceptualised as social practices which do not simply *reflect* differences, but actually *create* differences through action. What is needed, I would argue, is a more sophisticated approach to the problem, one that acknowledges the complexities of culture contact in a globalised world and, one that does not isolate tourism from other forms of external and internal change. If cultures are conceptualised as systems, which continuously borrow and adapt from each other, then a more dynamic and complex picture emerges. In turn, such an approach will need take to account of reverse flows, indigenisation, political circumstances, internal cultural dynamics, and the ways in which tourism itself can become a resource for creating and maintaining cultural distinctiveness.

As some readers will have noticed, most of the examples used in this chapter are broadly speaking anthropological in both approach and method. There is also a related methodological issue here, in terms of contextualisation. Tourism cannot be 'lifted out' or simply isolated from other processes, nor simply squashed into the catch-all category of culture. If we are to account for localised change, then rigorous micro-ethnographic techniques will need to be employed as much as macro analyses of the global context. But this is an issue I will return to in the concluding chapter.

Traditional forms of life and material culture were thus confined to other times and other places in both popular and academic discourses, and were increasingly viewed as survivals to be conserved, treasured and saved. Given the nature and scope of changes that occurred in the nineteenth century it is hardly surprising that this should be so, and that the dominant analytical paradigms should seek to explain such changes. We can also see how such categorisations can still be discerned and are perhaps still central in popular forms of discourse surrounding heritage, the past, and other cultures. There is little doubt that notions of an earthly and primitive paradise are fundamental cultural categories in developed western societies. It could also be argued that such categories are constructed through a series of mutually exclusive oppositions, each defining itself in contrast to some 'other', as if for example, the only choice was either modernity or tradition. Now if such categorisations were simply confined to popular forms of discourse, or the history of the social sciences this would hardly be a problem, and they could adequately be accounted for. Yet what is problematic are the ways in which they are still used, often in implicit forms, as analytical paradigms.

As I have argued, the debates surrounding commodification have tended to view it *a priori* in negative terms which, drawing on the distinction between sign value and use value, views commodification as that which causes alienation. In turn this is seen to destroy or corrupt the presumed 'depths' of non-commodified forms of authentic social relations. Within such a paradigm commodification is the handmaiden of capitalism and the result of its insidious spread is the shallow, inauthentic and dystopian shadow-land of modernity. By contrast, the utopian world of non-alienated relationships is to be found where commodification and modernity are not, either amongst the unalienated 'primitive others' or through the recovery of past traditions and heritage. Tourism, involving as it does the commodification of people and place is therefore either seen as a symptom of some malaise caused by modernity, or as a compensatory mechanism for such ills. Now, to argue that tourism is a response to this presumed or perceived state of affairs, as a quest for the 'other', is to reduce the complexities of social interaction to a crude form of social causation: we act the way we do because the structure compels us to do so. It is these factors that may well explain why some discussions and analyses of tourism have often adopted a censorious moral tone condemning the corruption and imminent collapse of tradition in relation to 'other' people and cultures, and view modern society as depthless.

Yet the logic of such reasoning can only lead to an impasse, where traditions need to be maintained simply because they are traditions. But appeals to tradition are also appeals against change, and it should always be borne in mind that traditional forms of social organisation may be perceived by some living within them as stifling and oppressive, rather than being cause for celebration (McDowell 1999: 220). It should hardly be surprising that tourism as an industry, which relies on the commodification of people and places, should draw on such generalised categories, for after all, these are what are generally recognised and accepted, and these are what the tourist gazes also draw from. Yet there is a difference between viewing these as the raw materials out of which the commodity is forged, and viewing them as categories that can be used in analytical terms.

The central problem here, I would suggest, is a result of seeing modernity as an end product or a steady state, as being that which 'we' have, and 'others' should avoid. In turn, this can imply a static model of equilibrium in which cultures are classified as either modern or non-modern, and the intrusion of the former into the latter through the medium of tourism can only result in destabilisation and the erosion of authentic ways of life. Any changes to traditional forms of culture and social organisation are then taken as *prima facie* evidence of loss and corruption. Even attempts to account for change that rely on notions of linear development, of modernity as a single route to progress, do not resolve this problem. If we propose that cultures change, but do so on a given trajectory from the non-modern to the modern, change will occur, but this will inevitably sweep aside tradition and authenticity as these factors in themselves are seen as barriers to progress. It is also interesting to note that the fiercest criticisms of such change are most usually applied to 'other' non-western cultures. I would argue that this is a result of the ways that the pre-modern, or the underdeveloped, is assumed as a state where social identities and cultures are considered to be 'natural' and hence unproblematic.

In such cases what we are dealing with are notions of loss, with the causal factor being outside pressures and influences. In turn, such approaches view cultures as self-contained systems without history or internal dynamics that exist in some inherent state of equilibrium. As I have argued, it is no longer possible on theoretical and empirical grounds to view cultures as bounded, self-contained units which are passively subjected to external forces of change. As Nash points out, accounting for such change is both theoretically and methodologically complex, but this complexity is often overlooked 'Mostly, one gets some statements about social development which are loosely associated with the advent of tourism in the host society' (Nash 1996: 26). Such approaches, although long abandoned by anthropologists and sociologists, still return to haunt us. R.E. Wood's comments, although concerned with development theory, could equally be applied to many of the ways that cultural change in tourism analyses has been assessed: 'Long after... modernisation theorists had abandoned the earlier formulations about culture and development, less sophisticated adherents continued to simplify and popularise them' (R.E. Wood 1993: 53).

Many of the examples I have used point to the ways in which the internal dynamics of cultures and places have influenced the direction of change in relation to tourism, both at the macro level of policy making and to the micro level of localised practices. In short, change is neither so unilinear in its forms, nor as inevitable in its consequences as may first appear. I would suggest that many forms of tourism analysis have not fully grasped or adequately formulated this problem of accounting for cultural change in a shifting and now globalised world.

Accounting for globalisation

There is little doubt that globalisation, inasmuch as it refers to the increasing interconnections between places, is having profound effects in terms of politics, the economy, culture and, of course, tourism. Yet we must also be wary of viewing it as a singular condition that has uniform effects. In some respects, globalisation appears to be paradoxical. We can point to trends in the global political economy such as policies of deregulation and the championing of the free market as the prevailing orthodoxy. Also, there is a need to account for the changes within localities as investment capital becomes less tied to specific locales and more mobile, and the role of the state is seemingly diminished by the power of MNCs, or at least must take them into account. At the same time, we can also point to the ways in which national governments are instituting policy measures in attempts to control, if not actually regulate, these global flows. The material presented here also shows how specific locales are asserting differences through commodified forms in order to compete in the global market. This assertion of differences, of singularity, appears to run counter to the notion of linear development leading to the homogenisation of cultural forms or the emergence of a globally homogeneous 'world culture'. I would argue that it is best to view globalisation as changing the context in which old certainties are being reforged, not as a singular process but as a combination of different influences. In turn, this can be conceptualised as a form of de-territorialisation in which the flows of capital, commodities and people are less confined within the boundaries of nation states than has hitherto been the case.

That new forms of political, economic, social and cultural organisation are emerging, and doing so in the context of a globalised political economy, cannot be denied. The influences which are realised in specific localities are not only the result of outside changes, but also in part due to internal pressures for change which may not have anything to do with tourism as such, and may involve a dynamic interplay between factors such as ethnicity, gender and socioeconomic status, and also perhaps between modernisers and traditionalists. It may also be tied into national or regional economic policy developments. On the one hand, culture and cultural forms are more mobile, yet on the other they can still be rooted in particular localities. As the material used here indicates, the notion of outside influences simply intruding or 'impacting' on localities often ignores processes better described as a mutual transformation and reconfiguration in both material and symbolic terms.

For example, the commodification of cultures is assumed to debase them, while the passive consumers are likewise fooled into thinking that what they get is the authentic article. As I noted, one of the problems with such approaches is that they tend to neglect the symbolic value of commodities, and the ways that such values are derived from commodified forms. In short, there is a tendency to assume that the consumption of commodities can be simply inferred from the logic of their production. On closer examination though, it would seem that consumption is more than a passive response. It is not simply the end point of a commodity chain, but rather, is part of wider processes related to the construction of meanings and values. In short, people are not passive but active agents, and this applies equally to host populations as to guests. There is plenty of ethnographic evidence, which I have drawn on here, that points to the indigenisation of commodities and other cultural forms, and the transformations in values and meanings that this entails. As Oakes argues, people do not simply respond to the logic of the global political economy, but engage with and act upon it (1993: 63). In other words, accounting for tourism and change and cultural transformation can only be apprehended through a focus on the practices involved in the creation of representational spaces.

A symbolic economy of space

As I have argued, a distinguishing and fundamental feature of tourism is the commodification of place. The production of tourist space involves both the material environment and the socio-economic circumstances which give rise to it, and is as much a symbolic order of meaning as a form of material production. I also suggested that the triad of spatial practice, representations of space and representational spaces suggested by Lefebvre (1991) could be adapted as follows. First, the material order of space is also a social order, which encapsulates both material and symbolic elements. Secondly, tourism is irreducibly associated with the production and consumption of specific socio-spatial forms. Thirdly, the production of tourist spaces is a general process of commodification mediated at various spatial and institutional levels, from the global and transnational to the national, regional and local. Lastly, such processes need to be considered as dynamic systems of change.

I also argued that the representational spaces, those of lived experience, were localised forms of knowledge encompassing not only a set of values and meanings derived from the environment but also sets of norms governing practices. I also suggested that these forms of knowledge, far from being fixed, were constantly open to reinterpretation and transformation. It is here that we can locate the contested nature of the symbolic construction of space, in the form of the struggle to objectify meanings, to impose upon, or appropriate from the environment a particular order. Accounting for localised forms of knowledge must do so in the context of such changes. The production and consumption of space must be grasped through the dynamic practices that give rise to it.

In sum, we can conceptualise space as both a material and a social order mediated by symbolic forms that are both imposed on, and derived from it. Tourism or tourisms are forms of commodification and consumption of these socio-spatial forms. In turn the general processes of commodification involved in the production of tourists spaces are mediated at various spatial and institutional levels, from the macro level of globalised institutions to the micro level of people's day-to-day lives. Finally, analytical approaches need to see such processes as dynamic, as transforming both social and spatial relations. Local forms of knowledge are not necessarily corrupted by tourism, rather tourism is one element that needs to be dealt with, perhaps to be resisted, perhaps to be incorporated, perhaps to be changed and modified in the process.

Towards a future research agenda

What I am arguing for then are transformative paradigms of social action, which acknowledge that the material and the symbolic are mediated and changed by social practices, and that both constitute a symbolic economy in which spaces and their associated meanings are produced for consumption. In chapter one I stated that it was time to subject the analytical frameworks, most commonly employed in tourism, to serious scrutiny. As I have argued, subsequently, there are a number of elements that need rejecting or reformulating which in turn implies a conceptual as much as a practical reorientation, and that many of these are simply accepted as given unproblematic categories whereas they contain implicit value judgements.

Let me begin with mutually exclusive dualisms. I have probably already said enough about the problems of thinking in terms of either/or, but it does strike me as being both a fundamental and widespread problem, especially when dealing with tourism impacts, authenticity and cultural change. Tourism is perhaps not *the* agent of change, but rather, is indicative of other processes. Accounting for change must be able to deal with the complexity of global–local relationships, which must include internal as well as external dynamics of cultures and places. What this means is not that the problems have changed, but rather, the ways in which they have been framed must change, it means shifting the focus of the questions. If it is accepted that cultures are more dynamic than has hitherto been allowed for, then accounting for cultural change will need to be more firmly contextualised. Rather than trying to assess the impacts of tourism in terms of external intrusions, the question could be better reformulated by asking what are the processes of social change within localities, how are other external factors incorporated and mediated or even resisted, and what role does tourism play in these processes?

The idea of authenticity is a category that should be discarded, certainly in terms of its indiscriminate use. As I have pointed out, in itself it has no analytical utility except perhaps to those involved in activities where issues of provenance are important. As a general category though, its primary use appears to be as a large stick, which a cultural elite wield against the misguided cultural popularisers. Authenticity is not a universally valid category, and this needs to be recognised. This means focusing on its uses, which may be ideological or political, which in turn may be linked to perceived threats to ethnicity and cultural identity. Now this is not to say that it is unimportant, as it clearly is, and if people perceive that the authenticity of their culture is threatened then this must be treated seriously. If perceptions affect the way that people behave then they are none the less real for that, and are as valid in this sense as anything else. What this means though is that questions surrounding the nature of authenticity need to focus on who uses it, why they use it, and what they use it for. Also, a look at the ways in which certain aspects of cultures are selected for elevation to the status of authentic representations will reveal a lot about the value system of that culture.

Culture is another term that cannot be granted unproblematic status. As with authenticity, the differences between analytical and commonsense notions of culture will also need to be more fully articulated. There is also a need to be more precise about whether or not the term is used to describe total ways of life, or just some aspects of a particular society. There is also a need to focus on its uses in terms of policy developments and the relation between culture, identities and politics. To see both authenticity and culture in relational terms like this means not only focusing on the instrumental use of such categories but, by doing so, focusing on people as active agents of change, not passive recipients.

There are also clearly a number of issues regarding the creation and formation of boundaries and other forms of differentiation. Although these are not new concerns within tourism literature, there is room for further development. Adopting a transformative approach means that, rather than asking what boundaries do tourists transgress it is more useful to look at the ways in which both hosts and guests contribute to the creation and maintenance of boundaries, and how these are renegotiated in the process. Again, the case study material shows that this often occurs. In turn this would require a full understanding not only of local forms of knowledge, of local models of society, but also of those that the tourists bring with them.

The fact that negotiations occur also casts doubt on forms of analysis that privilege the text, discourse, or gaze, bearing in mind that these terms are often used indiscriminately. Creating representations of space, either in textual or visual forms may appear to be the exercise of power, and in certain cases may be. Yet the problem here lies in assuming that there is only one way in which these gazes or discourses can be decoded, that the intent of the producers is simply transferred, as if by osmosis, to the consumers without any sort of transformation in meaning. The idea of the gaze is certainly a useful metaphor, but mostly its analytical uses have tended to focus on the production of images, and too often they are assumed to have a single causative effect. Less attention has been focused on the ways that individuals consume and interpret them, and whether or not such interpretations can then be matched, for example, to differences in gender, socio-economic status, ethnicity, and so on. I would suggest that this would be a useful avenue for further exploration, but one which focuses on the consumption of such representations, not their production, and one that also needs to be fully grounded in empirical investigation, not theoretically driven speculation cloaked as social criticism.

Although there are a number of studies that focus on issues of gender in relation to tourism, especially in relation to work and changing gender roles, it still remains a largely underdeveloped area. Although it is not unreasonable to suppose that there are differential patterns of tourist consumption according to gender, this is yet to be fully examined. In chapter four, I made reference to some studies that analysed what, for want of a better term, could be called identity work. That is, they focused on the ways that individuals created narratives of the self through particular patterns of consuming time and place. Again, this is an area that could be developed.

Overall, these suggestions amount to a focus on both cultural and individual change and consumption as forms of practice in which people are actively engaged. Many of the suggestions outlined here

also mean that there is a need to question the idea of commodification as a priori negative, and to begin to see commodities not as
possessing fixed attributes but attributes which can be reworked past
the immediate point of consumption. Although this book is primarily
concerned with the development of a more theoretically informed
approach to the study of tourism, there is also the need to at least
consider some of the methodological implications of the approach I
have outlined, as each must inform the other. To think beyond
dualisms in theoretical terms also requires thinking about the methods that will enable this.

A methodological note

In chapter one I raised the possibility that an uncritical eclecticism
may result in the more problematic areas of disciplines, rather than
the best, coming together, and the same applies to methodology. The
first point to consider here is whether or not tourism requires a
different methodology or range of methodologies from other disciplines. I think that the immediate response to this is no, but there
are a range of methods which could be usefully applied to the issues I
have raised above. Although there are a number of books that are
specifically aimed at methodology for tourism, they do not, I feel,
amount to a new methodological paradigm (Brunt 1997, Ritchie and
Gouldner 1994, Ryan 1995, Veal 1997). If anything, they tend to be
dominated by positivist approaches, that is, they are concerned with
the gathering of quantifiable data for the testing of hypotheses and
purposes of measurement. While there are certainly aspects of tourism that can only be addressed by using such methods, less attention
is being paid to other qualitative techniques other than the use of
interviews that have been, or could be successfully employed.

First let's look at ethnography, which is not a method as such, but
an approach that can combine a number of methods, most usually
participant observation, interviews and documentary analysis. Ethnography is particularly suited for micro-level analysis especially in
teasing out the complexities involved in localised forms of practice
and knowledge, and contextualising these in terms of transformation.
(E. Cohen 1984, 1988b, Graburn and Moore 1994, Nash 1996,
Selwyn 1994). Second, biographical narratives and life histories,
techniques often used in ethnographic research, could also be use-

fully employed in for example, assessing changes over an extended period of time in terms of both localities as much as individual patterns of consumption (R. Atkinson 1998). Third, the use of time diaries, which has been touched on, could be a very useful way of assessing, in both quantitative as well as qualitative terms, the ways in which both time and space are consumed. Fourth, visual techniques other than observation, such as photographs and videos either as forms of documentation, or to provide the stimulus for either individual or group discussion (Banks and Morphy 1999). Fifth, the use of focus groups is another method that has been widely adopted in the social sciences, and is a means of accessing group norms and values (Barbour and Kitzinger 1999).

Now, it is not my intention to provide a detailed commentary on the above, but what applies to theoretical approaches should also be applied to methods. There is a need then to scrutinise both conceptual and methodological frameworks and, *if necessary*, modify them in the light not only of theory, but also by examining empirical data from both primary and secondary sources. Now this is *not* to argue for eclecticism, rather that both theory and method should inform the other (Wacquant 1992: 30). There is a need here, I would argue, for some critical but constructive reflexivity which does not slip into theorising for the sake of it, nor for that matter into a dogged form of empiricism as if facts are facts and that is that, but rather takes a closer look at underlying principles.

To conclude, what I am suggesting above all else is that tourism analysis should stop relying on uncritical borrowings from different disciplines as if this were a strength, and begin to engage in a more critical appraisal of theoretical frameworks, in particular those which rely on mutually exclusive dualisms such as the modern versus the primitive, the inauthentic versus the authentic and so on. I would also argue that, if tourism analysis is to move forward, there is a need to adopt and develop transformative analytical frameworks that account for the dynamics of change at both a macro and a micro level, and the interactions that inform local knowledge and practices in the context of a globalised world. On a final note, I also realise that the material and arguments presented in this book will not be to everyone's taste. There are those, I am sure, who will still wish to argue for eclecticism, and others who may regard my dismissive treatment of certain approaches as unwarranted, but these are matters for further debate. The important thing, however, is to move on.

Chapter 3

The voluminous work by Held et al. (1999) is a very good source of both empirical material and theoretical debate concerning globalisation, and looks set to become a standard reference work. A more focused set of readings can be found in Sklair (1994), while the book edited by Harrison (1992) provides some interesting case studies of development, as does the collection edited by Wahab and Pigram (1997) which examines development in relation to sustainability. Mowforth and Munt's (1997) book on sustainability is also worth a look. Hall and Jenkins' *Tourism and Public Policy* (1995) is a clearly written introduction to issues of planning and policy.

Chapter 4

There is growing literature on issues of consumption. As an introductory text, Miles (1998) is a good place to start. Don Slater's *Consumer Culture and Modernity* (1997) is also worth a read, as is the book edited by du Gay (1997) The edited collection by Miller, *Acknowledging Consumption*, provides an interesting view of approaches to consumption from a variety of disciplinary approaches, and the collection edited by Martinez (1998) gives a view from the Japanese perspective.

Chapter 5

There is a wealth of writing on heritage, and the usual suspects are Wright (1985) and Hewison (1987). Raphael Samuel's (1994) reassessment and overview of the field is probably the best. Despite his polemical approach, he raises a number of very important issues. The book by Corner and Harvey (1991) links issues of heritage into wider issues of politics and economics. Merriman's (1991) study of consumption is also worth a read as he actually provides an analysis grounded in empirical data.

Chapter 6

Tomlinson (1999) gives a comprehensive account of globalisation and cultural change. The book edited by Richards (1996b) provides some interesting case studies of cultural tourism as does that by Robinson and Boniface (1999). From a more anthropological perspective, Hannerz (1996) is also worth looking at, as are the ethnographies in the collection edited by Abram, Waldren and Macleod (1997). Picard's study of tourism in Bali (1996) is an excellent example of both historical and ethnographic work focusing on the complexities of cultural change and is highly recommended.

Chapter 7

Many of the examples used in this chapter are ethnographic case studies. The collections edited by Lanfant et al. (1995), Boissevain (1996) and Selwyn (1996) are highly recommended, while those who wish to know more about ritual and performance should also look at the books edited by Boissevain (1992), Hughes-Freeland (1998) and Hughes-Freeland and Crain (1998). Van Den Berghe's book, *The Quest for the Other* (1994) is also worth reading. This book also provides some useful insights into anthropological methods.

Bibliography

Abercrombie, N. (1991) 'The Privilege of the Producer'. In Keat, R. and Abercrombie, N. (eds) *Enterprise Culture*. London: Routledge.

Abram, S. (1998) 'Introduction: Anthropological perspectives on local development'. In Abram, S. and Waldren, J. (eds) *Anthropological Perspectives on Local Development: Knowledge and sentiments in conflict*. London: Routledge.

Abram, S., Waldren, J. and MacLeod, D.V. (eds) (1997) *Tourists and Tourism: identifying with people and places*. Oxford: Berg.

Abu-Lughod, L. (1995) 'The Objects of Soap Opera: Egyptian television and the cultural politics of modernity'. In Miller, D. (ed.) *Worlds Apart: Modernity through the Prism of the Local*. London: Routledge.

Adler, J. (1989) 'Origins of Sightseeing'. In *Annals of Tourism Research*, **16, 1**: 7–29.

Agnew, J.A., Mercer, J. and Sopher, D.E. (eds) (1984) *The City in Cultural Context*. Boston: Allen and Unwin.

Aitchison, C. (1999) 'New Cultural Geographies: The spatiality of leisure, gender and sexuality'. In *Leisure Studies*, **18, 1**: 19–40.

Albrow, M., Eade, J., Dürrschmidt, J. and Washbourne, N. (1997) 'The Impact of Globalization on Sociological Concepts: Community, culture and milieu'. In Eade, J. (ed.) *Living the Global City*. London: Routledge.

Aldridge, D. (1989) 'How the Ship of Interpretation was Blown Off Course in the Tempest: Some philosophical thoughts'. In Uzzell, D. (ed.) *Heritage Interpretation Volume 1: The natural and built environment*. London: Belhaven Press.

Alfino, M., Caputo, J.S. and Wynyard, R. (eds) (1998) *McDonaldization Revisited: Critical Essays on Consumer Culture*. Westport: Praeger.

Allcock, J. (1995) 'International Tourism and the Appropriation of History in the Balkans'. In Lanfant, M.F., Allcock, J.B. and Bruner, E.M. (eds) *International Tourism: Identity and Change*. London: Sage.

Allen, J. (1992) 'Fordism and Modern Industry'. In Allen, J., Braham, P. and Lewis, P. (eds) *Political and Economic Forms of Modernity*. Cambridge: Polity Press.

Amin, A. and Thrift, N. (1994) 'Living in the Global'. In Amin, N. and Thrift, N. (eds) *Globalization, Institutions and Regional Development in Europe*. Oxford: Oxford University Press.

Anderson, B. (1983) *Imagined Communities: Reflections on the origin and spread of nationalism*. London: Verso.

Andrews, H. (1999) 'Landscapes of Consumption: The examples of Palmanova and Magaluf'. Unpublished conference paper presented at the 1st International Conference on Consumption and Representation, University of Plymouth, September 1999.

Apostolopous, Y., Leivadi, S. and Yiannakis, A. (eds) (1996) *The Sociology of Tourism: Theoretical and empirical investigations*. London: Routledge.

Appadurai, A. (ed.) (1986) *The Social Life of Things: Commodities in cultural perspective*. Cambridge: Cambridge University Press.

Appadurai, A. (1990) 'Disjuncture and Difference in the Global Cultural Economy'. In Featherstone, M. (ed.) *Global Culture: Nationalism, Globalisation and Modernity*. London: Sage.

Appadurai, A. (1995) The Production of Locality. In Fardon, R. (ed.) *Counterworks: Managing the diversity of knowledge*. London: Routledge.

Archer, B. and Cooper, C. (1998) 'The Positive and Negative Impacts of Tourism'. In Theobald, W. (ed.) (2nd edn) *Global Tourism: The next decade*. Oxford: Butterworth Heinemann.

Ashworth, G. J. (1994) 'From History to Heritage – From Heritage to Identity'. In Ashworth, G. and Larkham, P. (eds) *Building a New Heritage: Tourism culture and identity in the new Europe*. London: Routledge.

Ashworth, G. and Dietvorst, A. (1995) *Tourism and Spatial Transformations: Implications for policy and practice*. Wallingford: CABI Publishing.

Ashworth, G. and Goodall, B. (eds) (1990) *Marketing Tourism Places*. London: Routledge.

Ashworth, G. and Larkham, P. (eds) (1994) *Building a New Heritage: Tourism culture and identity in the new Europe*. London: Routledge.

Ashworth, G. and Tunbridge, J. (1990) *The Tourist–Historic City*. London: Belhaven Press.

Atkinson, C.Z. (1997) 'Whose New Orleans? Music's place in the packaging of New Orleans for tourism'. In Abram, S., Waldren, J. and MacLeod, D.V. (eds) *Tourists and Tourism: Identifying with people and places*. Oxford: Berg.

Atkinson, R. (1998) *The Life Story Interview*. Thousand Oaks: Sage.

Australian Heritage Commission (1997) http://www.environment.gov.au.heritage/environments/index.htm

Bagguley, P., Mark-Lawson, J., Shapiro, D., Urry, J., Walby, S and Warde, A. (1990) *Restructuring: Place, class and gender*. London: Sage.

Banks, M. and Morphy, H. (eds) (1999) *Rethinking Visual Anthropology*. New Haven: Yale University Press.

Barber, B. (1982) 'Municipal Government in Leeds 1835–1914'. In Fraser, D. (ed.) *Municipal Reform and the Industrial City*. Leicester: Leicester University Press.

Barber, K. and Waterman, C. (1995) 'Traversing the Global and the Local: Fújì music and praise poetry in the production of contemporary Yorùbá culture'. In Miller, D. (ed.) *Worlds Apart: Modernity through the Prism of the Local.* London: Routledge.

Barbour, R.S. and Kitzinger, J. (eds) (1999) *Developing Focus Group Research: Politics, theory and practice.* London: Sage.

Barker, C. (1999) *Television, Globalization and Cultural Identities.* Buckingham: Open University Press.

Baudrillard, J. (1988) *Selected Writings.* Cambridge: Polity Press.

Bauman, Z. (1992) *Intimations of Postmodernity.* London: Routledge.

Beazley, M., Loftman, P. and Nevin, B. (1997) 'Downtown Redevelopment and Community Resistance: An international perspective'. In Jewson, N. and MacGregor, S. (eds) *Transforming Cities: Contested governance and new spatial divisions.* London: Routledge.

Belk, R.W. (1995) 'Studies in the New Consumer Behaviour'. In Miller, D. (ed.) *Acknowledging Consumption: A review of new studies.* London: Routledge.

Bender, B. (1993) 'Stonehenge – Contested Landscapes (Medieval to present day)'. In Bender, B. (ed.) *Landscape: Politics and perspectives.* Oxford: Berg.

Benson, J. (1994) *The Rise of Consumer Society in Britain 1880–1980.* Harlow: Longman.

Bessière, J. (1998) 'Local Development and Heritage: Traditional food and cuisine in tourist attractions in rural areas'. In *Sociologica Ruralis*, **38**, 1: 21–34.

Bianchini, F. (1993) 'Culture, Conflict and Cities: issues and prospects for the 1990s'. In Bianchini, F. and Parkinson, M. (eds) *Cultural Policy and Urban Regeneration: The West European experience.* Manchester: Manchester University Press.

Bianchini, F. and Parkinson, M. (eds) (1993) *Cultural Policy and Urban Regeneration: The West European experience.* Manchester: Manchester University Press.

Bird, J., Curtis, B., Putnam, T., Robertson, G. and Tickner, L. (eds.) (1994) *Mapping the Futures: Local cultures, global change.* London: Routledge.

Bleasdale, S. and Tapsell, S. (1999) 'Social and Cultural Impacts of Tourism Policy in Tunisia'. In Robinson, M. and Boniface, P. (eds) *Tourism and Cultural Conflicts.* Wallingford: CABI Publishing.

Bocock, R. (1992a) 'Consumption and Lifestyles'. In Bocock, R. and Thompson, K. (eds) *Social and Cultural Forms of Modernity.* Cambridge: Polity Press.

Bocock, R. (1992b) 'The Cultural Formation of Modern Society'. In Hall, S. and Gieben, B. (eds) *Formations of Modernity.* Cambridge: Polity Press.

Bocock, R. (1993) *Consumption.* London: Routledge.

Bohlin, A. (1998) 'The Politics of Locality: memories of District Six in Cape Town'. In Lovell, N. (ed.) *Locality and Belonging.* London: Routledge.

Boissevain, J, (ed.) (1992) *Revitalising European Rituals*. London: Routledge.
Boissevain , J. (1994) 'Towards an Anthropology of European Communities?' In Goddard, V., Llobera, J. and Shore, C. (eds) *The Anthropology of Europe*. Oxford: Berg.
Boissevain, J. (1996) 'Introduction'. In Boissevain, J (ed.) *Coping With Tourists: European reactions to mass tourism*. Oxford: Berghahn Books.
Boissevain, J. and Theuma, N. (1998) 'Contested Space: Planners, tourists, developers and environmentalists in Malta'. In Abram, S. and Waldren, J. (eds) *Anthropological Perspectives on Local Development: Knowledge and sentiments in conflict*. London: Routledge.
Boniface, P. and Fowler, P.J. (1993) *Heritage and Tourism in the 'global village'*. London: Routledge.
Booth, P. and Boyle, R. (1993) 'See Glasgow, See Culture'. In Bianchini, F. and Parkinson, M. (eds) *Cultural Policy and Urban Regeneration: The West European experience*. Manchester: Manchester University Press.
Borja, J., Castells, M., Belil, M. and Benner, C. (1997) *Local and Global: Management of cities in the information age*. London: Earthscan.
Borley, L. (1994) 'Cultural Diversity in a Changing Europe'. In Fladmark, J.M. (ed.) (1994) *Cultural Tourism*. London: Donhead.
Bornschier, V. (1999) 'Hegemonic Transition, West European Unification and the Future Structure of the Core'. In Bornschier, V. and Chase-Dunn, C. (eds) *The Future of Global Conflict*. London: Sage.
Bornschier, V. and Chase-Dunn, C. (1999) 'Technological Change, Globalization and Hegemonic Rivalry'. In Bornschier, V. and Chase-Dunn, C. (eds) *The Future of Global Conflict*. London: Sage.
Böröcz, J. (1996) *Leisure Migration: A sociological Study*. Oxford: Pergamon Press.
Bouquet, M. and Winter, M. (eds) (1987) *Who From Their Labours Rest? Conflict and practice in rural tourism*. Aldershot: Avebury.
Bourdieu, P. (1977) *Outline of a Theory of Practice*. Cambridge: Cambridge University Press.
Bourdieu, P (1984) *Distinction: A social critique of the judgement of taste*. London: Routledge and Kegan Paul.
Bourdieu, P. (1985) The Market of Symbolic Goods. In *Poetics*, **14**: 13–44
Bourdieu, P. (1991) *Language and Symbolic Power*. Cambridge: Polity Press.
Bourdieu, P. (1993) *The Field of Cultural Production*. Cambridge: Polity Press.
Bovin, M. (1998) 'Nomadic Performance – Peculiar culture? "Exotic" ethnic performances of WoDaaBe nomads of Niger'. In Hughes-Freeland, F. and Crain, M (eds) *Recasting Ritual: Performance, media and identity*. London: Routledge.
Bowman, G. (1992) 'The Politics of Tour Guiding: Israeli and Palestinian tour guides in Israel and the Occupied Territories'. In Harrison, D (ed.) *Tourism and the Less Developed Countries*. Chichester: Wiley.

Brewer, J. and Porter, R. (eds) (1994) *Consumption and the World of Goods*. London: Routledge.

British Council (1998) *Sharing Common Ground Overseas*. British Council News 28/7/98, http://www.britcoun.org/uk/uknews.htm

British Tourist Authority/English Tourist Board (1996) *Tourism – Backing a Winner*. London: BTA/ETB.

British Tourist Authority (1997) *BTA Media Briefs*, 3/10/97, http://www.visitbritain.com/news/media-brief3.htm

British Tourist Authority (2000) Movie Map. http://www.visitbritain.com/uk/links/ visitbritain/moviemap.htm

Britton, S. (1982) 'The Political Economy of Tourism in the Third World'. In *Annals of Tourism Research*, **9**, **3**, 311–58.

Britton, S. (1991) 'Tourism, Capital and Place: Towards a critical geography of tourism'. In *Environment and Planning D: Society and Space*, **9**, **4**: 451–78.

Browne, S. (1994) 'Heritage in Ireland's Tourism Recovery'. In Fladmark, J.M (ed.) (1994) *Cultural Tourism*. London: Donhead.

Bruner, E.M. (1995) 'The Ethnographer/Tourist in Indonesia'. In Lanfant, M.F., Allcock, J.B. and Bruner, E.M. (eds) *International Tourism: Identity and Change*. London: Sage.

Brunt, P. (1997) *Market Research in Travel and Tourism*. Oxford: Butterworth Heinemann.

Buck, N., Gordon, I., Pickvance, C. and Taylor-Gooby, P. (1988) 'The Isle of Thanet: Restructuring and municipal conservatism'. In Cooke, P. (ed.) *Localities: The changing face of urban Britain*. London: Unwin Hyman.

Buckley, P.J. and Witt, S.F. (1985) Tourism in Difficult Areas: Case studies of Bradford, Bristol, Glasgow and Hamm. In *Tourism Management* **6, 3**: 205–13

Buckley, P.J. and Witt, S.F. (1989) 'Tourism in Difficult Areas II: Case studies of Calderdale, Leeds, Manchester and Scunthorpe'. In *Tourism Management*. **10, 2**: 138–52.

Burns, P. (1998) 'Tourism In Russia: background and structure'. In *Tourism Management* **19, 6**: 555–65.

Burns, P. and Holden, A. (1995) *Tourism: A new perspective*. London: Prentice Hall.

Butcher, J. (1997) 'Sustainable Development or Development?' In Stabler, M.J. (ed.) (1997) *Tourism and Sustainability: Principles to Practice*. Wallingford: CABI Publishing.

Butler, R., Hall, C.M. and Jenkins, J. (eds) (1998) *Tourism and Recreation in Rural Areas*. Chichester: Wiley.

Callinicos, A. (1999) *Social Theory: A historical introduction*. Cambridge: Polity Press.

Cannadine, D. (1989) *The Pleasures of the Past*. London: Collins.

Carr, N. (1999) 'A Study of Gender Differences: Young tourist behaviour in a UK coastal resort'. In *Tourism Management* **20**, **2**: 223–8.

Carrier, J.G. (1995) *Gifts and Commodities: Exchange and western capitalism since 1700*. London: Routledge.

Carter, S. (1998) 'Tourists' and Travellers' Social Construction of Africa and Asia as Risky Locations'. In *Tourism Management* **19**, **4**: 349–58.

Casey, B., Dunlop, R. and Selwood, S. (1996) *Culture as Commodity? The economics of the arts and built heritage in the UK*. London: Policy Studies Institute.

Castells, M. (1996) *The Information Age: Economy, society and culture*. Oxford: Blackwell.

CDL Hotels International (1999) *Annual Report*.
http:/www.irasia.com/listco/hk/cdl/annual/98/res.htm

Chang, T.C. (1997) 'Heritage as a Tourism Commodity: Traversing the tourist–local divide'. In *Singapore Journal of Tropical Geography*, **18**, **1**: 46–68.

Chant, S. (1992) 'Tourism in Latin America: Perspectives form Mexico and Costa Rica'. In Harrison, D (ed.) *Tourism and the Less Developed Countries*. Chichester: Wiley.

Chon, K-S. and Singh, A. (1995) 'Marketing Resorts to 2000: A review of trends in the USA'. In *Tourism Management*, **16**, **6**: 463–9.

Choy, D.J.L. (1984) 'Tourism Development: The case of American Samoa'. In *Annals of Tourism Research*, **11**, **4**: 573–90.

Chua, B-H. (1998) 'World Cities, Globalisation and the Spread of Consumerism: A view from Singapore'. In *Urban Studies* **35**, **5/6**: 981–1000.

Clancy, M.J. (1999) 'Tourism and Development: Evidence from Mexico'. In *Annals of Tourism Research*, **26**, **1**: 1–20.

Classen, C. and Howes, D. (1996) 'Epilogue: The dynamics and ethics of cross–cultural consumption'. In Howes, D. (ed.) *Cross-Cultural Consumption: Global markets. local realities*. London: Routledge.

Cleere, H.F. (ed.) (1989) *Archaeological Heritage Management in the Modern World*. London: Unwin Hyman.

Clifford, J. (1992) 'Travelling Cultures'. In Grossberg, L., Nelson, C. and Treichler, P. (eds) *Cultural Studies*. London: Routledge.

Clifford, J. (1997) *Routes: Travel and translation in the late twentieth century*. Cambridge, MA.: Harvard University Press.

Clift, S. and Forrest, S. (1999) 'Gay Men and Tourism: Destination and Holiday Motivations'. In *Tourism Management*, **20**, **5**: 615–25.

Cohen, A. (1982) 'Drama and Politics in the Development of a London Carnival'. In Frankenberg, R. (ed.) *Custom and Conflict in British Society*. Manchester: Manchester University Press.

Cohen, E. (1982) 'Thai Girls and Farang Men. The edge of ambiguity'. In *Annals of Tourism Research*, **9**, **4**: 403–28.

Cohen, E. (1984) 'The Sociology of Tourism: Approaches, issues, and findings'. In *Annual Review of Sociology*, **10**: 373–92.

Cohen, E. (1985) 'The Tourist Guide: The origins, structures and dynamics of a role'. In *Annals of Tourism Research*, **12, 1**: 5–29.

Cohen, E. (1988a) 'Authenticity and Commoditization in Tourism'. In *Annals of Tourism Research*, **15, 3**: 371–86.

Cohen, E. (1988b) 'Traditions in the Qualitative Sociology of Tourism'. In *Annals of Tourism Research*, **15, 1**: 29–46.

Cohen, E. (1995) 'Contemporary Tourism – Trends and Challenges: Sustainable authenticity or contrived post- modernity?' In Butler, R. and Pearce, D. (eds) *Change in Tourism: People, places, processes*. London: Routledge.

Cohen, S. (1997) 'More than the Beatles: Popular music, tourism and urban regeneration'. In Abram, S., Waldren, J. and MacLeod, D.V. (eds) *Tourists and Tourism: identifying with people and places*. Oxford: Berg.

Coleman, S. and Elsner, J. (1998) 'Performing Pilgrimage: Walsingham and the ritual construction of irony'. In Hughes- Freeland, F. (ed.) *Ritual, Performance, Media*. London: Routledge.

Conway, D. (1993) 'The New Tourism in the Caribbean: Reappraising market segmentation'. In Gayle, D.J. and Goodrich, J.N. (eds) *Tourism Marketing and Management in the Caribbean*. London: Routledge.

Cooper, C. (1997) 'Parameters and Indicators of the Decline of the British Seaside Resort'. In Shaw, G. and Williams, A. (eds) *The Rise and Fall of British Coastal Resorts: Cultural and economic perspectives*. London: Mansell.

Cooper, C., Fletcher, J., Gilbert, D. and Wanhill, S. (1998) (2nd edn) *Tourism Principles and Practice*. Harlow: Longman.

Cooper, M. (1993) 'Access to the Waterfront: Transformation of meaning on the Toronto Lakeshore'. In Rotenberg, R. and McDonogh, G. (eds) *The Cultural Meaning of Urban Space*. Westport: Bergin and Garvey.

Corbin, A. (1994) *The Lure of the Sea*. Cambridge: Polity Press.

Corner, J. and Harvey, S. (eds) (1991) *Enterprise and Heritage: Crosscurrents of national culture*. London: Routledge.

Cornford, J. (1999) 'Counting Computers – or why we are not well informed about the information society'. In Dorling, D. and Simpson, S. (eds) *Statistics in Society: The arithmetic of politics*. London: Arnold.

Corrigan, P. (1997) *The Sociology of Consumption*. London: Sage.

Cosgrove, D. and Daniels, S. (eds) (1988) *The Iconography of Landscape: Essays on the symbolic representation, design and use of past environments*. Cambridge: Cambridge University Press.

Council of Europe (1999a) *Council of Europe Launches 'Europe, a common heritage' campaign*. http://culture.coe.fr/infocentre/press/eng/99/epress99.06.30.html

Council of Europe (1999b) *Guide to the European Cultural Co- operation*. http://culture.coe.fr/ welcome/eng/ecop.mem.html

Council of Europe (1999c) *Report: Cultural routes – History of the Project (1987 – 1996)* http://culture.coe.fr/routes/eng/eitin2.1.htm

Craib, I. (1997) *Classical Social Theory: An introduction to the thought of Marx, Weber, Durkheim, and Simmel.* Oxford: Oxford University Press.

Crick, M. (1989) 'Representations of International Tourism in the Social Sciences: Sun, sex, sights, savings and servility'. In *Annual Review of Anthropology*, **18**: 307–44.

Crick. M. (1992) 'Life in the Informal Sector: Street guide in Kandy, Sri Lanka'. In Harrison, D (ed.) *Tourism and the Less Developed Countries.* Chichester: Wiley.

Crow, G. and Allan, G. (1994) *Community Life: An introduction to social relations.* Hemel Hempstead: Harvester Wheatsheaf.

Curtin, S. and Busby, G. (1999) 'Sustainable Destination Development: The tour operator perspective', In *International Journal of Tourism Research*, **1, 1**: 135–47.

Dahles, H. (1996) 'The Social Construction of Mokum: Tourism and the quest for local identity in Amsterdam'. In Boissevain, J. (ed.) *Coping With Tourists: European reactions to mass tourism.* Oxford: Berghahn Books.

Daniels, P.W. (1993) *Service Industries in the World Economy.* Oxford: Blackwell.

Dann, G. (1996) 'The People of Tourist Brochures'. In Selwyn, T. (ed.) *The Tourist Image: Myths and myth making in tourism.* Chichester: Wiley.

Dann, G. and Cohen, E. (1991) 'Sociology and Tourism'. In *Annals of Tourism Research*, **18, 1**: 155–69

Das, V. (1995) 'On Soap Opera: What kind of anthropological object is it?' In Miller, D. (ed.) *Worlds Apart: Modernity through the Prism of the Local.* London: Routledge.

Davies, C.A. (1998) ' "A oes heddwch?" Contesting meanings and identities in the Welsh National Eisteddfod'. In Hughes-Freeland, F. (ed.) *Ritual, Performance, Media.* London: Routledge.

Debbage, K.G. and Ioannides, D. (1998) 'Conclusion: The commodification of Tourism'. In Ioannides, D. and Debbage, K.G. (eds) *The Economic Geography of the Tourist Industry: A supply-side analysis.* London: Routledge.

de Kadt, E. (1979) *Tourism: Passport to Development?* Oxford: Oxford University Press/ World Bank/Unesco.

Delanty, G. (1997) *Social Science: Beyond constructivism and realism.* Buckingham: Open University Press.

Dellaert, B.G.C., Ettema, D.F. and Lindh, C. (1998) 'Multi–faceted Tourist Travel Decisions: A constraint based conceptual framework to describe tourist's sequential choices of travel components'. In *Tourism Management*, **19, 4**: 313–20.

Department for Culture, Media and Sport (1999) *Tomorrow's Tourism: A growth industry for the new Millennium.* London: Department for Culture, Media and Sport.

Department of National Heritage (1997) *Chris Smith Welcomes New Name For His Department.* DNH Press Release 178/97, 14/6/97, http://www.coi.gov.uk/coi/depts

Department of the Environment (1975) *What is Our Heritage? United Kingdom Achievements for European Architectural Heritage Year 1975.* London: HMSO.

Din, K.H. (1989) 'Islam and Tourism: Patterns, issues and options'. In *Annals of Tourism Research,* **16, 4**: 542–63.

Din, K.H. (1997) 'Indigenization of Tourism Development: Some constraints and possibilities'. In Oppermann, M. (ed.) *Pacific Rim Tourism.* Wallingford: CABI Publishing.

Dirlik, A. (1999) 'Globalisation and the Politics of Place'. In Olds, C., Dicken, P., Kelly, P.F., Kong, L. and Yeung, H. (eds) *Globalisation and the Asia Pacific: Contested territories.* London: Routledge.

Dodd, N. (1994) *The Sociology of Money: Economics, reason and contemporary society.* Cambridge: Polity Press.

Douglas, M. and Isherwood, B. (1978) *The World of Goods: Towards an anthropology of consumption.* Harmondsworth: Penguin.

Douglass, M. (1994) 'The "Developmental State" and the Newly Industrialised Economies of Asia'. In *Environment and Planning A: Society and Space,* **26, 4**: 543–66.

du Gay, P. (ed.) (1997) *Production of Culture/Cultures of Production.* London: Sage.

du Gay, P. and McFall, L. (1999) 'Reappraising the Culture/Economy Dualism: Critique/meaning/history'. Unpublished conference paper presented at the 1st International Conference on Consumption and Representation, University of Plymouth, September 1999.

Eade, J. (1997) (ed.) *Living the Global City.* London: Routledge.

Eckholm-Friedman, K. and Friedman, J. (1995) 'Global Complexity and the Simplicity of Everyday Life'. In Miller, D. (ed.) *Worlds Apart: Modernity through the Prism of the Local.* London: Routledge.

Edensor, T. (1998) *Tourists at the Taj: Performance and meaning as symbolic site.* London: Routledge.

Edgell, S. and Hetherington, K. (1996) 'Introduction: Consumption matters'. In Edgell, S., Hetherington, K. and Warde, A. (eds) *Consumption Matters: The production and experience of consumption.* Oxford: Blackwell.

Edgell, S., Hetherington, K. and Warde, A. (eds) (1996) *Consumption Matters: The production and experience of consumption.* Oxford: Blackwell.

Ehrlich, H. and Dreier, P. (1999) 'The New Boston Discovers the Old: Tourism and the struggle for a livable city'. In Judd, D.R. and Fainstein, S.S. (eds) *The Tourist City.* New Haven: Yale University Press.

Eidsvik, H. (1993) 'Cultural Landscapes: The need for a political perspective'. In Fladmark, J.M. (ed.) (1993) *Heritage: Conservation, Interpretation, Enterprise.* London: Donhead.

Ellen, R. (1988) 'Persistence and Change in the Relationship Between Anthropology and Human Geography'. In *Progress in Human Geography* **12, 2**: 229–62.

Elliott, J. (1997) *Tourism: Politics and public sector management.* London: Routledge.

Elliott, A. (1999) 'Introduction'. In Elliott, A. (ed.) *Contemporary Social Theory.* London: Blackwell.

Elsrud, T. (1998) 'Time Creation in Travelling: The taking and making of time among women backpackers'. In *Time and Society*, **7, 2**: 309–34

Elsrud, T. (1999) 'Risk Creation in Travelling: Risk-taking as narrative and practice in backpacker culture'. Unpublished conference paper presented at the 1st International Conference on Consumption and Representation, University of Plymouth, September 1999.

Espino, M.D. (1993) 'Tourism in Socialist Cuba'. In Gayle, D.J. and Goodrich, J.N. (eds) *Tourism Marketing and Management in the Caribbean.* London: Routledge.

European Union (1998) *Investing in Culture: An asset for all regions.* Luxembourg: Office for the Official Publications of the European Communities.

Evans-Pritchard, D. (1989) 'How "They" see "Us": Native American images of tourists'. In *Annals of Tourism Research*, **16, 1**: 89–105.

Fainstein, S. and Campbell, S. (eds) *Readings in Urban Theory.* Oxford: Blackwell.

Fainstein, S. and Gladstone, D. (1997) 'Tourism and Urban Transformation: Interpretations of urban tourism'. In Källtorp, O., Elander, I., Ericsson, O. and Franzén (eds) *Cities in Transformation – Transformation in Cities: Social and symbolic change of urban space.* Aldershot: Avebury.

Fardon, R. (ed.) (1995) *Counterworks: Managing the diversity of knowledge.* London: Routledge.

Faulkner, H.W. (1998) 'Developing Strategic Approaches to tourism Destination Marketing: The Australian experience'. In Theobald, W. (ed.) (2nd edn) *Global Tourism: The next decade.* Oxford: Butterworth Heinemann.

Featherstone, M. (ed.) (1990) *Global Culture: Nationalism, Globalisation and Modernity.* London: Sage.

Featherstone, M. (1991) *Consumer Culture and Postmodernism.* London: Sage.

Featherstone, M. and Lash, S, (eds) (1999) *Spaces of Culture: City, nation, world.* London: Sage.

Fees, C. (1996) 'Tourism and the Politics of Authenticity in a Cotswold Town'. In Selwyn, T. (ed.) *The Tourist Image: Myths and myth making in tourism.* Chichester: Wiley.

Feifer, M. (1986) *Tourism in History: From imperial Rome to the present.* New York: Stein and Day.

Fennel, D.A. (1999) *Ecotourism: An introduction.* London: Routledge.

Fine, B. (1995) 'From Political Economy to Consumption'. In Miller, D. (ed.) *Acknowledging Consumption: A review of new studies*. London: Routledge.

Finlayson, A. (1999) 'Culture'. In Ashe, F., Finlayson, A., Lloyd, M., MacKenzie, I., Martin, J. and O'Neill, S. *Contemporary Social and Political Theory*. Buckingham: Open University Press.

Foreign and Commonwealth Office (1998), Foreign Office Press Conference, London, Wednesday 1 April 1998. http://www.fco.gov.uk/news/newstxt.asp?130

Frey, W.H. (1994) 'The New Urban Revival in the United States'. In Paddison, R., Money, J. and Lever, B. (eds) *International Perspectives in Urban Studies 2*. London: Jessica Kingsley.

Friedman, J. (1995) 'Global System, Globalisation and the Parameters of Modernity'. In Featherstone, M., Lash, S. and Robertson, R. (eds) *Global Modernities*. London: Sage.

Friedman, J. (1999a) 'Class Formation, Hybridity and Ethnification in Declining Global Hegemonies'. In Olds, C., Dicken, P., Kelly, P.F., Kong, L. and Yeung, H. (eds) *Globalisation and the Asia Pacific: Contested territories*. London: Routledge.

Friedman, J. (1999b) 'The Hybridization of Roots and the Abhorrence of the Bush'. In Featherstone, M. and Lash, S, (eds) *Spaces of Culture: City, nation, world*. London: Sage.

Frow, J. (1997) *Time and Commodity Culture: Essays in cultural theory and postmodernity*. Oxford: Clarendon Press.

Game, A. (1991) *Undoing the Social: Towards a deconstructive sociology*. Milton Keynes: Open University Press.

Garcia-Ramon, M.D., Canoves, G. and Valdovinos, N. (1995) 'Farm Tourism, Gender and The Environment in Spain'. In *Annals of Tourism Research*, **22, 2:** 267–82.

Gayle, D.J. (1993) 'The Jamaican Tourist Industry'. In Gayle, D.J. and Goodrich, J.N. (eds) *Tourism Marketing and Management in the Caribbean*. London: Routledge.

Gayle, D.J. and Goodrich, J.N. (1993) 'Caribbean Tourism Marketing, Management and Development'. In Gayle, D.J. and Goodrich, J.N. (eds) *Tourism Marketing and Management in the Caribbean*. London: Routledge.

Giddens, A. (1971) *Capitalism and Modern Social Theory: An Analysis of the writings of Marx, Durkheim and Max Weber*. Cambridge: Cambridge University Press.

Giddens, A. (1991) *Modernity and Self Identity: Self and Society in the late modern age*. Cambridge: Polity Press.

Gilligan, H. (1987) 'Visitors, Tourists and Outsiders in a Cornish Town'. In Bouquet, M. and Winter, M. (eds) *Who From Their Labours Rest? Conflict and practice in rural tourism*. Aldershot: Avebury.

Gillis, J.R. (ed.) (1994) *Commemorations: The politics of national identity.* Princeton: Princeton University Press.

Glasson, J., Godfrey, K. and Goodey, B. (1995) *Towards Visitor Impact Management: Visitor impacts, carrying capacity and management responses in Europe's historic towns and cities.* Aldershot: Avebury.

Go, F.M. (1994) 'Globalization and Emerging Tourism Education Issues'. In Theobald, W. (ed.) (2nd edn) *Global Tourism: The next decade.* Oxford: Butterworth Heinemann.

Go, F.M. (1997) 'Asian and Australasian Dimensions of Global Tourism Development'. In Go, F.M. and Jenkins, C.L. (eds) *Tourism and Economic Development in Asia and Australia.* London: Pinter.

Goddard, V., Llobera, J. and Shore, C. (eds) (1994) *The Anthropology of Europe.* Oxford: Berg.

Gordon, I. (1999) 'Internationalisation and Urban Competition'. In *Urban Studies*, **36, 5/6**: 1001–16.

Gore, C. (1998) 'Ritual, Performance and the Media in Urban Shrine Configurations in Benin City, Nigeria'. In Hughes–Freeland, F. (ed.) *Ritual, Performance, Media.* London: Routledge.

Gottdeiner, M. and Lagopoulous, A. (eds) (1986) 'The City and the Sign: An introduction to urban semiotics'. New York: Columbia University Press.

Graburn, N. (1983) 'The Anthropology of Tourism'. In *Annals of Tourism Research* **10, 1**: 9–33.

Graburn, N. (1989) 'Tourism: The Sacred Journey'. In Smith, V. L. (ed.) (2nd edn) *Hosts and Guests: The anthropology of tourism.* Philadelphia: University of Pennsylvania Press.

Graburn, N, and Moore, S. (1994) 'Anthropological Research on Tourism'. In Ritchie, J.R.B. and Goeldner, C.R. (eds) (1994) (2nd edn) *Travel, Tourism, and Hospitality Research: A handbook for managers and researchers.* New York: Wiley.

Graham, B.J. (1994) 'Heritage Conservation and Revisionist Nationalism in Ireland'. In Ashworth, G. and Larkham, P. (eds) *Building a New Heritage: Tourism culture and identity in the new Europe.* London: Routledge.

Greenwood, D. J. (1989) 'Culture by the Pound: An anthropological perspective on tourism as cultural commoditization'. In Smith, V. L. (ed.) (2nd edn) *Hosts and Guests: The anthropology of tourism.* Philadelphia: University of Pennsylvania Press.

Gregory, D. (1994) *Geographical Imaginations.* Oxford: Blackwell.

Gregory, D. and Urry, J. (eds) (1985) *Social Relations and Spatial Structures.* Basingstoke: Macmillan.

Griffiths, J. (ed.) (1998) *Key Note Market Report Plus: Hotels.* Hampton: Key Note.

Gurnah, A. (1997) 'Elvis in Zanzibar'. In Scott, A. (ed.) *The Limits of Globalization.* London: Routledge.

Gusfield, J.R. and Michalowicz, J. (1984) 'Secular Symbolism: Studies of ritual, ceremony and the symbolic order in modern life'. In *Annual Review of Sociology*, **10**: 417–35.

Hall, C.M. (1992) 'Sex Tourism in South East Asia'. In Harrison, D (ed.) *Tourism and the Less Developed Countries*. Chichester: Wiley.

Hall, C.M. (1994) *Tourism and Politics: Policy, power and place*. Wiley: Chichester.

Hall, C.M (1998) 'The Institutional Setting – Tourism and the state'. In Ioannides, D. and Debbage, K.G. (eds) *The Economic Geography of the Tourist Industry: A supply-side analysis*. London: Routledge.

Hall, C.M. and Jenkins, J.M. (1995) *Tourism and Public Policy*. London: Routledge.

Hall, D.R. (1991) 'Introduction'. In Hall, D.R. (ed.) *Tourism and Economic Development in Eastern Europe and the Soviet Union*. London: Belhaven Press.

Hall, P. (1988) *Cities of Tomorrow: An intellectual history of urban planning and design in the twentieth century*. Oxford: Blackwell.

Hall, S. (2000) 'Cultural Identity and Diaspora'. In Mirzoeff, N. (ed.) *Diaspora and Visual Culture: Representing Africans and Jews*. London: Routledge.

Handler, R. (1988) *Nationalism and the Politics of Culture in Quebec*. Madison: University of Wisconsin Press.

Hannerz, U. (1992) 'The Global Ecumene as a Network of Networks'. In Kuper, A. (ed.) *Conceptualizing Society*. London: Routledge.

Hannerz, U. (1996) *Transnational Connections: Culture, people, places*. London: Routledge.

Hannigan, J. (1998) *Fantasy City: Pleasure and profit in the postmodern metropolis*. London: Routledge.

Harrell, H. and Chon, K-S. (1997) 'Hotel and resort Industry Trends in Asia-Pacific'. In Oppermann, M. (ed.) *Pacific Rim Tourism*. Wallingford: CABI Publishers.

Harrison, D. (1992a) 'Tourism to Less Developed Countries: The social consequences'. In Harrison, D (ed.) *Tourism and the Less Developed Countries*. Chichester: Wiley.

Harrison (1992b) 'Tradition, Tourism and Modernity in Swaziland'. In Harrison, D (ed.) *Tourism and the Less Developed Countries*. Chichester: Wiley.

Harrison, D. (1994) 'Tourism, Capitalism and Development in Less Developed Countries'. In Sklair, L. (ed.) (1994) *Capitalism and Development*. London: Routledge.

Harrison, D. (1997) 'Globalization and Tourism: Some themes from Fiji'. In Oppermann, M. (ed.) *Pacific Rim Tourism*. Wallingford: CABI Publishing.

Harron, S. and Weiler, B. (1992) 'Review, Ethnic Tourism'. In Weiler, B. and Hall, C.M. (eds) *Special Interest Tourism*. London: Belhaven Press.

Harvey, D. (1985) *Consciousness and the Urban Experience*. Oxford: Blackwell.

Harvey, D. (1989a) *The Condition of Postmodernity: An enquiry into the origins of cultural change*. Oxford: Blackwell.

Harvey, D. (1989b) *The Urban Experience*. Oxford: Blackwell

Harvey, D. (1993) 'From Place to Space and Back Again: Reflections on the condition of postmodernity'. In Bird, J., Curtis, B., Putnam, T., Robertson, G., and Tickner, L. (eds.) *Mapping the Futures: Local cultures, global change*. London: Routledge.

Hawkins, D. E. and Khan, M.M. (1994) 'Ecotourism opportunities for developing countries'. In Theobald, W. (ed.) (2nd edn) *Global Tourism: The next decade*. Oxford: Butterworth Heinemann.

Healey, P., Cameron, S., Davoudi S., Graham, S. and Madani Pour, A. (eds) (1995) *Managing Cities*. London: Wiley.

Held, D., McGrew, A., Goldblatt, D. and Perraton, J. (1999) *Global Transformations: Politics, economics and culture*. Cambridge: Polity Press.

Henderson, K. (1994a) 'Broadening an Understanding of Women, gender and Leisure'. In *Journal of Leisure Research* **26**: 1–7.

Henderson, K. (1994b) 'Perspectives on Analysing Gender, Women and Leisure'. In *Journal of Leisure Research* **26**: 119–37.

Henrici, J. (1999) 'Trading Culture: Tourism and Tourist Art in Pisac, Peru'. In Robinson, M. and Boniface, P. (eds) *Tourism and Cultural Conflicts*. Wallingford: CABI Publishing.

Herbert, D.H. (ed.) (1995) *Heritage, Tourism and Society*. London: Mansell.

Herrmann, J. (1989) 'World Archaeology: The world's cultural heritage'. In Cleere, H.F. (ed.) (1989) *Archaeological Heritage Management in the Modern World*. London: Unwin Hyman.

Herzfeld, M. (1995) 'It Takes One to Know One: Collective resentment and mutual recognition among Greeks in local and global contexts'. In Fardon, R. (ed.) *Counterworks: Managing the diversity of knowledge*. London: Routledge.

Hewison, R. (1987) *The Heritage Industry: Britain in a climate of decline*. London: Methuen.

Hewison, R. (1989) 'Heritage: An interpretation'. In Uzzell, D. (ed.) (1989a) *Heritage Interpretation Volume 1: The natural and built environment*. London: Belhaven Press.

Hitchcock, M. (1999) 'Tourism and Ethnicity: Situational perspectives'. In *International Journal of Tourism Research*, **1, 1**: 17–32.

Hitchcock, M., King, V.T and Parnwell, M.J.G. (1993) 'Tourism in South-East Asia: Introduction'. In Hitchcock, M., King, V.T and Parnwell, M.J.G. (eds) *Tourism in South East Asia*. London: Routledge.

Hobart, M. (1995) 'As I Lay Laughing: Encountering global knowledge in Bali'. In Fardon, R. (ed.) *Counterworks: Managing the diversity of knowledge*. London: Routledge.

Hobsbawm, E. and Ranger, T. (eds) (1983) *The Invention of Tradition*. Cambridge: Cambridge University Press.

Holcomb, B. (1999) 'Marketing Cities for Tourism'. In Judd, D.R. and Fainstein, S.S. (eds) *The Tourist City*. New Haven: Yale University Press.

Hoogvelt, A. (1997) *Globalisation and the Postcolonial World: The new political economy of development*. Basingstoke: Macmillan.

Howell, S. (1995) 'Whose Knowledge and Whose Power?: A new perspective on cultural diffusion'. Fardon, R. (ed.) *Counterworks: Managing the diversity of knowledge*. London: Routledge.

Howes, D. (ed.) (1996) *Cross-Cultural Consumption: Global markets, local realities*. London: Routledge.

Hoyle, B.S., Pinder, D.A. and Husain, M.S. (eds) (1988) *Revitalising the Waterfront: International dimensions of dockland development*. London: Belhaven Press.

Hughes, H. (1997) 'Holidays and Homosexual Identity'. In *Tourism Management*, **18, 1**: 3–8.

Hughes-Freeland, F (1998) 'From Temple to Television'. In Hughes-Freeland, F. and Crain, M (eds) *Recasting Ritual: Performance, media and identity*. London: Routledge.

Hughes-Freeland, F. and Crain, M (eds) (1998) *Recasting Ritual: Performance, media and identity*. London: Routledge.

Hunter, M. (1981) 'The Preconditions of Preservation: A historical perspective'. In Lowenthal, D. and Binney, M. (eds) *Our Past Before Us: Why do we save it?* London: Temple Smith.

Ioannides, D. and Debbage, K. (1997) 'Post-Fordism and flexibility: the travel industry polyglot'. In *Tourism Management* **18, 4**: 229–41.

Ioannides, D. (1998) 'Tour Operators: The gatekeepers of tourism'. In Ioannides, D. and Debbage, K.G. (eds) *The Economic Geography of the Tourist Industry: A supply-side analysis*. London: Routledge.

Jackson, P. and Penrose, J. (eds) (1993) *Constructions of Race, Place and Nation*. London: UCL Press.

Jameson, F. (1991) *Postmodernism or the Cultural Logic of Late Capitalism*. Durham, NC.: Duke University Press.

Jamison, D. (1999) 'Tourism and Ethnicity: The Brotherhood of coconuts'. In *Annals of Tourism Research*, **26, 4**: 944–67.

Jeffries, S. (1999) 'Globalizing Sexual Exploitation: sex tourism and the traffic in women'. In *Leisure Studies*, **18, 3**: 179–96.

Jessop, B. (1999) 'Reflections on Globalisation and its (il)logic(s)'. In Olds, C., Dicken, P., Kelly, P.F., Kong, L. and Yeung, H. (eds) *Globalisation and the Asia Pacific: Contested territories*. London: Routledge.

Jones, M. (1993) 'The Elusive Reality of Landscape: Concepts and approaches'. In Fladmark, J.M (ed.) *Heritage: Conservation, Interpretation, Enterprise*. London: Donhead.

Josiam, B.M., Hobson, J.S., Dietrich, U.C. and Smeaton, G. (1998) 'An Analysis of the Sexual, Alcohol and Drug Related Behavioural Patterns of Students on Spring Break'. In *Tourism Management*, **19, 6**: 501–13.

Judd, D. (1995) 'Promoting Tourism in US Cities'. In *Tourism Management*, **16, 3**: 175–87.

Judd, D.R. and Fainstein, S. S. (eds) (1999) *The Tourist City*. New Haven: Yale University Press.

Judd, D. and Parkinson, M. (eds) (1990) *Leadership and Urban Regeneration: Cities in North America and Europe*. Newbury Park: Sage.

Kahn, J.S. (1997) 'Culturalizing Malaysia: Tourism, heritage and the city in Georgetown'. In Picard, M. and Wood, R.E. (eds) (1997) *Tourism, Ethnicity and the State in Asian and Pacific Societies*. Honolulu: University of Hawaii Press.

Kapferer, J-N (1997) (2nd edn) *Strategic Brand Management: Creating and sustaining brand equity long term*. London: Kogan Page.

Kearns, G. and Philo, G. (eds) (1993) *Selling Places: The city as cultural capital, past and present*. Oxford: Pergamon Press.

Keily, R. (1998) 'Introduction: Globalisation (post)modernity and the Third World'. In Keily, R. and Marfleet, P. (eds) *Globalisation and the Third World*. London: Routledge.

Kelly, J.D. (1999) 'Time and the Global: Against the homogeneous, empty communities in contemporary social theory. In Meyer, B. and Gerschiere, P. (eds) *Globalization and Identity: Dialectics of flow and closure*. Oxford: Blackwell.

Kinnaird, V. and Hall, D. (1994) *Tourism: A Gender analysis*. Chichester: Wiley.

Kofman, E. and Youngs, G. (1996) 'Introduction: Globalization – the second wave'. In Kofman, E. and Youngs, G. (eds) *Globalization: Theory and Practice*. London: Pinter.

Kong, L. (1999) 'Globalisation, Transmigration and the Renegotiation of Ethnic Identity'. In Olds, C., Dicken, P., Kelly, P.F., Kong, L. and Yeung, H. (eds) *Globalisation and the Asia Pacific: Contested territories*. London: Routledge.

Kopytoff, I. (1986) 'The Cultural Biography of things: Commoditization as process'. In Appadurai, A. (ed.) *The Social Life of Things: Commodities in cultural perspective*. Cambridge: Cambridge University Press.

Kristiansen, K. (1989) 'Perspectives on the Archaeological heritage: history and future'. In Cleere, H.F. (ed.) *Archaeological Heritage Management in the Modern World*. London: Unwin Hyman.

Kruhse-Mount-Burton, S. (1995) 'Sex Tourism and Traditional Australian Male Identity'. In Lanfant, M.F., Allcock, J.B. and Bruner, E.M. (eds) *International Tourism: Identity and Change*. London: Sage.

Kumar, K. (1995) *From Post-Industrial to Post-Modern Society: New theories of the contemporary world*. Oxford: Blackwell.

Kuper, A. (1999) *Culture: The anthropologists' account*. Cambridge, MA.: Harvard University Press.

Laenen, M. (1989) 'Looking for the Future Through the Past'. In Uzzell, D. (ed.) (1989a) *Heritage Interpretation Volume 1: The natural and built environment*. London: Belhaven Press.

Lagopoulus, A.P. (1993) 'Postmodernism, Geography and the Social Semiotics of Space'. in *Environment and Planning D: Society and Space*, **11**, 3: 255–78.

Lanfant, M.F. (1995) 'Introduction'. In Lanfant, M.F., Allcock, J.B. and Bruner, E.M. (eds) *International Tourism: Identity and Change*. London: Sage.

Lash, S. and Urry, J. (1994) *Economies of Signs and Space*. London: Sage.

Law, C.M. (1993) *Urban Tourism: Attracting visitors to large cities*. London: Mansell.

Laxson, J. (1991) 'How "We" See "Them": Tourism and native American Indians'. In *Annals of Tourism Research*. **18**, 3: 365–89.

Lefebvre, H. (1991) *The Production of Space*. Oxford: Blackwell.

Lefebvre, H. (1996) *Writings on Cities*. Oxford: Blackwell.

Le Gales, P (1993) *Rennes: Catholic humanism and urban entrepreneurialism. In Bianchini and Parkinson (eds) Cultural Policy and Urban Regeneration: The West European Experience*. Manchester: Manchester University Press.

Leontidou, L. (1990) *The Mediterranean City in Transition: Social change and urban development*. Cambridge: Cambridge University Press.

Lévi-Strauss, C. (1968) *Structural Anthropology*. London: Allen Lane.

Lewandowski, S.J. (1984) 'The Built Environment and Cultural Symbolism in Post-Colonial Madras'. In Agnew, J.A., Mercer, J. and Sopher, D.E. (eds) *The City in Cultural Context*. Boston: Allen and Unwin.

Ley, D. (1985) 'Cultural/Humanistic Geography'. In *Progress in Human Geography*, **9**, 3: 415–423

Ley, D. (1989) 'Modernism, Post-Modernism and the Struggle for Place'. In Agnew, J. and Duncan, J (eds) *The Power of Place*. Boston: Unwin Hyman.

Light, D. and Prentice, R.C. (1994) 'Who Consumes the Heritage Product? Implications for European Heritage Tourism'. In Ashworth, G. and Larkham, P. (eds) *Building a New Heritage: Tourism culture and identity in the new Europe*. London: Routledge.

Lindknud, C. (1998) 'When Opposite Worldviews Attract: A case of tourism and local development in Southern France'. In Abram, S. and Waldren, J. (eds) *Anthropological Perspectives on Local Development: Knowledge and sentiments in conflict*. London: Routledge.

Linnekin, J. (1997) 'Consuming Cultures: Tourism and the commoditization of cultural identity in the island Pacific'. In Picard, M. and Wood, R.E. (eds) (1997) *Tourism, Ethnicity and the State in Asian and Pacific Societies*. Honolulu: University of Hawaii Press.

Löfgren, O. (1999) *On Holiday: A history of vacationing*. Berkeley: University of California Press.

Long, N. and Villareal, M. (1999) 'Small Product, Big Issues: Value contestations and cultural identities in cross-border commodity networks'.

In Meyer, B. and Gerschiere, P. (eds) *Globalization and Identity: Dialectics of flow and closure.* Oxford: Blackwell.

Longhurst, B. and Savage, M. (1996) 'Social Class, Consumption and the Influence of Bourdieu: Some critical issues'. In Edgell, S., Hetherington, K. and Warde, A. (eds) *Consumption Matters: The production and experience of consumption.* Oxford: Blackwell.

Lovell, N (1998) 'Introduction: belonging in need of emplacement?' In Lovell, N. (ed.) *Locality and Belonging.* London: Routledge.

Lowenthal, D. (1985) *The Past is a Foreign Country.* Cambridge: Cambridge University Press.

Lowenthal, D. (1990) 'Conclusion: Archaeologists and others'. In Gathercole, P. and Lowenthal, D. (eds) *The Politics of the Past.* London: Unwin Hyman.

Lowenthal, D. (1993) 'Landscape as Heritage: National scenes and global changes'. In Fladmark, J.M. (ed.) *Heritage: Conservation, Interpretation, Enterprise.* London: Donhead.

Lowenthal, D. (1994) 'Identity, Heritage and History'. In Gillis, J.R. (ed.) (1994) *Commemorations: The politics of national identity.* Princeton: Princeton University Press.

Luhmann, N. (1999) 'The Concept of Society'. In Elliot, A. (ed.) *Contemporary Social Theory.* Oxford: Blackwell.

Lunt, P.K. and Livingstone, S.M. (1992) *Mass Consumption and Personal Identity: Everyday economic experience.* Buckingham: Open University Press.

Lyon, D. (1999) (2nd edn) *Postmodernity.* Buckingham: Open University Press.

MacCannell, D. (1976) *The Tourist: A new theory of the leisure class.* New York: Schocken Books.

MacCannell, D. (1992) *Empty Meeting Grounds: The tourist papers.* London: Routledge.

Macdonald, S. (1997a) 'A people's Story: Heritage, identity and authenticity'. In Rojek, C. and Urry, J (eds) (1997) *Touring Cultures: Transformations of travel and theory.* London: Routledge.

Macdonald, S. (1997b) *Reimagining Culture: Histories, identities and the Gaelic renaissance.* Oxford: Berg.

Machor, J. L. (1987) *Pastoral Cities: Urban ideals and the symbolic landscape of America.* Madison: University of Wisconsin Press.

Macleod, D.V.L. (1997) '"Alternative" tourists on a Canary Island'. In Abram, S., Waldren, J. and MacLeod, D.V. (eds) *Tourists and Tourism: identifying with people and places.* Oxford: Berg.

Mangion, G. and Tamen, I. (1998) *European Cultural Routes.* Strasbourg: Council of Europe.

March, R, (1997) 'An Exploratory Study of Buyer-Supplier Relationships in International Tourism: The case of Japanese wholesalers and Australian suppliers'. In *Journal of Travel and Tourism Marketing,* **6, 1**: 55–68.

Marien, C. and Pizam, A. (1997) 'Implementing Sustainable Tourism Development Through Citizen Participation in the Planning Process'. In Wahab, S. and Pigram, J. (eds) *Tourism Development and Growth: The challenge of sustainability.* London: Routledge.

Martinez, D.P. (1996) 'The Tourist as Deity: Ancient continuities in modern Japan'. In Selwyn, T. (ed.) *The Tourist Image: Myths and myth making in tourism.* Chichester: Wiley.

Martinez, D.P. (1998) 'Introduction: Gender, shifting boundaries and global cultures'. In Martinez, D.P. (ed.) *The Worlds of Japanese Popular Culture: Gender, shifting boundaries and global cultures.* Cambridge: Cambridge University Press.

Massey, D. (1994) *Space, Place and Gender.* Cambridge: Polity Press.

Massey, D. and Allen, J. (eds) (1984) *Geography Matters!: A reader.* Cambridge: Cambridge University Press.

Mathieson, A. and Wall, G. (1982) *Tourism: Economic, physical and social Impacts.* Harlow: Longman.

Matthews, H.G. and Richter, L.K. (1991) 'Political Science and Tourism'. In *Annals of Tourism Research,* **18, 1**: 120–35.

May, J. (1996) 'In Search of Authenticity Off and *On* the Beaten Track'. In *Environment and Planning D: Society and Space,* **14, 4**: 709–36.

Mazanec, J.A., Zins, A. and Dolnicar, S. (1988) 'Analysing Tourist Behaviour with Lifestyle and Vacation Style Typologies'. In Theobald, W. (ed.) (2nd edn) *Global Tourism: The next decade.* Oxford: Butterworth Heinemann.

McCracken, G. (1988) *Culture and Consumption: New approaches to the symbolic character of consumer goods and activities.* Bloomington, IN. Indiana University Press.

McDowell, L. (1999) *Gender Identity and Place: Understanding feminist geographies.* Cambridge: Polity Press.

McGuigan, J. (1996) *Culture and the Public Sphere.* London: Routledge.

McGuigan, J. (1999) *Modernity and Postmodern Culture.* Buckingham: Open University Press.

McGrew, A. (1992) 'The State in Advanced Capitalist Societies'. In Allen, J. Braham, P. and Lewis, P. (eds) *Political and Economic Forms of Modernity.* Cambridge: Polity Press.

McMichael, P. (1996) *Development and Social Change: A global perspective.* Thousand Oaks: Pine Forge Press.

Meethan, K. (1996a) 'Consuming (in) the Civilized City'. In *Annals of Tourism Research,* **23, 2**: 322–40

Meethan, K. (1996b) 'Place, Image and Power: Brighton as a resort'. In Selwyn, T. (ed.) *The Tourist Image: Myths and myth making in tourism.* Chichester: Wiley.

Meethan, K. (1997) 'York: Managing the tourist city'. In *Cities,* **14, 6**: 333–42.

Meethan, K. (1998) 'New Tourism for Old? Policy developments in Cornwall and Devon'. In *Tourism Management*, **19, 6**: 583–93.

Mellor, A. (1991) 'Enterprise and Heritage in the Dock'. In Corner, J. and Harvey, S. (eds) *Enterprise and heritage: Crosscurrents of national culture.* London: Routledge.

Mercer, D. (1989) 'The Uneasy Relationship Between Tourism and Native People'. In Theobald, W. (ed.) (2nd edn) *Global Tourism: The next decade.* Oxford: Butterworth Heinemann.

Merriman, N. (1991) *Beyond the Glass Case: The past, the heritage and the public in Britain.* Leicester: Leicester University Press.

Meyer, B. and Gerschiere, P. (eds) (1999) *Globalization and Identity: Dialectics of flow and closure.* Oxford: Blackwell.

Middleton, V. (1988) *Marketing in Travel and Tourism.* Oxford: Heinemann.

Miles, S. (1998) *Consumerism – as a Way of Life.* London: Sage.

Miles, S. and Paddison, R. (1998) 'Urban Consumption: An historographical note'. In *Urban Studies*, **35, 5/6**: 815–23.

Miller, A. (1994) 'The Whisky Experience: Interpretation and brand identity'. In Fladmark, J.M (ed.) *Cultural Tourism.* London: Donhead.

Miller, D. (ed.) (1995a) *Acknowledging Consumption: A review of new studies.* London: Routledge.

Miller, D. (1995b) 'Consumption as the Vanguard on History: A polemic by way of an introduction'. In Miller, D. (ed.) (1995) *Acknowledging Consumption: A review of new studies.* London: Routledge.

Miller, D. (1995c) 'Introduction: Anthropology, Modernity and Consumption'. In Miller, D. (ed.) *Worlds Apart: Modernity through the Prism of the Local.* London: Routledge.

Mittelman, J.H. (1997) 'How Does Globalization Really Work?' In Mittelman, J.H. (ed.) *Globalization: Critical reflections.* Boulder: Lynne Rienner.

Morgan, M. (1998) 'Homogenous Products: The future of established resorts'. In Theobald, W. (ed.) (2nd edn) *Global Tourism: The next decade.* Oxford: Butterworth Heinemann.

Morphy, H. (1995) 'Aboriginal Art in a Global Context'. In Miller, D. (ed.) *Worlds Apart: Modernity through the Prism of the Local.* London: Routledge.

Mort, F (1989) 'The Politics of Consumption'. In Hall, S. and Jacques, M. (eds) *New Times: the changing face of politics in the 1990s.* London: Lawrence and Wishart.

Mowforth, M. and Munt, I. (1997) *Tourism and Sustainability: New tourism in the third world.* London: Routledge.

Mullins, P. (1991) 'Tourism Urbanization'. In *International Journal of Urban And Regional Research*, **15, 3**: 326–42.

Mullins, P. (1999) 'International Tourism and the Cities of Southeast Asia'. In Judd, D and Fainstein, S. (eds) *The Tourist City.* New Haven: Yale University Press.

Munt, I. (1994) 'The "Other" Postmodern Tourism'. In *Theory, Culture Society*, **11**, **3**: 101–23.

Muroi, H. and Sasaki, N. (1997) 'Tourism and Prostitution in Japan'. In Sinclair, T. (ed.) *Gender, Work and Tourism*. London: Routledge.

Murphy. P. (1998) 'Tourism and Sustainable Development'. In Theobald, W. (ed.) (2nd edn) *Global Tourism: The next decade*. Oxford: Butterworth Heinemann.

Murray, R. (1989) 'Fordism and Post-Fordism'. In Hall, S. and Jacques, M. (eds) *New Times: The changing face of politics in the 1990s*. London: Lawrence and Wishart.

Nash, D. and Smith, V.L. (1991) 'Anthropology and Tourism'. In *Annals of Tourism Research*, **18**, **1**: 12–25.

Nash, D. (1996) *Anthropology of Tourism*. Oxford: Pergamon Press.

Nederveen-Pieterse, J. (1995) 'Globalization as Hybridization'. In Featherstone, M., Lash, S. and Robertson, R. (eds) *Global Modernities*. London: Sage.

Nettleford, R. (1993) 'Heritage Tourism and the Myth of Caribbean Paradise'. In Gayle, D.J. and Goodrich, J.N. (eds) *Tourism Marketing and Management in the Caribbean*. London: Routledge.

Oakes, T.S. (1993) 'The Cultural Space of Modernity: Ethnic tourism and place identity in China'. In *Environment and Planning D: Society and Space*, **11**, **1**: 47–66.

Oakes, T.S. (1997) 'Ethnic Tourism in Rural Guizhou: Sense of place and the commerce of authenticity'. In Picard, M. and Wood, R.E. (eds) *Tourism, Ethnicity and the State in Asian and Pacific Societies*. Honolulu: University of Hawaii Press.

O'Connor, B. (1993) 'Myths and Mirrors: Tourist images and national identity'. In O'Connor B. and Cronin, M (eds) *Tourism in Ireland: A critical analysis*. Cork: University of Cork Press.

Ohnuki-Tierney, E. (1997) 'McDonald's in Japan'. In Watson, J.L. (ed.) *Golden Arches East: McDonald's in East Asia*. Stanford CA.: Stanford University Press.

Olivier, G. (1995) (4th edn) *Marketing Today*. Hemel Hempstead: Prentice Hall.

Oppermann, M. (1997) 'The Outbound Tourist Cycle and the Asian Tourism Tigers'. In Oppermann, M. (ed.) *Pacific Rim Tourism*. Wallingford: CABI Publishing.

Oppermann, M. and McKinley, S. (1997) 'Sexual Imagery in the Marketing of Pacific Tourism Destinations'. In Oppermann, M. (ed.) *Pacific Rim Tourism*. Wallingford: CAB International.< Organisation for Economic Co-operation and Development. (1990) *Implementing Change: Entrepreneurship and Local Initiative*. Paris: OECD.

Ottino, A. (1998) 'Origin and Ritual Exchange as Transformative Belonging in the Balinese Temple'. In Lovell, N. (ed.) *Locality and Belonging*. London: Routledge.

Page, S. (1995) *Urban Tourism*. London: Routledge.

Palmer, R.W. (1993) 'Tourism and Taxes: The case of Barbados'. In Gayle, D.J. and Goodrich, J.N. (eds) *Tourism Marketing and Management in the Caribbean*. London: Routledge.

Parker, M. (1998) 'Nostalgia and Mass Culture: McDonaldization and cultural elitism'. In Alfino, M., Caputo, J.S. and Wynyard, R. (eds) *McDonaldization Revisited: Critical Essays on Consumer Culture*. Westport: Praeger.

Parker, P.L. and King, T.F. (1995) *Guidelines for Evaluating and Documenting Traditional Cultural Properties*. National Register Bulletin, US Department of the Interior, National Park Service:
http://www.cr.nps.gov/nr/ bulletins/nr38_toc.html

Pearce, D. (1989) (2nd edn) *Tourist Development*. Harlow: Longman.

Pearce, P.L. (1998) 'The Relationship Between Residents and Tourists: The research literature and management directions'. In Theobald, W. (ed.) (2nd edn) *Global Tourism: The next decade*. Oxford: Butterworth Heinemann.

Pedersen, R. (1995) 'Scots Gaelic as a Tourism Asset'. In Fladmark, J.M (ed.) *Sharing the Earth: Local identity in global culture*. London: Donhead.

Philp, J. and Mercer, D. (1998) 'Commodification of Buddhism in Contemporary Burma'. In *Annals of Tourism Research*, **26, 1**: 21–54.

Picard, M. (1993) 'Cultural Tourism' in Bali: National integration and regional differentiation. In Hitchcock, M., King, V.T and Parnwell, M.J.G (eds) (1993) *Tourism in South East Asia*. Routledge: London.

Picard, M. (1996) (2nd edn) *Bali: Cultural Tourism and Touristic Culture*. Archipelago Press: Singapore.

Picard, M. (1997) Tourism, Nation Building and Culture. In Picard, M. and Wood, R.E. (eds) (1997) *Tourism, Ethnicity and the State in Asian and Pacific Societies*. University of Hawaii Press: Honolulu.

Picard, M. and Wood, R.E. (eds) (1997) *Tourism, Ethnicity and the State in Asian and Pacific Societies*. University of Hawaii Press: Honolulu.

Pigram, J. and Wahab, S. (1997) 'The Challenge of Sustainable Tourism Growth'. In Wahab, S. and Pigram, J. (eds) *Tourism, Sustainability and Growth: The challenge of sustainability*. London: Routledge.

Piercy, N. (1997) (2nd edn) *Market led Strategic Change: Transforming the process of going to market*. Oxford: Butterworth Heinemann.

Pitchford, S.R. (1995) 'Ethnic Tourism and Nationalism in Wales'. In *Annals of Tourism Research*, **22, 1**: 35–52.

Plimoth-on-Web (1999) *Living History and Authenticity*.
http://www/plimoth.org/library/liveh3.htm

Poon. A, (1993) *Tourism, Technology and Competitive Strategies*. Wallingford: CABI Publishing.

Pretes, M. (1995) 'Postmodern Tourism: The Santa Claus Industry'. In *Annals of Tourism Research*, **22, 1**: 1–15.

Priestley, G.K. (1995) 'Evolution of Tourism on the Spanish Coast'. In Ashworth, G.J. and Dietvorst, A.G.J. (eds) *Tourism and Spatial Transformations: Implications for policy and planning*. Wallingford: CABI Publishing.

Pritchard, A. and Morgan, N.J. (1997) 'The Gay Consumer: A meaningful market segment?' In *Journal of Targeting Measurement and Analysis for Marketing*, **6, 1**: 9–20.

Pritchard, A., Morgan, N. and Sedgely, D. (1998) 'Reaching out to the Gay Tourist: Opportunities and threats in an emerging market segment'. In *Tourism Management*, **19, 3**: 273–82.

Qiu Zhang, H., Chong, K. and Ap, J. (1999) 'An Analysis of Tourism Policy Development in Modern China'. In *Tourism Management*, **20, 4**: 471–85.

Reisinger, V. (1995) 'Social Contact Between Tourists and Hosts of Different Cultural Backgrounds'. In Seaton, A.V. (ed.) *Tourism: The state of the art*. Chichester: Wiley.

Richards, G. (1996a) 'Production and Consumption of European Cultural Tourism'. In *Annals of Tourism Research*, **23, 2**: 261–83.

Richards, G. (1996b) 'The Social Context of Cultural Tourism'. In Richards, G. (ed.) *Cultural Tourism in Europe*. Wallingford: CABI Publishing.

Richter, K.L. and Richter, W.L. (1985) 'Policy Choices in South Asian Tourism Development'. In *Annals of Tourism Research*, **12, 4**: 201–17.

Richter, K.L. (1993) 'Tourism Policy-Making in South-East Asia'. In Hitchcock, M., King, V.T and Parnwell, M.J.G. (eds) (1993) *Tourism in South East Asia*. London: Routledge.

Richter, K. L. (1998) 'Exploring the Political Role of Gender in Tourism Research'. In Theobald, W. (ed.) (2nd edn) *Global Tourism: The next decade*. Oxford: Butterworth Heinemann.

Ritchie, J.R.B. and Gouldner, C.R. (eds) (1994) (2nd edn) *Travel, Tourism, and Hospitality Research: A handbook for managers and researchers*. New York: Wiley.

Ritzer, G. (1993) *The McDonaldization of Society*. Newbury Park: Pine Forge Press.

Ritzer, G. and Liska, A. (1997) 'McDisneyization' and 'Post-Tourism': Complementary perspectives on contemporary tourism. In Rojek, C. and Urry, J. (eds) *Touring Cultures: Transformations of travel and theory*. London: Routledge.

Robertson, R. (1992) *Globalization: Social theory and global culture*. London: Sage.

Robertson, R. (1995) Glocalization: Time-space and homogeneity- hetero-geneity. In Featherstone, M., Lash, S. and Robertson, R. (eds) *Global Modernities*. London: Sage.

Robins, K. (1993) 'Prisoners of the City: Whatever could a postmodern city be?' In Carter, E., Donald, J. and Squires, J. (eds) *Space Place: Theories of identity and location*. London: Lawrence and Wishart.

Robinson, M. (1999) 'Cultural Conflicts in Tourism: Inevitability and inequality'. In Robinson, M. and Boniface, P. (eds) *Tourism and Cultural Conflicts*. CABI Publishing: Wallingford.

Robinson, M. and Boniface, P. (eds) (1999) *Tourism and Cultural Conflicts*. Wallingford: CABI Publishing.

Roche, M. (1996) 'Mega-Events and Micro-Modernization: On the sociol-ogy of the new urban tourism'. In Apostolopous, Y., Leivadi, S. and Yiannakis, A. (eds) *The Sociology of Tourism: Theoretical and empirical investiga-tions*. London: Routledge.

Rojek, C (1985) *Capitalism and Leisure Theory*. London: Tavistock.

Rojek, C. (1993) *Ways of Escape: Modern transformation in leisure and travel* Basingstoke: Macmillan.

Rojek, C (1995) *Decentring leisure: Rethinking leisure theory*. London: Sage.

Rojek, C. and Urry, J (eds) (1997) *Touring Cultures: Transformations of travel and theory*. London: Routledge.

Rose, M.A. (1991) *The Post-modern and the Post-industrial: A critical analysis*. Cambridge: Cambridge University Press.

Rotenberg, R. (1995) *Landscape and Power in Vienna*. Baltimore: John Hop-kins University Press.

Rotenberg, R and McDonogh, G. (eds) (1993) *The Cultural Meaning of Urban Space*. Westport: Bergin and Garvey.

Ryan, C. (1991) *Recreational Tourism: A social science perspective*. London: Rou-tledge.

Ryan, C, (1995) *Researching Tourist Satisfaction: Issues, concepts, problems*. London: Routledge.

Sahlins, M. (1976) *Culture and Practical Reason*. Chicago: University of Chi-cago Press.

Sahlins, M. (1985) *Islands of History*. London: Tavistock.

Salaman, R. (1985) (revised edn) *The History and Social Influence of the Potato*. Cambridge: Cambridge University Press.

Sampath, N. (1997) '*Mas'* Identity: Tourism and Global and Local Aspects of Trinidad Carnival'. In Abram, S., Waldren, J. and MacLeod, D.V. (eds) (1997) *Tourists and Tourism: identifying with people and places*. Oxford: Berg.

Samuel, R. (1994) *Theatres of Memory*. London: Verso.

Sassen, S. and Roost, F (1999) 'The City: Strategic site for the global entertainment industry'. In Judd, D and Fainstein, S. (eds) *The Tourist City*. New Haven: Yale University Press.

Savage, M., Barlow, J., Dickens, P. and Fielding, T. (1992) *Property, Bureaucracy and Culture: Middle-class formation in contemporary Britain.* London: Routledge.

Savage, M. and Warde, A. (1993) *Urban Sociology, Capitalism and Modernity.* Basingstoke: Macmillan.

Sayer, A. (1989) 'Post-Fordism in Question'. In *The International Journal of Urban and Regional Research*, **13, 4**: 666–95.

Schama, S. (1995) *Landscape and Memory.* London: Harper Collins.

Scholte, J.A. (1996) 'Towards a Critical theory of Globalization'. In Kofman, E. and Youngs, G. (eds) *Globalization: Theory and Practice.* London: Pinter.

Schülter, R.G. (1998) 'Tourism Development: A Latin America persepctive'. In Theobald, W. (ed.) (2nd edn) *Global Tourism: The next decade.* Oxford: Butterworth Heinemann.

Scott, A. (1997) 'Globalization: Social Process or Political Rhetoric?' In Scott, A. (ed.) *The Limits of Globalization: Cases and Arguments.* London: Routledge.

Scott, J. (1995) 'Sexual and National Boundaries in Tourism'. In *Annals of Tourism Research*, **22, 2**: 385–403.

Scott, J. (1997) 'Chances and Choices: Women and Tourism in Northern Cyprus'. In Sinclair, T. (ed.) *Gender, Work and Tourism.* London: Routledge.

Seaton, A.V. and Palmer, C. (1997) 'Understanding VFR Tourism Behaviour: The first five years of the United Kingdom tourism survey'. In *Tourism Management*, **18, 6**: 345–55.

Selänniemi, T. (1994) 'Touristic Reflections on a Marine Venus: An anthropological interpetation of Finnish tourism to Rhodes'. In *Ethnologica Fennica*, **22**, 35–42.

Selwyn, T. (1993) 'Peter Pan in South East Asia: Views from the brochures'. In Hitchcock, M., King, V.T and Parnwell, M.J.G (eds) (1993) *Tourism in South East Asia.* London: Routledge.

Selwyn, T. (1994) 'The Anthropology of Tourism: Reflections on the state of the art'. In Seaton, A.V. (ed.) *Tourism: The state of the art.* Chichester: Wiley.

Selwyn, T. (ed.) (1996) *The Tourist Image: Myths and myth making in tourism.* Chichester: Wiley.

Sennett, R. (1999) 'Growth and Failure: The new political economy and its culture'. In Featherstone, M. and Lash, S, (eds) *Spaces of Culture: City, nation, world.* London: Sage.

Shachar, A and Shoval, N. (1999) 'Tourism in Jerusalem: A place to pray'. In Judd, D and Fainstein, S. (eds) *The Tourist City.* New Haven: Yale University Press.

Shackley, M. (1999) 'Cultural Impact of Religious Tourism in the Himalayas'. In Robinson, M. and Boniface, P. (eds) *Tourism and Cultural Conflicts.* Wallingford: CABI Publishing.

Sharpley, R. (1994) *Tourism, Tourists and Society*. Huntingdon: Elm Publications.

Shaw, B.J. and Jones, R. (1997) 'Introduction: Contested urban heritage'. In Shaw, B.J. and Jones, R (eds) *Contested Urban Heritage: Voices from the periphery*. Aldershot: Ashgate.

Shaw, G. and Williams, A. (1994) *Critical Issues in Tourism: A geographical perspective*. Oxford: Blackwell.

Shaw, G. and Williams, A. (1997) 'The Private Sector: Tourism entrepreneurship – a constraint or a resource?' In Shaw, G. and Williams, A. (eds) *The Rise and Fall of British Coastal Resorts: Cultural and economic perspectives*. London: Mansell.

Shaw, G. and Williams, A. (1998) 'Entrepreneurship, Small Business Culture and Tourism Development'. In Ioannides, D. and Debbage, K.G. (eds) *The Economic Geography of the Tourist Industry: A supply-side analysis*. London: Routledge.

Shenav–Keller, S. (1995) 'The Jewish Pilgrim and the Purchase of a Souvenir in Israel'. In Lanfant, M.F., Allcock, J.B. and Bruner, E.M. (eds) *International Tourism: Identity and Change*. London: Sage.

Shields, R. (1991) *Places on the Margin*. London: Routledge.

Short, J.R. (1991) *Imagined Country: Society, culture and the environment*. London: Routledge.

Sieber, R.T. (1993) 'Public Access on the Urban Waterfont: A question of vision'. In Rotenberg, R and McDonogh, G. (eds) (1993) *The Cultural Meaning of Urban Space*. Westport: Bergin and Garvey.

Simpson, P. and Wall, G. (1999) 'Consequences of Resort Development: A comparative study'. In *Tourism Management*, **20, 3**: 283–96

Sinclair, M.T. and Stabler, M. (eds) (1997) *Economics of Tourism*. London: Routledge.

Sinclair, T. and Vokes, R.W.A. (1993) 'The Economics of Tourism in Asia and the Pacific'. In Hitchcock, M., King, V.T and Parnwell, M.J.G. (eds) (1993) *Tourism in South East Asia*. London: Routledge.

Sinclair, T. (ed.) (1997) *Gender, Work and Tourism*. London: Routledge.

Skeggs, B. (1999) 'Matter out of Place: Visibility and sexualities in leisure spaces'. In *Leisure Studies*, **18, 3**: 213–32.

Sklair, L. (1991) *Sociology of the Global System: Social change in global perspective*. Hemel Hempstead: Harvester Wheatsheaf.

Sklair, L. (ed.) (1994a) *Capitalism and Development*. London: Routledge.

Sklair, L. (1994b) 'Capitalism and Development in Global Perspective'. In Sklair, L. (ed.) (1994) *Capitalism and Development*. London: Routledge.

Slater, D. (1997) *Consumer Culture and Modernity*. Cambridge: Polity Press.

Smith, A.D. (1991) *National Identity*. Harmondsworth: Penguin.

Smith, M.P. (1988) *City, State, and Market: The political economy of urban society*. Oxford: Blackwell.

Smith, V. L. (ed.) (1989) (2nd edn) *Hosts and Guests: The anthropology of tourism.* Philadelphia: University of Pennsylvania Press.

Smith, V. L. (1994) 'Privatization in the Third World: Small- scale tourism enterprises'. In Theobald, W. (ed.) (2nd edition) *Global Tourism: The next decade.* Oxford: Butterworth Heinemann.

Smyth, H. (1994) *Marketing the City: The role of flagship developments in urban regeneration.* London: E&FN Spon.

Soane, J.V.N. (1993) *Fashionable Resort Regions: Their evolution and transformation.* Wallingford: CABI Publishing.

Soja, E. (1989) *Postmodern Geographies: The reassertion of space in critical social theory.* London: Verso.

Squires, S.J. (1993) 'The Cultural Values of Literary Tourism'. In *Annals of Tourism Research,* **21, 2**: 103–20.

Stabler, M.J. (ed.) (1997) *Tourism and Sustainability: Principles to Practice.* Wallingford: CABI Publishing.

Stevenson, M. (1995) 'Silk and Textile Routes: Council of Europe Cultural Itineraries'. Fladmark, J.M. (ed.) *Sharing the Earth: Local identity in global culture.* London: Donhead.< Storey, J. (1999) *Cultural Consumption and Everyday Life.* London: Arnold.

Street, J. (1997) ' "Across the Universe": The limits of popular global culture'. In Scott, A. (ed.) *The Limits of Globalization: Cases and Arguments.* London: Routledge.

Swarbrooke, J. (1995) 'The Future of the Past: Heritage tourism into the 21st century'. In Seaton, A.V. (ed.) *Tourism: The state of the art.* Chichester: Wiley.

Swingewood, A. (1977) *The Myths of Mass Culture.* London: Macmillan.

Swingewood, A. (1998) *Cultural Theory and the Problem of Modernity.* Basingstoke: Macmillan.

Talle, A. (1998) 'Sex for Leisure: Modernity among female bar workers in Tanzania'. In Abram, S. and Waldren, J. (eds) *Anthropological Perspectives on Local Development: Knowledge and sentiments in conflict.* London: Routledge.

Taylor, G. and Davis, D. (1997) 'The Community Show: A mythology of resident responsive tourism'. In Stabler, M.J. (ed.) (1997) *Tourism and Sustainability: Principles to Practice.* Wallingford: CABI Publishing.

Teague, K. (1997) 'Representations of Nepal'. In Abram, S., Waldren, J. and MacLeod, D.V. (eds) *Tourists and Tourism: identifying with people and places.* Oxford: Berg.

Theobald, W. (ed.) (1998) (2nd edn) *Global Tourism: The next decade.* Oxford: Butterworth Heinemann.

Therond, D. (1999) *The Cultural Heritages of Tourism and Travel: An asset for development?* Strasbourg: C of E.
http://culture.coe.fr/postsummit/pat/en/epatourismart01.htm

Thompson, K. (1997) 'Regulation, De-regulation and Re- regulation'. In Thompson, K. (ed.) *Media and Cultural Regulation*. London: Sage.

Thornton, P.R., Shaw, G. and Williams, A. M. (1997) 'Tourist Group Holiday Decision Making and Behaviour: The influence of children'. In *Tourism Management*: **18, 5**: 287–97.

Tomlinson, J. (1999) *Globalization and Culture*. Cambridge: Polity Press.

Tonkin, E., McDonald, M. and Chapman, M. (1989) *History and Ethnicity*. London: Routledge.

Towner, J. (1994) 'Tourism History: Past, present and future'. In Seaton, A.V. *Tourism: the state of the art*. Chichester: Wiley.

Tramposch, W.J. (1994) 'Heritage Recreated in the USA: Colonial Williamsburg and other sites'. In Fladmark, J.M. (ed.) *Cultural Tourism*. London: Donhead.

Tribe, J. (1997) 'The Indiscipline of Tourism'. *In Annals of Tourism Research*, **24, 3**: 638–57.

Tucker, H. (1997) 'The Ideal Village: Interactions through tourism in central Anatolia'. In Abram, S., Waldren, J. and MacLeod, D.V. (eds) (1997) *Tourists and Tourism: identifying with people and places*. Oxford: Berg.

Turner, L. and Ashe, J. (1975) 'The Golden Horde: International tourism and the pleasure periphery'. London: Constable.

UNESCO (1999a) *World Heritage*.
http://www.unesco.org/whc/ pages/home/pages/homepage.htm

UNESCO (1999b) *Report of the Director General 1996–97: General conference, 30th session 1999, 30 C3*.http://unesdoc.unesco.org/ulis/default.htm

Urry, J. (1990a) 'The Consumption of Tourism'. In *Sociology*, **24, 1**: 23–35

Urry, J. (1990b) *The Tourist Gaze: Leisure and travel in contemporary societies*. London: Sage.

Urry, J. (1992) 'The Tourist Gaze "Revisited"'. In *American Behavioural Scientist*, **36, 2**: 172–86.

Urry, J. (1995) *Consuming Places*. London: Routledge.

Urry, J. (1997) 'Cultural Change and the Seaside resort'. In Shaw, G. and Williams, A. (eds) *The Rise and Fall of British Coastal Resorts: Cultural and economic perspectives*. London: Mansell.

Urry, J. (1999) 'Sensing the City'. In Judd, D.R. and Fainstein, S.S. (eds) *The Tourist City*. New Haven: Yale University Press.

US Department of Housing and Urban Development (1995) *Atlantic City, N.J. Consolidated Plan for 1995: Executive Summary*.
http://www.hud.gov/cpes/nj/atlantnj.html

US Department of the Interior, National Park Service (1998) *Places Where Women Made History*.
http://www.cr.nps.gov/nr/travel/pwwmh/intro.htm

US Department of the Interior, National Park Service (1999a) *Register of Historic Places*. http://www.cr.nps.gov/nr/welcome.htm

US Department of the Interior, National Park Service (1999b) *We Shall Overcome: Historic places of the civil rights movement.* http://www.cr.nps.gov/nr/travel/civilrights/intro.htm

Uzzell, D. (ed.) (1989a) *Heritage Interpretation Volume 1: The natural and built environment.* London: Belhaven Press.

Uzzell, D. (ed.) (1989b) *Heritage Interpretation Volume 2: The visitor experience.* London: Belhaven Press.

Van Den Berghe, P. L. (1994) *The Quest for the Other: Ethnic tourism in San Cristóbal, Mexico.* Seattle and London: University of Washington Press.

Van Den Berghe, P. L. and Keyes, C.F. (1984) 'Introduction: Tourism and recreated ethnicity'. In *Annals of Tourism Research*, **1, 3**: 343–52.

Van der Hoeven, R. and Sziracki, G. (1997) *Lessons From Privatization: Labour issues in developing and transitional countries.* Geneva: International Labour Organization.

Var, T. and Ap, J. (1998) 'Tourism and World Peace'. In Theobald, W. (ed.) (2nd edn) *Global Tourism: The next decade.* Oxford: Butterworth Heinemann.

Veal, A.J. (1997) (2nd edn) *Research Methods for Leisure and Tourism: A practical guide.* London: Pitman.

Vellas, F. and Bécherel, L. (1995) *International Tourism: An economic perspective.* Basingstoke: Macmillan.

von Droste, B. (1995) 'Cultural landscapes in a Global World Heritage Strategy'. In von Droste, et al. (eds) *Cultural Landscapes of Universal Value.* New York and Jena: Gustav Fischer Verlag.

von Droste, B., Plachter, H. and Rössler M. (eds) (1995) *Cultural Landscapes of Universal Value.* New York and Jena: UNESCO/Gustav Fischer Verlag.

Wahab, S. (1997) 'Sustainable Tourism in the Developing World'. In Wahab, S. and Pigram, J. (eds) *Tourism, Sustainability and Growth: The challenge of sustainability.* London: Routledge.

Wacquant, L.J.D. (1992) 'Toward A Social Praxeology: The structure and logic of Bourdieu's sociology'. In Bourdieu, P. and Wacquant, L.J.D. *An Invitation to Reflexive Sociology.* Cambridge: Polity Press.

Waitt, G. (1999) 'Playing Games With Sydney: Marketing Sydney for the 2000 Olympics'. In *Urban Studies*, **36, 7**: 1055–78.

Waldren, J. (1998) 'The Road To Ruin: The politics of development in the Balearic Isles'. In Abram, S. and Waldren, J. (eds) *Anthropological Perspectives on Local Development: Knowledge and sentiments in conflict.* London: Routledge.

Wall, G. (1997) 'Sustainable Tourism – Unsustainable Development'. In Wahab, S. and Pigram, J.J. (eds) *Tourism, Development and Growth.* London: Routledge.

Wall, G. and Nuryanti, W. (1997) 'Marketing Challenges and Opportunities Facing Indonesian Tourism'. In *Journal of Travel and Tourism Marketing*, **6, 1**: 69–84

Walton, J. (1983) *The English Seaside Resort: A social history 1750–1914*. Leicester: Leicester University Press.

Walton, J. (1993) 'Tourism and Economic Development in ASEAN'. In Hitchcock, M., King, V.T. and Parnwell, M.J.G. (eds) (1993) *Tourism in South East Asia*. London: Routledge.

Walton, J. (1997) 'The Seaside Resorts of England and Wales 1900–1950: Growth, diffusion and the emergence of new forms of coastal tourism'. In Shaw, G. and Williams, A. *The Rise and Fall of British Coastal Resorts: Cultural and economic perspectives*. London: Mansell.

Wang, N. (1999) 'Rethinking Authenticity in Tourism Experience'. In *Annals of Tourism Research*, **26, 2**: 349–70.

Wanhill, S. (1998) 'The Role of Government Incentives'. In Theobald, W. (ed.) (2nd edn) *Global Tourism: The next decade*. Oxford: Butterworth Heinemann.

Watson, G.L. and Kopachevsky, J.P. (1994) 'Interpretations of Tourism as a Commodity'. In *Annals of Tourism Research*, **21, 3**: 643–60.

Watson, J.L. (1997) 'Introduction: Transnationalism, localization, and fast foods in East Asia'. In Watson, J.L. (ed.) *Golden Arches East: McDonald's in East Asia*. Stanford: Stanford University Press.

Weaver, D.B. (1998) *Ecotourism in the Less Developed World*. Wallingford: CABI Publishing.

Weinstein, A. (1994) *Market Segmentation: Using demographics, psychographics and other niche marketing techniques to predict consumer behaviour*. Chicago: Probus.

Welsch, W. (1999) 'Transculturality: The puzzling form of cultures today'. In Featherstone, M. and Lash, S, (eds) (1999) *Spaces of Culture: City, nation, world*. London: Sage.

Wheeler, B. (1994) 'Egotourism, Sustainable Tourism and the Environment: A symbiotic, symbolic or shambolic relationship?' In Seaton, A.V. (ed.) *Tourism: The state of the art*. Wiley: Chichester.

Wheeler, B. (1997) 'Here We Go, Here We Go, Here We Go Eco'. In Stabler, M.J. (ed.) (1997) *Tourism and Sustainability: Principles to Practice*. Wallingford: CABI Publishing.

Wilk, R. (1995) 'Learning to be Local in Belize'. In Miller, D. (ed.) *Worlds Apart: Modernity through the prism of the local*. London: Routledge.

Wilkinson, P.F. and Prativi, W. (1995) 'Gender and Tourism in an Indonesian Village'. In *Annals of tourism Research* **22, 2**: 283–99.

Williams, A. and Shaw, G. (1997) 'Riding the Big Dipper: The rise and decline of the British seaside resort in the twentieth century'. In Shaw, G. and Williams, A. (eds) (1997) *The Rise and Fall of British Coastal Resorts: Cultural and economic perspectives*. London: Mansell.

Williams, W. and Papamichael, E.M. (1995) 'Tourism and Tradition: Local control versus outside interests in Greece'. In Lanfant, M.F., Allcock,

J.B. and Bruner, E.M. (eds) *International Tourism: Identity and Change*. London: Sage.

Wilson, D. (1997) 'Paradoxes of Tourism in Goa'. In *Annals of Tourism Research*, **24, 1**: 52–75.

Wood, R.C. (1998) 'Old Wine in New Bottles: Critical limitations of the McDonaldization thesis – the case of hospitality services'. In Alfino, M., Caputo, J.S. and Wynyard, R. (eds) (1998) *McDonaldization Revisited: Critical Essays on Consumer Culture*. Westport: Praeger.

Wood, R.E. (1984) 'Ethnic Tourism, The State, and Cultural Change in Southeast Asia'. In *Annals of Tourism Research*, **11, 4**: 353–74

Wood, R.E. (1993) 'Tourism, Culture and the Sociology of Development'. In Hitchcock, M., King, V.T. and Parnwell, M.J.G. (eds) *Tourism in South East Asia*. London: Routledge.

Worden, N. (1997) 'Contesting Heritage in a South African City: Cape Town'. In Shaw, B.J. and Jones, R. (eds) *Contested Urban Heritage: Voices from the periphery*. Aldershot: Ashgate.

World Tourism Organisation. (1997) *Compendium of Tourist Statistics, 17th Edition*. Madrid: World Tourism Organisation.

Wright, P. (1985) *On Living in an Old Country: The national past in contemporary Britain*. London: Verso.

Wright, P. (1995) *The Village that Died for England: The strange story of Tyneham*. London: Jonathan Cape.

Youell, R. (1998) *Tourism: An introduction*. Harlow: Longman.

Zarkia, C. (1996) Philoxenia: Receiving tourists – but not guests – on a Greek island. In Boissevain, J (ed.) *Coping With Tourists: European reactions to mass tourism*. Oxford: Berghahn Books.

Zeppel, H. (1992) 'Case study: The Festival of the Pacific Arts: An emerging special interest tourism event'. In Weiler, B. and Hall, C.M. (eds) *Special Interest Tourism*. London: Belhaven Press.

Zeppel, H. (1997) 'Headhunters and Longhouse Adventure: Marketing of Iban culture in Sararwak, Borneo'. In Oppermann, M. (ed.) *Pacific Rim Tourism*. Wallingford: CABI Publishing.

Zeppel, H. and Hall, C.M. (1992) 'Arts and Heritage Tourism'. In Weiler, B. and Hall, C.M. (eds) *Special Interest Tourism*. London: Belhaven Press.

Zukin, S. (1990) 'Socio-Spatial Prototypes Of a New Organization of Consumption: The role of real cultural capital'. In *Sociology*, **24, 1**: 37–56.

Zukin, S. (1995) *The Cultures of Cities*. Oxford: Blackwell.

Zukin, S. (1998) 'Urban Lifestyles: Diversity and Standardisation in Spaces of Consumption'. In *Urban Studies* **35, 5/6**: 825–40.

Index